Civil Society

Civil Society

Measurement, Evaluation, Policy

Helmut K Anheier

CIVICUS
World Alliance for Citizen Participation

London • Sterling, VA

First published by Earthscan in the UK and USA in 2004

ISBN: 1-84407-885-3 paperback
       1-84407-923-X hardback

Typesetting by MapSet Ltd, Gateshead, UK
Printed and bound by Creative Print and Design Wales
Cover design by Yvonne Booth

For a full list of publications please contact:

Earthscan
8–12 Camden High Street, London, NW1 0JH, UK
Tel: +44 (0)20 7387 8558
Fax: +44 (0)20 7387 8998
Email: earthinfo@earthscan.co.uk
Web: **www.earthscan.co.uk**

22883 Quicksilver Drive, Sterling, VA 20166-2012, USA

Earthscan publishes in association with WWF-UK and the International Institute for
Environment and Development

A catalogue record for this book is available from the British Library

Library of Congress Cataloging-in-Publication Data

Anheier, Helmut K., 1954-.
   Civil society : measurement, evaluation, policy / by Helmut K. Anheier
      p. cm.
   Includes bibliographical references and index.
   ISBN 1-85383-885-3 (pbk.) – ISBN 1-85383-923-X (hardback)
      1. Civil society. I. Title

 JC337.A55 2003
 300–dc21

                                                                              2003018170

This book is printed on elemental chlorine-free paper

Contents

List of Illustrations

Boxes

Figures

Tables

Examples

Foreword

From its inception, the mission of CIVICUS: World Alliance for Citizen Participation[1] was to contribute to a better understanding of civil society around the world, and to help build a knowledge base that would assist practitioners, policy-makers and researchers, both nationally and internationally. As part of this mission, CIVICUS published the *New Civic Atlas* in 1997 and, expanding this work, began an international consultation phase about the possibility of developing an 'index system' for civil society. In 1999, CIVICUS contracted Dr Helmut Anheier, then the director of the Centre for Civil Society (CCS) at the London School of Economics and Political Science, to develop the conceptual and methodological framework of such a system. The results of this work are presented in this book, together with a series of country applications. Some of these were conducted in 2000 and 2001 with national partners in over ten countries around the world. Based on the experience gained in this initial pilot test, the approach presented in this book is to be further developed and implemented in some 50 countries between 2003 and 2005.

Reviewing the conceptual and operational development of the approach developed by Helmut Anheier over the last three years, several key lessons have emerged:[2]

Civil Society is a Complex and Multifaceted Concept

Civil society is probably one of the most elusive concepts used in the social sciences and in development discourse today. This certainly is a consequence of the vast heterogeneity of civil society actors and the location of civil society in the midst of multiple spheres of influence of the state, market and family. As Anheier shows in this book, only a multidimensional approach is able to detect the various kinds of interplay between the dimensions as well as the specific strengths and weaknesses of civil society.

'What know they of England, who only England know?'

In the spirit of Rudyard Kipling's adage, comparative knowledge provides the key to understanding, explaining and interpreting social phenomena. To fully understand the specific shape and underlying conditions of the civil society of a given country, identifying commonalities and differences with the civil societies of other countries is essential. Furthermore, if knowledge aims at transcending local boundaries, it has to be comparative in nature. For this reason, CIVICUS welcomes the comparative approach embraced in this book.

One Size Does Not Fit All

Civil society is the arena in which people associate voluntarily to advance common interests. The notion of an 'arena' renders it possible to account for country-specific variations. When operationalizing country-specific concepts of civil society, indicators and measures may vary significantly, which opens up the question of how to achieve comparability. The approach developed here deals with this challenge in recognizing that the use of *identical* indicators across countries might often not yield valid results. What is recommended, instead, is to search for indicators with an *equivalent* meaning.

Closing the Gap between Research and Action: Difficult but Essential

Building knowledge that is relevant for practitioners has always been a challenge for academic research. The approach proposed here tackles this challenge in making the engagement of the research results on the part of civil society stakeholders an integral part of the project design. The ultimate aim of the project is not only to gather information and provide analysis, but to create a forum for policy and debate about civil society.

Building Local Capacity: The Key to Strengthening Civil Society

This publication presents an important contribution to the methodological and conceptual issues around the assessment of civil society. It proves that a thorough and accurate understanding of the terrain of civil society is of interest not only for the research community, but also for civil society practitioners and policy-makers who are engaged in strengthening citizen action towards the common good. For this reason, building local capacity for analysing civil society is a key to its future strength.

Volkhart 'Finn' Heinrich and Kumi Naidoo
Washington, DC, and Capetown[3]

Acknowledgements

This book owes its origins to a seminar hosted by CIVICUS: World Alliance for Citizen Participation at the Commonwealth Foundation in London in 1999, and a lunch with Kumi Naidoo at St Giles Café in Oxford a few weeks later. At the London meeting, I first proposed the initial idea that led to the concept of the Civil Society Diamond; an idea that was judged to be something worthy of further discussion by a number of the participants. Several of those attending continued to have a keen interest in the development of the approach presented in this book – in particular, Colin Ball and Barry Knight. At the Oxford lunch, Kumi and I discussed the way forward and how a project could be developed around the idea. I am grateful to him and CIVICUS for their trust, and for giving me the opportunity to develop what became the Civil Society Diamond.

In the course of the next two years, many contributed to this effort; but certain people stand out: Lisa Carlson, then at the Centre for Civil Society at the London School of Economics (LSE), carried out much of the background work on data systems and graphical representations; she also helped with logistics and generally held the project together and on track. The other person is Volkhart 'Finn' Heinrich, who served as the liaison officer between the team at the LSE and CIVICUS. Finn also coordinated the case studies we use in Chapter 6, and I am deeply indebted to him, as well as to the other staff members at CIVICUS.

Thanks are owed to Marcus Lam for editorial assistance and pulling together the various country studies; Jane Schiemann and Sue Roebuck of the Centre for Civil Society at the LSE for administrative support and to Laurie Spivak at UCLA's Center for Civil Society; Richard Holloway, Rajesh Tandon, Mark Lyons, Richard Bothwell, Alan Fowler and members of the CIVICUS board for solid feedback on drafts and ideas; and the entire staff at Social Watch for introducing me to the Equity Diamond. I also thank the individual authors of the pilot studies, in particular for their permission to make use of their studies in Chapter 6.

List of Acronyms and Abbreviations

CCS	Centre for Civil Society
CEMEFI	Mexican Centre for Philanthropy
CEO	chief executive officer
CERANEO	Centre for Development of Non-profit Organizations (Croatia)
CPI	Corruption Perceptions Index
CSD	Civil Society Diamond
CSO	civil society organization
CSR	corporate social responsibility
EKAK	Estonian Civil Society Development Concept
EU	European Union
EUROSTAT	Statistical Office of the European Union
FAO	Food and Agriculture Organization
FCI	Fulfilled Commitment Index
FTE	full-time equivalent
FWCW	Fourth World Conference on Women in Beijing
GDP	gross domestic product
GNP	gross national product
HDI	Human Development Index
HRO	human rights organization
ICNPO	International Classification of Non-profit Organizations
IFDO-net	International Federation of Data Organizations
IMF	International Monetary Fund
IMV	imputed monetary valuation
IPDC	International Programme for the Development of Communication
ISO	intermediary support organization
IT	information technology
JHCNSP	Johns Hopkins Comparative Non-profit Sector Project
JHU	Johns Hopkins University
LSE	London School of Economics
NAFTA	North American Free Trade Agreement
NATO	North Atlantic Treaty Organization
NGO	non-governmental organization
NPO	non-profit organization
NPOE	non-profit operating expenditures
OECD	Organization for Economic Cooperation and Development

PEAI	public benefit, environment, animal and international
PFI	Political Freedom Index
PGI	Philanthropic Giving Index
POW	production of welfare framework
PPP	purchasing power parity
SANGOCO	South African Nongovernmental Organisation Council
SCAF	Belarus Support Centre for Associations and Foundations
TI	Transparency International
UIA	Union of International Associations
UK	United Kingdom
UN	United Nations
UN-Habitat	United Nations Human Settlements Programme
UNCTAD	United Nations Commission on Trade and Development
UN-DESA	United Nations Department for Economic and Social Affairs
UNDP	United Nations Development Programme
UNEP	United Nations Environment Programme
UNESCO	United Nations Educational, Scientific and Cultural Organization
UNHCHR	United Nations High Commission for Human Rights
UN-POPIN	United Nations Population Information Network
UNSD	United Nations Statistics Division
UNU-WIDER	World Institute for Development Economics Research
US	United States
USAID	United States Agency for International Development
VAT	value-added tax
VSI	Voluntary Sector Initiative (Canada)
WFP	World Food Programme
WHO	World Health Organization
WSSD	World Summit on Social Development
WTO	World Trade Organization
WVS	World Values Survey

Chapter 1

Measuring Civil Society:
Why and How

Thought takes the form of visual images.
Really, to impress the mind a concept
first has to take visible shape.

J Huizinga (1954, p284)

This book is about civil society and how to measure, analyse and interpret it. The book's basic premise is that social scientists, policy-makers and practitioners alike have not yet found the conceptual and methodological repertoire adequate for discussing civil society in ways similar to how they would debate the state of the economy or the performance of government. Whereas most readers would have an intuitive understanding of such abstract concepts as 'market' and 'state', would, indeed, be able to attach meaning to the 'language' of market experts and political analysts alike, and, what is more, even be quite capable of engaging in ongoing debates, little such understanding and capacity exists for civil society.

To a great extent, and irrespective of its present currency, civil society remains 'uncharted territory' in a world long dominated by a two-sector view of market versus state. The major social science theories and political ideologies from Marxism to neo-liberalism relate to them, and the world's statistical information systems are designed to privilege data on the economy, demographics and politics, leading to a benign neglect of data on civil society. This lack of systematic information on civil society is, of course, a function of basic conceptual deficiencies in social science when it comes to describing phenomena that are neither market- nor state-related. These two weaknesses have reinforced each other for much of modern social science history, creating an underdeveloped conceptual, methodological and statistical repertoire for describing and analysing civil society.

However, in the course of the last decade, following the events of 1989 in Central and Eastern Europe, and democratization processes in many parts of the world, civil society has become an important concept in the social sciences (Keane, 1998; Kaviraj and Khilnani, 2001; Anheier et al, 2001; Kaldor, 2003). What was once a rather obscure term of interest to historians and political philosophers has emerged as a central term in modern social science discourse that straddles the boundaries of policy-making, advocacy and the academy (Kaldor, 2003). Whether in the US, Europe or other parts of the world, a 'strong and vibrant civil society characterized by a social infrastructure of dense networks of face-to-face relationships that cross-cut existing social cleavages such as race, ethnicity, class, sexual orientation and gender that will underpin strong and responsive democratic government' (Edwards, Foley and Diani, 2001, p17) is seen as a desirable policy objective.

Civil society has thus emerged as a central topic among policy-makers and practitioners alike (Naidoo and Tandon, 1999), from civic renewal projects in the US to counteract increased social isolation and distrust among citizens (Sirianni and Friedland, 2000), efforts by the German parliament to revitalize voluntarism (Enquettekommission, 2002), and attempts by the UK Cabinet Office to modernize the voluntary sector (Strategy Unit, 2002) to the World Bank's new approach to economic development, the European Union's encouragement of a Citizens' Europe, and NATO's programme to seek ways of constructing a 'civil society' in countries torn apart by civil war – all of these are indications of heightened policy relevance.

> ... civil society has emerged as a central topic among policy-makers and practitioners ...

With such prominence comes a need for information and ways to position civil society and its various dimensions in a wider policy dialogue. Unfortunately, no such system exists at present, and civil society leaders, academics and policy-makers alike are frequently frustrated by the absence of a common language and the lack of basic data that could be as easily communicated and understood as economic growth rates, electoral returns or information on government spending and budget priorities. In this respect, the purpose of this book is to introduce, develop and illustrate the basic elements of such a system for presenting the major contours of civil society in a systematic and user-friendly way.

The development of an information system on civil society is as difficult as it is challenging. There are major conceptual and methodological issues involved in developing an approach for measuring and assessing civil society that would apply across countries and regions, but may differ significantly in terms of culture, economy and politics. Therefore, at the most basic level, the book has to reach at least some initial agreement on aspects that are still unsettled and continue to be debated among experts. Such issues include questions such as what is meant by civil society? What characteristics are significant for measurement purposes, and how should relevant data be presented and analysed? Establishing such agreements is no small task and the academic literature on the concept of civil society alone, leaving aside issues of measurement and aspects of policy, easily fills several bookshelves (see, among others, Cohen and Arato, 1997; Keane, 1998; Kaviraj and Khilnani, 2001; Kaldor, 2003).

> ...this book is about civil society and how to measure, analyse and interpret it...

At the risk of great oversimplification, one could say that work on civil society tends to be of two kinds: conceptual and policy-related. By contrast, due to the frequently abstract nature of current work in the field, there is a relative absence of systematic empirical analysis of what civil society actually is and what its contours are – that is, dimensions or measures similar to those with which one would describe an economic or political system. Moreover, given the bias in official statistics described above, there are significant technical challenges in terms of data coverage and availability. Many of the data items that would be part of a future civil society reporting system are simply not readily available at the levels of quantity and quality needed. Therefore, any approach developed must be able to deal with the very complexity of the task, while aiming to preserve a high degree of simplicity and practicality.

Yet, while the task may ultimately be too immense to accomplish in a single book, there can be little doubt that even the rudiments of such a systematic information and reporting system on civil society are very much needed. For one, as suggested above, the topic has come to occupy much attention across academic disciplines and across the political spectrum. Second, while it is regarded as a major component of what makes modern society possible, it is also increasingly seen as something 'problematic' and changing, and as something that can no longer be taken for granted. The recent debate about the decline in social capital and the increase in social disengagement in the US and other countries is one indication of this trend (Putnam, 2000; 2002).

Civil Society and the Non-profit or Voluntary Sector

In many countries, the (re)discovery of civil society coincided with renewed emphasis on the role of non-profit organizations (Deakin, 2001). In the course of the last decade, most developed market economies in Europe, North America and Asia-Pacific have seen a general increase in the economic importance of non-profit organizations as providers of health, social, educational and cultural services of many kinds. On average, the non-profit sector accounts for about 6 per cent of total employment in Organization for Economic Cooperation and Development (OECD) countries, or nearly 10 per cent with volunteer work factored in (Salamon et al, 1999).

Prompted, in part, by growing doubts about the capacity of the state to cope with its own welfare, developmental and environmental problems, analysts across the political spectrum (see Anheier and Kendall, 2001; Deakin, 2001) have come to see non-profit and community-based organizations as strategic components of a middle way between policies that put primacy on 'the market' and those that advocate greater reliance on the state (see Edwards and Gaventa, 2001). Likewise, institutions such as the World Bank, the United Nations or the European Union (UNDP, 2002), together with bilateral donors and many developing countries, are searching for a balance between state-led and market-led approaches to development, and are allocating more responsibility to NGOs (see Clark, 2003).

The basic argument for a greater non-profit role in both developing and developed countries is based on public administration (Salamon, 1995), which suggests that non-profits or NGOs are efficient and effective providers of social and other services that governments may find costlier and more ineffectual to offer themselves. As a result, cooperative relations between governments and non-profits in welfare provision have become a prominent feature in countries such as the US (Salamon, 2002), Germany (Anheier and Seibel, 2001), France (Archambault, 1996) or the UK (Plowden, 2001; Strategy Unit, 2002).

Where such partnerships with government emerged, the role of non-profit organizations is more pronounced than in countries where collaboration did not prevail (Anheier and Salamon, 2003). As part of public sector reform in many developed and developing countries, this partnership is opened up and seen in the context of privatization. The rise of quasi-markets and public–private partnerships under the heading of 'new public management' stresses the role of non-profits as providers of services, typically as contractors of services paid for, at least in part, by government (Ferlie, 1996; McLaughlin, Osborne and Ferlie, 2002). As a broad label, new public management includes several related characteristics that draw in the non-profit sector, specifically:

> ... the political discourse about non-profit provision has expanded from the welfare state paradigm to include pronounced civil society elements.

- a move from third-party government (Salamon, 1995), where non-profits served as either extension agents or partners of governments in service delivery, to a mixed economy of social care and welfare that includes businesses and public agencies next to non-profit providers (Knapp, Hardy and Forder 2001); and
- a move from simple contracts and subsidies to 'constructed markets' (Le Grand, 1999), particularly in health care and social services, with a premium on managed competition. For example, the long-term care insurance in Germany and services for the frail elderly in the UK are based on competition among alternative providers through competitive bidding for service contracts.

With the rise of new public management, the emphasis on non-profits as service providers and instruments of privatization casts non-profit organizations essentially in a neo-liberal role. Examples of this include Germany's efforts to modernize its subsidiarity policy by introducing competitive bidding into social service contracting (Anheier and Seibel, 2001); New Labour's Compact in Britain in the UK (Mulgan, 1999; Plowden, 2001), or France's unemployment policy of 'insertion' (Archambault, 1996).

The political discourse about the role of non-profit provision has expanded from the welfare state paradigm that long characterized the field to include pronounced civil society elements today. While their economic function, particularly in terms of welfare provision, has been a common, though often overlooked, feature of non-profits in most developed countries, the emphasis on civil society, however, is new and reflects profound changes in the wider political environment. The non-profit or voluntary sector is seen as the social infrastructure of civil society, creating as well as facilitating a sense of trust and social inclusion that is seen as essential for the functioning of modern societies (see, for example, Putnam, 2000; Anheier and Kendall, 2002). The explicit or implied joint emphasis on service provision and civil society, however, brings with it many theoretical and policy-related challenges.

More generally, we have to address anew 'the proper role and appropriate balance of state, market and civil society in public life' (Naidoo and Tandon, 1999, p4). With the end of the Cold War, a 'global associational revolution' (Salamon, 1994) began to gather momentum, aided by the expansion of a more confident middle class, and the introduction and spread of new information technologies such as the internet, among other factors (Anheier and Salamon, 2003). Within a short period of time, the world changed from a place dominated by the monologues of autocrats to the cacophony of conversations among individuals and groups of many different kinds (Naidoo and Tandon, 1999).

> What is the proper role and appropriate balance of state, market and civil society in public life?

At least to some extent, these conversations – however diverse or similar, shrill or soft, poignant or comforting, effective or ineffective they might be – are, ultimately, expressions of democracy and citizenship, and are about individual freedom, social participation and responsibility. While the individual voices of civil society are part of a democratic social order, they are not necessarily democratic themselves – nor are they necessarily responsible or tolerant, let alone supportive, of freedom or citizenship for some group or another. Many of the voices are; but civil society includes a great diversity of views, as the sometimes grey area between some civil society groups and organized violence demonstrates (Glasius and Kaldor, 2002; Clark, 2003). The crucial point, however, is that such voices are being expressed and heard when, for most of the 20th century, they were not.

The cacophony of civil society that Naidoo and Tandon (1999) describe, and the diversity of voices it expresses, is a relatively new phenomenon in many parts of the world. Yet, how can we know how many voices there are, what their strengths and weaknesses might be, or their potential for democracy and greater social equity, and what impact they could potentially have? What are the contours of civil society? How large or how small is it, and relative to what? How can we understand civil society conceptually, how and where can we locate it empirically, and with what measures and techniques?

> How can we understand civil society conceptually, how can we locate it empirically, and with what measures and techniques?

These are some of the questions that motivate the present effort to develop an information system for civil society. Indeed, one of the first impressions one gains from examining civil society is this: the diverse voices of civil society at local, regional, national and, increasingly, international levels have neither a common map nor a compass and a set of instruments that could frame and guide the conversation.

An Impossible Task?

Even though civil society has become an important topic, there is, at the same time, little in terms of a systematic empirical basis for, and conceptually grounded information on, what civil society actually is 'in the real world'. At present, we have no systematic way to answer the questions posed above. Moreover, little is known about how policy-makers and practitioners could anticipate, track and address trends in civil society over time, and how they could explore the impact of actual and potential policies in the context of such changes and developments. Put simply, civil society is a term without much of the methodological and empirical underpinnings needed to make it a useful and fruitful concept in the long term. To provide this infrastructure for researchers, practitioners and policy-makers is the ultimate goal to which this book is meant to contribute.

> The diverse voices of civil society have neither a common map nor a compass and a set of instruments to guide them.

More specifically, the objective of the civil society information system proposed here is to provide a tool for describing the empirical contours of civil society in a systematic way. In turn, this would enable the assessment of the 'health' of civil society by providing indications of strengths and weaknesses with a view to suggesting policy options. What is more, the information system should help to assess the impact or contributions of civil society at large and in particular fields, and suggest measures for improvement and further development.

> The approach developed here provides a tool for describing the empirical contours of civil society in a systematic way.

The ultimate aim of the system proposed here is to enable a structured dialogue about civil society nationally, as well as internationally. This includes raising awareness about civil society across different stakeholders and the population at large; assisting civil society representatives in developing a vision and policy position; and improving standards of transparency and accountability throughout. To this end, the information system is designed to:

- Describe the state of civil society according to a number of core characteristics and dimensions.
- Serve as an assessment and 'vision-guidance' tool for policy-makers and civil society representatives.
- Meet the interests of researchers in the field by encouraging systematic analysis that is empirically grounded, conceptually informed and relevant for policy purposes.
- Encourage constructive exchange among civil society representatives, policy-makers and researchers.

- Lend itself to rich narrative interpretations, thereby contributing to the development of policy options and strategies.
- Be useful for national-, regional- and local-level applications and comparisons.

These are important and ambitious goals, and it helps to put them in perspective in order to understand the long-term implications of the system proposed here. In other words, in order to comprehend the import of the approach introduced in this book, it is useful to take a brief look at how the social sciences have developed over time in relation to civil society, particularly in the context of the data collection systems that generate empirical information.

> The ultimate aim is to enable a structured dialogue about civil society nationally, as well as internationally

Civil Society and the Social Sciences

How helpful, we ask, are the social sciences in offering civil society organizations and their representatives the map and compass needed for self-reflection, debate and policy dialogue, let alone for the 'orchestration' of some of their many voices? Unfortunately, the answer is not very reassuring, although there are signs of change in the sense that more and more social scientists are beginning to realize the limitations of standard measurement and reporting systems. Examples include Eisner's (1994) critique of standard economic reporting; the United Nations Development Programme's (UNDP's) Human Development Index (2000; see also www.undp.org/hdro for all *Human Development Reports*); the World Bank's governance project (Kaufamnn et al, 1999a; 1999b; World Bank, 1999) and social capital measures (Dasgupta and Serageldin, 2000); the OECD's Paris 21 Initiative (Development Cooperation Directorate, OECD, 2001); the World Values surveys (Inglehart et al, 1998; World Values Study Group, 1994; 1999); and more specific efforts, such as the Johns Hopkins Comparative Non-profit Sector Project (Salamon and Anheier, 1996); the Independent Sector's Measurement Project (www.independent sector.org); Desai's (1994) measure of political freedom (see also UNDP, 1992); the *Global Civil Society Yearbook* (Anheier et al, 2001; Glasius et al, 2002); and the UN's *Handbook on Nonprofit Institutions* (2002), among many others (see Chapter 5). Yet, despite these developments, the social sciences still have much catching up to do.

Why is this the case? The answer is simple, yet full of implications. For a long time, as mentioned above, social scientists and most policy-makers alike believed that we lived in a two-sector world. There was the market or the economy, on one hand, and the state or government, on the other. The great social science theories addressed them, and virtually all of the social science efforts were dedicated to exploring the two institutional complexes of market and state. In particular, the statistical machinery and instruments of data collection, analysis and reporting were primarily oriented to cover and serve the economy and the state, including military needs. This is where investment took place, and this is where significant progress was made over the last few decades – from the system of national income accounts, population census methods and public-sector statistics, to election studies and consumer surveys. Nothing else seemed to matter much.

Did civil society figure in social science data efforts? The answer is, clearly, no. Some historians remind us that the term civil society had been in vogue during the 18th and 19th centuries; but it had long since fallen into disuse by the early 20th century. Civil society, it seemed, was a term of interest primarily to those studying the history of ideas rather than those interested in contemporary societies. Not surprisingly, civil society was pushed to the sidelines and, ultimately, became a very abstract notion, relegated to the confines of sociological theorizing, not fitting the two-sector worldview that has dominated the social sciences for over 50 years. Civil society was simply not 'on the agenda'.

...for a long time, we lived in a two-sector world: the market and the state... nothing else seemed to matter...

In retrospect, such a short-sighted approach had disastrous consequences, of which the inability of the social sciences to predict and understand the fall of communism in Central and Eastern Europe is just one of many examples. One of the most important events of the 20th century escaped the attention of mainstream social science until after the fact! Even the emergence or re-emergence of civil society as a major political phenomenon in many parts of the world went largely unnoticed. One could probably think of other similar major social and political events – from South Africa to Yugoslavia, and from the anti-globalization protests that first coalesced in Seattle at the 1998 meeting of the World Trade Organization (WTO) to the formation of resistance movements against large-scale dam projects in India and other developing countries. The emergence of a pro-terrorist movement industry in part of the Middle East and South Asia is as much a failure of local civil society to develop, as it is the long-term result of misguided international diplomacy. These events – the collapse of state socialism, the rise of micro-nationalisms, and the surge in global terrorism epitomized by the tragedy of 11 September 2001 – unfolded outside the attention of social science reporting. The social sciences – to paraphrase a critique Dahrendorf (1959) expressed long ago – are left with too many events of immense historical importance that remain unexplained, and with too many developments that proceed unnoticed and uncharted.

Of course, dissenting voices have always been present in the social sciences. Yet, it is essential for the purpose of this book to keep in mind that such voices were rarely heard, and that they certainly had little influence on the types of measures social scientists and statistical offices developed and the kinds of data they collected. One of the few exceptions is the area of social indicators (see *Journal of Social Indicators Research*). Measures of social participation, subjective and objective well-being and other aspects of society enjoyed a relatively short period of interest during the 1970s (see Diener and Suh, 1999). Yet, these efforts failed to maintain momentum and, in the end, could neither expand the repertoire of social science statistics in a significant way, nor change the emphasis on economic reporting around the world. The revival of social indicators happened only during the 1990s, aided by landmark publications such as the UNDP's *Human Development Report*, which challenged the dominance of economic reporting at the international level.

Likewise, the notion that a non-profit or 'third' sector might exist between the market and the state got lost in the two-sector worldview. Of course, there are many private institutions that serve public purposes and do not fit the state–market dichotomy: voluntary associations, charities, non-profits, foundations and NGOs. Yet, until quite recently, such third-sector institutions were neglected if not ignored outright by all social sciences, particularly economics. While the System of National Accounts recognizes a separate economic sector of 'Non-profit institutions serving households' (United Nations, 1993), it is basically treated as a residual, and very few countries collect data on this sector (Anheier and Salamon, 1998).

> The notion that a 'third sector' might exist between the market and the state got lost in the two-sector worldview.

Only through separate individual efforts such as the Johns Hopkins Comparative Non-profit Sector Project (Salamon and Anheier, 1996), the World Values surveys (Inglehart et al, 1998), the databases of the Union of International Associations (2000), studies such as EUROVOL (Gaskin and Davis Smith, 1997), or projects conducted by the Commonwealth Foundation (www.commonwealthfoundation.com/programmes), and the Civil Society and Governance Programme at Sussex University (www.ids.ac.uk/ids/civsoc/home.html), to name a few, was it possible to begin approaching the task of collecting information on civil society. Some efforts, such as the project at Johns Hopkins, have successfully engaged the UN Division of Statistics to develop the *Handbook of Nonprofit Institutions* as part of the 1993 System of National Accounts. Over time, this will likely lead to a major improvement of non-profit statistics in many countries.

The Task Ahead

The challenges and the tasks ahead are clear: the social sciences need to develop a measurement and reporting system for civil society – a system that can put in place, at least initially, a systematic and potentially comprehensive mechanism for data collection, analysis and dissemination. Such a system could assist the dialogue among civil society organizations and policy-makers, and help stakeholders to locate and position themselves in the policy process. It could support the social science community in developing a more adequate understanding of civil society than has been possible under the predominant 'two-sector worldview'. Moreover, it could locate civil society relative to the economy and politics, as well as in relation to society at large. Ultimately, a reporting system that targets civil society and incorporates this information in regular statistics could help to bring about better policy advice and impact.

At the very least, it would serve as an 'early warning system' for social, political and cultural changes that may have repercussions for society as a whole. For example, in most countries, the current debate about the decline of social capital in advanced market economies (see Putnam, 2000; 2002) is handicapped by the absence of a systematic and high-quality data system that tracks changes in social participation, trust and other relevant variables on a regular basis. Likewise, discussions about the role of NGOs in Africa or parts of Central Asia are complicated by a lack of systematic understanding of how these institutions fit into local societies and what their potential for social self-organization and resource mobilization consequently might be. The democratic deficit and social stagnation in much of the Middle East is made worse by inadequate knowledge about the contours and potential of civil society institutions. The political reform of Japan's third sector after the Kobe earthquake was made more complicated by a lack of concepts and information on aspects such as volunteering and civic engagement (Deguchi, 2001). To mention one more example from the many, one could add the 'Citizen Dialogue' initiated by the European Union (EU), which aims to increase a sense of 'ownership' that citizens have in the EU (www.europa.eu.int/citizens/). Yet, the effort continues to be frustrated by a low awareness of what civil society is and means in the various member states.

> The challenge ahead is clear: the social sciences need to develop a measurement and reporting system for civil society.

The Civil Society Diamond (CSD) approach, which finds its intellectual heritage in the work of Social Watch (2000), encourages data collection, improved coverage and a concern for data quality. It involves a structured dialogue among users such as civil society representatives, policy-makers and researchers. This dialogue, as we will suggest in Chapter 6, is a crucial part of the CSD approach. It can involve, for example, a workshop among these groups to assess the state of civil society and to explore a policy agenda based on the results of CSD applications. Such a workshop could also increase the common self-understanding of civil society. By bringing together a broad range of civil society stakeholders, the CSD can provide a meeting ground for debate and joint policy dialogue. Importantly, the CSD invites users to take on a comparative perspective and encourages them to examine the phenomenon of civil society across fields, regions and countries, as well as over time.

> The CSD presents and interprets information about various aspects of civil society in a systematic way.

Challenges

No doubt, as mentioned at the beginning of this chapter, developing the CSD approach poses significant challenges. One of the major challenges in developing a reporting system on civil society is the sheer complexity of the concept and the diversity of organizations, groups, networks and individuals that constitute the sphere between the market, the state and the family. Many definitions of civil society have been proposed, and many are culture-bound and inherently normative. Civil society is both an old and a new concept, and therefore carries with it much conceptual and ideological 'baggage'. To cut across this conceptual challenge is the first formidable hurdle for the effort proposed here.

A second challenge arises from the previously mentioned fact that conventional social science methodology has largely bypassed the field of civil society, as have statistical offices in most countries. As a result of this long neglect, civil society institutions and organizations are among the least studied, and frequently constitute the *terra incognito* of economic, social, political and cultural statistics. Moreover, while extended time series data exist for many aspects of economic and social behaviour, such information is very limited for virtually all aspects of civil society. Basic data on social participation, membership, community, volunteering and value dispositions are much less systematic and grounded in terms of validity and reliability than standard economic measures.

> Civil society institutions and organizations are among the least studied, and constitute the *terra incognito* of statistical reporting.

Thus, conceptual and methodological challenges stand in the way of developing an information system for civil society. Yet, there is also a strong lesson to be learned from similar attempts at developing indicators in economics, sociology and political science. The lesson, also supported by the case studies in Chapter 6, is that only persistent and systematic efforts lead to better measurements and improved data coverage – efforts that would bring about not only greater sophistication in terms of validity and reliability, but also greater and more sustained demand for data from a range of different user groups. Ultimately, this combination of supply and demand for high-quality data and wider coverage is the key to having this information provided as part of the regular 'statistical menu' of national and international institutions.

Plan of the Book

The main body of this book is divided into six chapters. As some chapters, notably Chapters 3 and 5, involve some level of technical detail and data presentations, we have moved some of this material to separate appendices in an effort to keep the overall book more readable and user friendly. These appendices are located towards the end of the book. Importantly, readers primarily interested in basic applications of the CSD methodology may refer to Holloway's (2001) 'toolkit' on how to use the CSD in different contexts and for different purposes.

Chapter 2 introduces the background and methodology of the CSD. It offers an overview of the objectives, assumptions, definition, indicators and approaches. Importantly, Chapter 2 introduces a working definition of civil society.

Chapter 3 presents the CSD approach in full. It reveals the structure and range of the CSD at different levels of complexity and for a variety of purposes – in particular, cross-national and longitudinal analysis. This chapter is the methodological heart of the CSD approach. Because of the visual approach taken in developing and presenting the CSD, this chapter requires only a basic background in methodology or statistics on behalf of the reader.

Chapter 4 deals with applications. The CSD is applied across a broad range of countries that vary in economic development, political system, culture, religion and ethnicity. The purpose of these applications is less to test the methodology in any rigorous sense of the term, and more to demonstrate the variety of use and applicability of the approach across a wide range of different circumstances.

Chapter 5 addresses indicator selection and data issues. Without the right indicators and without sufficient data to measure them, much of the approach developed in these pages will remain little more than an intellectual exercise. In other words, for the CSD to become accepted among users, a systematic and sustained data collection effort will be indispensable.

Chapter 6 presents a sequential overview of the steps that need to be taken in applying the CSD in actual situations. As is the case for applications presented in Chapter 4, this chapter, too, will illustrate the use of the CSD from a broad cross-section of countries, as well as applications.

Chapter 7 offers concluding comments and spells out the challenges ahead in terms of methodological and practical aspects. These challenges must be addressed if the system proposed here is to develop and flourish over the next few years. In this sense, it should be clear that the CSD approach is merely the first step towards a future information system on civil society – a task for the social science community to achieve.

Caveats

Several caveats are called for from the very beginning. First, not all of what this book argues and presents is new in the sense that nobody has dealt with it before, or that others have not made similar statements in the past. In particular, we are indebted to the idea of the Equity Diamond introduced by Social Watch (2000; see www.socialwatch.org). However, taken together, the overall conceptual and methodological approach introduced in the balance of this book covers new ground. Nonetheless, it ventures into methodological and data-specific areas that still require much work in the future. Specifically, some of the measures and tools presented in this book are in need of closer methodological scrutiny as more data becomes available and as experience in using the CSD continues to grow. Obviously, while some aspects of the system proposed here are straightforward, others need more thought and exploration. For these reasons, it is best to think of the CSD as an evolving project, and none of its underlying premises and principles preclude changes and modifications over time.

Conclusion

Across the world, civil society has become a major item on the political agenda – in the developed countries of the OECD, in the developing regions of Africa, Latin America, the Middle East and Asia, as well as in transition countries of Central and Eastern Europe. Yet, political agendas change, and the 'seat at the policy table' that has been gained in some countries may be more difficult to maintain for long unless civil society leaders have more and better information to support both their political positions and the policy arguments that they wish to put forward. Information is part of the voice function of civil society and without it – without a supporting pool of current and high-quality data – civil society leaders may find it even harder to be heard where it matters – in the policy process.

> The 'seat at the policy table' can only be maintained for long if civil society leaders have more and better information to support their positions and arguments.

In other words, through its representatives and organizations, civil society must be able to demonstrate repeatedly and decisively how, where and for whom it matters and how this relates to the impact of markets and states. It must be able to examine its current strengths and weaknesses; it must be able to point to policy options and future challenges. Civil society representatives not only must be equipped with the relevant information, but they also need to make effective use of such information as part of a systematic, ongoing and structured dialogue. The approach proposed and developed in this book represents an initial step towards this goal.

Chapter 2

The Civil Society Diamond:
The Basics

Two intellectual styles seem to dominate
social science activity…the story-tellers
and the pyramid-builders.
Johan Galtung (1992, p96)

In terms of Galtung's apt description, the Civil Society Diamond (CSD) approach would be an exercise in *story-telling*. It is a narrative that starts with different pieces of quantitative and qualitative information, combines them with descriptive accounts, and interprets the result by searching for patterns and relationships that culminate in some conclusion relevant to users. In other words, applying the CSD approach is to 'tell a story' about civil society with systematic information at hand. The CSD is not an effort to build mental pyramids by reflecting about the fundamentals of civil society at the conceptual and philosophical level.

Ultimately, the CSD is information-based and data-driven; it is applied rather than basic research, and is closer to action-oriented analysis than to pure social science. The CSD is not designed to serve as a methodological tool for rigorous hypothesis testing in the strict sense of social science research. Its primary purpose is to assist civil society representatives, analysts and policy-makers in examining different aspects of civil society. The CSD is first and foremost a method of presenting and interpreting information about civil society in a systematic and structured way.

This chapter will provide a summary of the background, methodology and different uses of the CSD. Specifically, the chapter offers an overview of the CSD's objectives, assumptions, definitions and approaches.

Objectives

The purpose of the CSD is to serve as a tool for civil society practitioners, policy-makers and researchers to:

Assess core facets of civil society.

The CSD provides indications of civil society's major contours, strengths and weaknesses, and thereby facilitates the identification and development of policy options. For example, the CSD can be used to gauge the capacity of civil society organizations relative to needs and resources available against the background of current tax laws and funding regulations.

Assess the impact and potential contributions of civil society.

The CSD makes it possible to assess the impact of civil society generally – for example, in terms of the overall well-being of a society – or economically and socially, with respect to human development indicators. The CSD can also be applied to selected fields as a way of examining the contributions of civil society organizations in areas such as health care, the environment or culture. Regardless of the impact level, however, interpreting the CSD leads to suggestions about possible interventions and options for improvement.

The ultimate aim of the CSD, therefore, is to:

- **Create a tool for an ongoing and systematic dialogue** about the strengths and weaknesses of civil society at local, regional, national and international levels. Much of the utility of the CSD comes with repeated use, particularly for applications across different levels and fields, and over time. For example, a systematic self-assessment of the effectiveness of civil society leaders in achieving policy aims becomes an important tool for charting progress in the context of other indicators about civil society's scale, scope and capacity. Similarly, stakeholder surveys provide indications of how expectations and achievement match in terms of particular policies and set objectives.
- **Raise awareness** across different population groups and stakeholders about civil society. Systematic and easily understandable, as well as communicable, information can facilitate both awareness and dialogue about the potentials, strengths and weaknesses, and the challenges and opportunities of civil society. Moreover, use of the CSD is not limited to one group of stakeholders alone; the relative ease and simplicity of the CSD makes it attractive to groups who would normally not apply social science methodology to describe and analyse complex phenomena.
- **Enhance the transparency and accountability** of civil society institutions, organizations and representatives nationally, as well as internationally. Examining and reporting the state of civil society from a variety of perspectives, and in a critical and constructive way, can contribute significantly to both the credibility and legitimacy that civil society enjoys among different stakeholders.
- **Enhance professionalism** and raise leadership standards within civil society organizations, as well as among corporations and government agencies dealing with civil society institutions. The CSD is by no means designed to emphasize the 'good' and 'convenient' aspects of civil society

alone. To the contrary, by making it possible to identify critical issues and developments, to point to shortcomings and problems, and to invite creative policy thinking, the CSD can, ultimately, contribute to professionalism and effective leadership.

More specifically, to help meet these objectives, the CSD:

- Offers a basic **description** of civil society along different dimensions; for example, the CSD displays the major contours of civil society in terms of scale and scope, both overall and for specific fields and areas.
- Serves as an **assessment** tool for policy-makers and civil society representatives. The CSD makes it possible to explore critical areas and to highlight strengths and weaknesses of civil society in a systematic and policy-oriented way.
- Lends itself to intuitive and useful **interpretations**. The graphical display of several indicators across different dimensions can open up dialogue among users, and invite constructive and creative 'readings' of complex information.
- Is useful for **applications** at national, regional and local levels. The CSD is not limited to any specific levels of application, nor to any particular field, institution or organization. In fact, the CSD methodology can be applied both at different levels and from the perspectives of different stakeholders.
- Provides the basis for **comparisons** within and across countries, and across different cultural and political settings. Even though the CSD is designed to allow for flexibility and adaptability to local, regional and national settings, the types of indicators used allow for systematic comparisons. Of course, over time, the potential and usefulness of cross-sectional and longitudinal comparisons will increase as more information becomes available.

Assumptions

Like any approach or method, the CSD rests on a number of basic understandings. There are four assumptions that form the conceptual and methodological foundation for developing and applying the CSD. Specifically, the approach is based on a:

Holistic conception

Because civil society is a multifaceted concept, the CSD incorporates multiple aspects of civil society, and takes into account different dimensions and orientations in assessing civil society issues and trends. For example, an indicator system that would focus primarily on economic aspects at the expense of social and legal information would violate the assumption that civil society requires a holistic measurement approach.

Normative platform

The CSD is not only based on a holistic assumption, it is expressly normative in its use. It goes beyond both descriptive and analytic aspects of various civil society dimensions by also incorporating expectations and commitments in achieving specified goals. The CSD enables civil society representatives and other stakeholders to set their own standards and measure progress accordingly. In this respect, the CSD is a normative tool to assess the strengths and weaknesses of civil society.

Strategic developmental dimension

Because civil society is a multifaceted and complex social phenomenon, specific dimensions can develop their own dynamics that either diverge or converge over time. These developments can affect other dimensions in a variety of ways, which may involve different opportunities and challenges. For this reason, the CSD views civil society and its component parts as an evolving system whose dimensions develop different ways and dynamics over time.

Operative dimension

The CSD should be easy to use for policy-makers, civil society representatives and other stakeholders across diverse social, cultural and political settings. While the complexity of civil society would perhaps require a highly sophisticated methodological approach and an equally refined measurement system, parsimony and user-friendliness are seen as overriding concerns for the development of the CSD.

In contrast, and by implication, the CSD is not designed to:

- **Emphasize only one dimension of civil society**, such as political or economic aspects or legal issues, at the expense of others – for example, social or cultural dimensions – as this would distort rather than inform debate.
- **Establish a rigid and fixed set of universal criteria** against which all countries, regions and organizations are to be judged, as this would divert from a more contextual, nuanced and culturally sensitive discussion.
- **Neglect the importance of changes and developments** over time in different aspects of civil society, as this would lead to a static view; instead, the CSD is designed to invite repeated applications for tracking changes over time.
- **Encourage 'naming and shaming,'** which is implicit in many report card systems and ranking of countries, such as the corruption index, growth figures or human rights measures.

Against this background, the CSD attempts to preserve four essential qualities:

- **The CSD is easy to use** by different types of users. The CSD is for use by civil society representatives, policy-makers, researchers and other interested parties for different purposes (planning, analysis, debate) that involve different levels of aggregation (local, regional, national and international), as well as different cultural, economic and political circumstances.
- **The CSD is easy to interpret** in both general dimensions and specific aspects in order to invite widespread use, fuller discussion and informed debate about civil society.
- **The CSD is enabling** to users in the sense that it is designed not as a controlling mechanism for management and policy-makers, but as a tool for assessment, reflection and forward-looking discussion.
- **The CSD is normative** in its implications for policy-making, governance and management by allowing users to set standards, goals and expectations and judge them against current trends and achievements.

Data Availability

Although data issues will be addressed more fully in Chapters 5 and 6, it is important to point out that some degree of data availability is an implicit assumption made throughout this book. In essence, the CSD approach assumes that data is available for its use. In fact, the CSD cannot function without data, and any CSD application requires as basic input some basic information for its different dimensions. Both quantitative data (for example, economic measures or size of membership) and qualitative data (such as legal information) can be used in actual CSD applications. In general, the richer and the more comprehensive the databases available across the various CSD dimensions (see below), the more valid, informed and useful applications ultimately become for different types of users and purposes. Therefore, an assessment of data availability, coverage and quality is the necessary first step towards applying the CSD.

Undoubtedly, countries, fields and organizations vary in the extent to which data and information are available for the various dimensions and indicators that compose the CSD. Therefore, a major part of the effort to encourage and maintain the use of the CSD across the world will be the development of a *basic information system on civil society*. Specifically, such efforts should focus on the type of data needed for the set of recommended indicators suggested below. This would refer to the following major data items and efforts (see also Appendix C):

- the basic economic data collected by the Johns Hopkins Comparative Non-profit Sector Project (Salamon and Anheier, 1996; Salamon et al, 1999a; 1999b) and similar efforts to map the basic contours of civil society;
- the large data bases on different types of international organizations maintained by the Union of International Associations (UIA, 1905–1999/2000);

- the legal indicator work carried out by the International Centre for Not-for-profit Law and the World Bank (ICNL and World Bank, 1997) or measures developed by Transparency International (1999–2000) to show the legal dimension;
- the World Bank's governance project (Kaufmann et al, 1999a; 1999b; World Bank, 1999) that collects a wide range of information on a country's political and administrative system;
- the Harvard Center for International Development–World Bank DataMart (2000) project, which includes data sets on political institutions, risk indicators and a mapping of political conflict and civil society;
- the University of California, San Diego Social Science Data Collection (UCSD, 2001a), which includes a searchable catalogue to over 440 data sites with data that can be downloaded, nearly 100 data libraries worldwide, and various other sources, including the Lijphart Election Archive (UCSD, 2001b).
- the United Nations Educational, Scientific and Cultural Organization's (UNESCO's) media and communication website and the CSD's CD-ROM on 'Trade in Cultural Goods' (UNSD, 2000), the International Programme for the Development of Communication (IPDC) (www.unesco.org/webworld/ ipdc/introduction.htm) and the Webworld-Communication, Information and Informatics (www.unesco.org/webworld/index.shtml), in particular.
- the data collected as part of the European and World Values Survey (Halman, 2001; Inglehart et al 1998; World Values Study Group, 1994; 1999), and similar projects and surveys to measure the values, norms and attitudes that characterize civil society, such as the Eurobarometer (www.gesis.org/en/data_service/eurobarometer/index.htm) or the Latinóbarometro (www.latinobarometro.cl); and
- the information based on the systematic application of impact surveys along the lines developed by Social Watch (2000), the United States Agency for International Development (USAID) NGO Sustainability Index (2000) or the impact approach developed by the London School of Economics (LSE) (Kendall and Knapp, 1999) to gauge the extent to which civil society, generally, and policy measures, specifically, 'make a difference'.

Of course, these are only some of the international data collection efforts that can be mined for purposes of CSD applications. Many more exist at national, regional and field-specific levels, though the data is typically not in a ready-made form and, therefore, requires some user input in terms of data modification and preparation. Fortunately, as Chapter 6 will demonstrate, the availability of even a minimal set of data and information makes CSD applications possible and useful, particularly when complemented with targeted surveys and focus group discussions. Nonetheless, in most countries additional and sustained efforts will be needed to collect and draw in information to fill in major data gaps.

Concepts of Civil Society: A Synopsis

Many different definitions of civil society exist and there is little agreement on its precise meaning, though much overlap exists among core conceptual components (see Keane, 1998; 2001; Kaldor, 2003). While civil society is a somewhat contested concept, definitions typically vary in the emphasis that they put on some characteristics of civil society over others. Some definitions primarily focus on aspects of state power, politics and individual freedom, and others more on economic functions and notions of social capital and cohesion. Nonetheless, most analysts would probably agree with the statement that civil society is the sum of institutions, organizations and individuals located between the family, the state and the market in which people associate voluntarily to advance common interests.

Civil society is primarily about the role of both the state and the market relative to that of citizens and the society they constitute. The intellectual history of the term is closely intertwined with the notion of citizenship, the limits of state power and the foundation, as well as the regulation, of market economies. The prevailing modern view sees civil society as a sphere located between state and market – a buffer zone strong enough to keep both state and market in check, thereby preventing each from becoming too powerful and dominating. In the words of Gellner, civil society is the set of 'institutions, which is strong enough to counterbalance the state and, whilst not preventing the state from fulfilling its role of keeper of peace and arbitrator between major interests, can, nevertheless, prevent the state from dominating and atomizing the rest of society' (Gellner, 1994, p5). Civil society is not a singular, monolithic, separate entity, but a sphere constituted in relation to both state and market, and permeating both.

Civil society is self-organization of society outside of the stricter realms of state power and market interests. For Habermas (1992, p443), 'civil society is made up of more or less spontaneously created associations, organizations and movements that find, take up, condense and amplify the resonance of social problems in private life, and pass it on to the political realm or public sphere' (own translation). Dahrendorf sees the concept of civil society as part of a classical liberal tradition, characterized by the existence of autonomous organizations that are neither state-run nor otherwise directed from the central political power (Dahrendorf, 1991, p262).

As a concept, civil society is essentially an intellectual product of 18th-century Europe, when citizens sought to define their place in society independently of the aristocratic state and when, simultaneously, the certainty of a status-based social order began to suffer irreversible decline. The early theorists of civil society welcomed these changes. For Adam Smith, trade and commerce among private citizens created not only wealth but also invisible connections among people: the bonds of trust and social capital in today's terminology. Others such as John Locke and Alexis de Tocqueville saw civil society less in relation to the market but more in political terms and emphasized the importance of democratic association in everyday life as a base of a functioning polity. Friedrich Hegel sounded a more cautionary note about the self-organizing and self-regulatory capacity of civil society, and emphasized the need of the state to regulate society. For Hegel, state and civil society depend upon each other; yet, their relation is full of tensions and requires a complicated balancing act. The role of the state relative to civil society was also emphasized in the writings of Montesquieu, von Stein and other thinkers, who saw the rule of law as the essence of state–society and society–market relations (see Cohen and Arato, 1997).

During the 20th century, civil society became associated with notions of civility (Elias, 1994), popular participation and civic mindedness (Verba et al, 1995), the public sphere (Habermas, 1992), social capital (Putnam, 2000; Coleman, 1990), culture (Gramsci, 1971) and community (Etzioni, 1971). The various concepts and approaches emphasize different aspects or elements of civil society: values and norms such as tolerance in the case of civility; the role of the media and the intellectual; connections among people and the trust they have in each other; the moral dimensions that communities create and need; and the extent to which people constitute a common public space through participation and civic engagement.

The complexity of civil society and the many relations and intersections it has with the economy, the state and institutions such as the family, the media or culture make it not only possible, but almost necessary to examine the concepts from different perspectives and orientations. Some analysts adopt an abstract, systemic view and see civil society as a macro-sociological attribute of societies, particularly in the way that state and society relate to each other. Others take on a more individualistic orientation and emphasize the notions of individual agency, citizenship, values and participation, using econometric and social network approaches in analysing civil society. There is also an institutional approach to studying civil society by looking at the size, scope and structure of organizations and associations, and the functions that they perform. Note that the different perspectives of civil society are not necessarily contradictory, nor are the various approaches to understanding it necessarily opposing. To the contrary, they are often complementary as they differ in emphasis, explanatory focus and policy implication rather than in principle.

Definition

The *definition of civil society* is a central part of the development of the CSD. Not surprisingly, a phenomenon as complex and multifaceted as civil society invites a variety of definitions and attempts to capture its 'conceptual essence' across time and space. Certainly, the concept of civil society will always be larger and more complex than any measurement of it; but this impossibility does not diminish the need for systematic measurement and assessment.

In the previous section we presented some background to the different conceptualizations of civil society. Even though the concept of civil society has become prominent in the social sciences, it remains somewhat unclear and even contested in terms of its actual meanings and uses. Ultimately, it may not be possible to develop a standard definition of civil society that would apply equally well to different settings. By contrast, an approach that views any *conceptual* definition as part and, indeed, the outcome of ongoing empirical efforts to understand civil society more fully appears as the more fruitful strategy. In this sense, any definition of civil society will evolve over time.

Nonetheless, a working definition that can serve as a platform for the methodological development and empirical applications of the CSD is needed. Therefore, we suggest the following formulation as the initial working or operational definition:

> Civil society is the sphere of institutions, organizations and individuals located between the family, the state and the market in which people associate voluntarily to advance common interests.

This is an operational definition of civil society for the purposes of the CSD; it does not attempt to define all aspects of civil society, nor does it necessarily fit different perspectives and approaches equally well. What the definition does, however, is list elements and components that most attempts to define civil society would identify as essential.

In methodological terms, definitions as such are neither true nor false, and their utility is judged by the extent to which they lead to new insights and improved understanding of such highly complex and diverse phenomena as civil society (see Box 2.1).

BOX 2.1 OPERATIONAL DEFINITIONS OF
COMPLEX PHENOMENA

Several examples may help to illustrate the difference between the complexity of a phenomenon and its operational definition:

- In medicine, a person's health status involves highly complex interactions among organs, fluids and chemical as well as neurological processes; yet, we take a series of simple tests (blood pressure, cardiovascular symptoms) as indicative of 'overall health'.
- In psychology, intelligence tests are used as empirical approximations to intelligence – a phenomenon that cannot be directly observed but needs an operational definition in the form of the IQ score to aproximate it.
- In economics, a set of 'leading economic indicators' is used to gauge the 'health' of the national economy; yet, as a system, the economy is more complex than what is captured by ten separate indicators, such as the index of consumer expectations, the index of stock prices or measures of money supply.
- In sociology, a person's social status is measured by combining indicators for educational attainment, household income and occupational prestige and projecting them into a common measurement metric ranging from 0 to 1000 (Duncan Socio-Economic Indicator), even though, conceptually, social class has other connotations that involve aspects of social and cultural capital, etc.

Thus, as with the examples presented in Box 2.1, the definition of CSD proposed here would represent essential conceptual aspects of civil society, but not claim to capture and measure civil society either as a totality or in all of its aspects. Specifically, the operational definition of civil society includes separate component parts: institutions, organizations and individuals.

Institutions

Institutions (for example, the rule of law) are structural patterns that address and regulate specific areas or tasks. For instance, an institution for political decision-making would be democracy, although there are different ways in which democratic decision-making can be organized, as is the case for parliamentary or presidential democracies. In the case of justice, the institution would be the legal system and the rule of law; in the case of social inclusion, a central institution would be citizenship; for reproduction, the family; and for information and communication needs, the media.

In each case, not all aspects of these institutions would be relevant for the CSD. For example, in the case of democracy, the entire electoral process and governance system of a country would not be important for CSD purposes. Instead, the CSD would focus on questions such as how civil society represents democratic values, how it influences or supports the democratic process, or the degree of internal democracy of civil society organizations. In the case of the legal system, not all laws, rules and regulations would come into play but only those bodies of law that address aspects of civil society (for example, association law, tax treatment, accountability requirements and government control of private organizations, etc).

Organizations

These comprise voluntary associations, non-governmental organizations, non-profit, foundations, charities, social movements, networks and informal groups that make up the infrastructure of civil society. They are the vehicles and forums for social participation, 'voice' processes, the expression of values and preferences, and service provision. Of particular interest are civil society organizations (CSOs), which are defined as self-organized groups characterized by:

- voluntary participation (which would exclude compulsory membership organizations);
- relative autonomy from family, market and state; and a
- capacity for collective action to advance common interests.

Civic action groups, networks, coalitions and other less formal organizations would also be included under this definition. Note that organizations do not have to be registered with the relevant authorities, or be formally established otherwise, in order to qualify as a civil society organization. Clearly, the degree of formality and informality in organizations varies across countries and

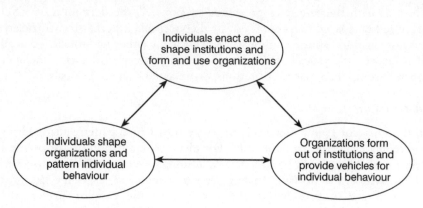

Figure 2.1 *Relations among Civil Society Elements*

cultures, and users of the CSD will have to establish guidelines on what can be regarded as a civil society organization and what is too close to family structures – in particular, the extended family system, as would be the case in many African countries.

Individuals

This category comprises citizens and participants in civil society, generally. This would include people's activities in civil society, such as membership, volunteering, organizing events or supporting specific causes; people's values, attitudes, preferences and expectations; and people's skills in terms of governance, management and leadership.

Institutions, organizations and individuals are analytic categories rather than empirically separate and unrelated entities. Institutions do not exist independently of social action; they need organizations and individuals to enact their rules, norms and expectations, thereby forming and maintaining institutions as regular structured patterns of society. Likewise, organizations do not act. It is the people who manage, work and participate in them that make organizations more than a legal form, structure or unit. Finally, people typically act within and through organizations, which, in turn, are shaped by a wider institutional context. Indeed, we are reminded by Perrow (2001) how little of modern life takes place outside of the organizational and institutional structures that they embody. Civil society, too, is largely organizational society. Figure 2.1 shows the relation between the three analytic elements that make up civil society, and Table 2.1 lists some of the major units or entities included and excluded from the approach taken here.

Thus, civil society includes multiple units, each with its own range of dimensions and characteristics. For each unit (institutions, organizations, individuals), we would be interested in their basic structural features, the values that the units represent, the activities they carry out, and the contributions they make. For example, an institution such as the media has institutional as well as organizational and individual characteristics attached to it (see Figure 2.2).

Table 2.1 *Types of Units Included and Excluded*

	Institutions	Organizations	Individuals
Included	• Freedom of expression, press, association, assembly, etc • Rule of law • Legislative process • Human rights • Democratic process • Philanthropy; charity • Accountability and transparency • Citizenship • Independent media	• Civil society organizations (CSOs) • Voluntary associations • Non-governmental organizations (NGOs) • Non-profit service providers • Foundations • Advocacy groups • Social movement organizations • Coalitions and networks among CSOs • Community groups • Self-help groups • Corporate responsibility programmes	• Activists • Volunteers • Members • Participants • Leaders • Managers • Employees • Users • Beneficiaries
Excluded	• Institutions not directly related to civil society (eg market exchange; political process and elections; family forms; etc)	• Government agencies and organizations • For-profit and commercial organizations • Organizations outside of the realm of civic rules and values	• Non members • Non participants etc • Individuals outside realm of civil rules and values

In each case, we look for specific characteristics. For example, in the case of the media (freedom of information) → organization (internet) → individual link (web users), the following characteristics would come into focus:

- number of users;
- frequency of use;
- number of sites visited by type;
- type of use (seeking information, sharing information, communicating, etc);
- social profile of users (age, gender, social and cultural background, occupation, etc);
- value profile of users;
- social participation profile of users; and
- political profile of users.

Of course, other aspects might be of importance as well, and the specific selection characteristics and the type of data needed are, ultimately, dictated by the question or problem that a particular CSD application addresses. More

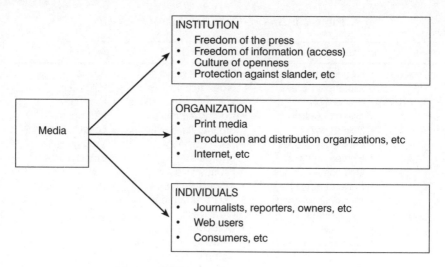

Figure 2.2 *Units Associated with the Media*

generally, as represented in Table 2.2a, the separate characteristics of
institutions, organizations and individuals have different measures and data
attached to them. Table 2.2b presents the same analytic approach for the
concept of philanthropy. In each case, the characteristics and measures
presented are examples only, and other empirical manifestations can certainly
be brought into the analysis.

What Table 2.2 illustrates is that civil society can be measured in various
ways and at different levels: as separate units, each with specific characteristics,
measures and data; or as a composite entity that combines individual
components. Moreover, as will become clear below, we can measure civil
society at local, regional, national and even international levels.

What Civil Society Is Not

Having put some effort into defining civil society and its component parts, it
is also useful to address what civil society is not – at least in the context of the
CSD – and the way in which it is understood for the purpose of measurement
and interpretation. Specifically, civil society:

- *Is not synonymous with the more general term of society.* A society includes
  economy, market, judiciary, family and other institutions, as well as civil
  society; in other words, civil society is part of the larger society.
- *Is not identical to the non-profit sector,* or other terms such as third, voluntary
  or NGO sectors, however defined. The third sector and civil society
  overlap in terms of organizations, and it would be fair to say that civil
  society includes large parts of the third sector, even though some non-
  profit organizations can be close to market firms or state agencies in
  constitution and behaviour.

Table 2.2a *Civil Society Elements, Characteristics, Measures and Data: Internet Example*

Elements	Sample Characteristics	Sample Measures	Sample Data
Institutions	Freedom of information	Extent to which freedom of information is granted by law	Scale of freedom of information
Organizations	Internet	Scale and scope of websites relating to civil society	Website traffic of civil society related sites
Individuals	Users	Use of web for civil society purposes	Number of users among members of civil society organizations

Table 2.2b *Civil Society Elements, Characteristics, Measures and Data: Philanthropy Example*

Elements	Sample Characteristics	Sample Measures	Sample Data
Institutions	Philanthropy	Extent to which philanthropy is an established cultural pattern	Index of philanthropic culture
Organizations	Philanthropic organizations	Scale and scope of foundations	Foundation assets per capita
Individuals	Philanthropic behaviour	Individual giving patterns	Giving per capita

- *Does not include the market and market firms*, even though some earlier theorists and neo-liberal thinkers see the market economy and its self-organizing and self-regulating capacity as an essential component of 'non-state' society. What is more, some institutions, such as the media, while essentially based on market organizations, nonetheless have significant civil society elements.
- *Does not include the state and public agencies* even though, through its judiciary and regulatory function, the state upholds the rule of law, social order and other essential components of society and civility. However, aspects of the legal system and specific laws that deal with civil society institutions and organizations can be included in the CSD. What is more, civil society organizations frequently work with government organizations, particularly in the field of service delivery, and examining such relationships and public–private partnership would fall within the realm of CSD applications.
- *Does not include the family.* Cross-cultural family forms vary significantly and tend to imply different demarcation lines between the private sphere of

the family, however defined, and the public sphere of the wider society. In either case, the family as an organizational unit (for example, households, extended family systems and dynasties) will be excluded from the CSD. However, in some parts of the world, such as Africa, establishing some kind of dividing line between familial and non-familial relations would require sound knowledge of local society and culture.

Of course, establishing 'rules' or 'principles' for including and excluding some element or another will involve 'grey areas' that require close scrutiny and qualitative judgement. Indeed, over time, users will have to establish guidelines on how to apply the operational definition in a specific context, and how to approach decisions on what elements and components to include or exclude (see Chapter 6).

Civil and Uncivil Civil Society

The operational definition of civil society proposed for the CSD does not establish any *a priori* and exclusionary emphasis on 'good' civil society. The definition also includes what could be regarded as 'uncivil' institutions (for example, encouraging disrespect of human rights), organizations (advocating violence) or individuals (nurturing ethnic or religious prejudice). This is so because the definition only specifies voluntary action and common purpose as constituting characteristics, but establishes neither the limit nor the intent of such purpose, nor does it privilege some over others. In this sense, the definition does not distinguish among causes and objectives, and does not pass judgement on them.

In many instances, the 'moral blindness' of the definition should be rather unproblematic; but in some instances, the differences between 'good' and 'bad' civil society could be of central importance. Users may decide to measure, contrast and compare 'civil' and 'uncivil' parts in an effort to gauge the overall health of civil society in terms of size, legitimacy, impact or some other dimension. In such cases, users of the CSD would have to establish some demarcation line to mark the inclusion or exclusion of such components from various 'camps'. Drawing such a line, however, is best done in the context of concrete situations rather than abstractly and *a priori*. In any case, it is important to keep in mind that the definition of civil society proposed here does not necessarily restrict CSD application to what is socially beneficial and positive. While much and perhaps most of civil society is private action for public benefit, not all of it is. Similarly, the CSD does not establish some form of presupposed consensus about civil society, or a 'harmony condition' about what civil society does, what it represents and what it achieves.

Unit of Analysis and Unit of Observation

We emphasized above that civil society can be examined from different perspectives and with different orientations in mind. The operational definition, too, allows for the measurement and interpretation of a range of components, focusing either on institutions, organizations or the characteristics of individuals. To help identify the level at which we approach civil society, we refer to the term unit of analysis. The *unit of analysis* is that entity whose characteristics are of central importance for observation and interpretation. In other words, it is the unit whose characteristics we want to analyse. Specifically, for the purpose of the CSD, there are three major units of analysis:

1 **Macro level.** At this level, the CSD is applied to countries, societies or regions. The perspective taken is that of civil society and its characteristics in the context of the larger society, perhaps even including the relationship between civil society, the economy and the state. For example, we would analyse French civil society in the context of France as a country, or Scottish civil society, as part of the UK, as a political unit. At the macro level, data is typically in aggregate form and report averages – for example, the average number of volunteer hours per capita – or share data, such as the percentage of adults holding membership in civil society organizations.

2 **Meso level.** At this level, the unit of analysis is no longer civil society but a particular segment or sub-field, such as human rights or community development. Typically, the CSD would deal with institutions, organizations and individuals of special relevance to the field of interest. For example, in the human rights area, the CSD would bring in information on the extent to which human rights legislation has been implemented in a country or region; how many human rights organizations there are; what resources they command; the degree to which they have been able to influence human rights policies; and how deeply ingrained respect for human rights is within the population or among members of particular groups that might be of interest. At the meso or field level, data typically comprises aggregates; but unlike the macro-case, they pertain to the area under investigation, and not to civil society as a whole.

3 **Micro level.** Finally, at the micro level, the CSD primarily applies to one organization or one specific setting. Here, for example, we would focus on one environmental organization and compare it with other environmental organizations in the context of the larger civil society and the parameters of local and regional environmental policies. Data of interest relates to the size and revenue structure of the organization; the profile of staff and volunteers; issues of governance, management and leadership; and measures of efficiency and effectiveness. At the micro level, the focus could be on a particular scenario, project or case – for example, in development planning, humanitarian assistance or human

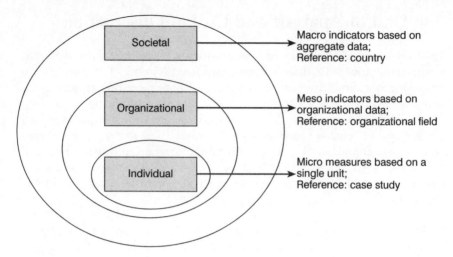

Figure 2.3 *Units of Analysis and Indicators*

rights campaigns. In either case, the data is most likely at the individual level – it reports on the relevant characteristics of a particular case.

Why is the distinction between units of analysis important? There are two basic reasons: to safeguard against fallacies of over-interpretation and misattribution, and to help identify the right set of indicators.

First, to avoid methodological fallacies and the misinterpretations that come with them, it is important to clearly specify the unit of analysis of any CSD application. The distinction is important for basic methodological reasons in the sense that characteristics of aggregates cannot be attributed to their component parts. For example, because a country has a democratic constitution and democratic political institutions, we cannot say that its civil society organizations are necessarily as democratic as the political system of which they are part. Vice versa, because particular civil society organizations happen to be democratic, it does not follow that they operate in a democratic society. Moreover, because a country has a pronounced presence of voluntary organizations in the field of human rights or some other area does not mean that it has a well-developed civil society overall.

The distinction between different units of analysis is also important because each level draws in different types of indicators (see Tables 2.4 and 2.5). Some indicators refer to the macro level – for example, the Human Development Index (HDI) (UNDP, 2000); others are aggregate measures of organizations – for example, the combined economic size of civil society organizations. Still others are individual-level characteristics – for example, value dispositions and attitudinal aspects, such as tolerance or religiosity held among members of a given population. Significantly, within one CSD application, all indicators must be at the same level or 'unit' of measurement. This is indicated in Figure 2.3, which shows the three units of analysis and the relationship among indicators.

In some cases, the unit of analysis may involve separate *units of observation* (the origin of actual data or information). For example, in order to measure the decision-making culture of civil society organizations in terms of accountability and openness, data can come form a variety of sources, such as documents and records of board meetings, the executive leadership, individual members, volunteers or employees. In this case, the organization – or micro level – is the unit of analysis. The documents, records and the opinions and assessments of the board, the management, members, volunteers and employees represent units of observation. Together, they provide information about the characteristics of interest for a given unit of analysis.

Approach

Grounding the CSD

Defining society as 'the sphere of institutions, organizations and individuals located between the family, the state and the market, in which people associate voluntarily to advance common interests' has important consequences for measurement for two reasons. First, the 'sphere' of civil society is an analytic category and does not typically exist as a separate, identifiable element like a physical infrastructure or geographic feature. While there might be pure expressions of civil activism and engagement, civil society, like the market or the state, is usually intermingled with other aspects of human and organizational behaviour.

Second, understanding civil society as a sphere is different from a concept of civil society as a sector. While terms such as non-profit, voluntary or third sector have become increasingly acceptable among social scientists and policy-makers, civil society does not constitute a separate sector. The non-profit sector reaches into civil society and is, largely, part of it; but as a sphere, civil society extends beyond it and transcends the notion of 'sectors' in important ways. In other words, civil society is grounded in different components of economy, polity and society, and does not exist in isolation.

What are the 'moorings' or 'grounding' of civil society? Most current writers on civil society would probably agree that civil society is closely linked to a democratic *polity* based on the rule of law and a corresponding *value system* that encourages civic virtue and social participation; the development of a *mixed economy* of market firms, non-profits and government providing goods and services; and social networks and *associations* that are outside family structures and relatively independent of state power (see Keane, 1998; 2001; Dahrendorf, 1995; Gellner, 1994). Civil society exists within and between these other components and sectors of society. In abstract terms, civil society is grounded in a society's polity, economy, laws and values, while at the same time providing the connecting tissue among them.

The fact that civil society is grounded or embedded in polity, economy, legal systems and values means that, as an analytic concept, civil society can be measured and analysed across four different dimensions:

1 **structural**, in terms of size, composition and sources of support of the civil society unit under consideration;
2 **legal and political space**, in terms of the regulatory environment in which civil society operates;
3 **impact-related** or functional, in terms of the contributions of civil society, generally, or in particular fields; and
4 **value-related**, in terms of norms and cultural elements.

In more simple terms, at the macro level, the four dimensions describe:

• How large in scale and scope is civil society in economic, social and organizational terms (**structure**)?
• What legal and political 'space' does civil society have within the regulatory 'environment' of the country or region in which it operates (**space**)?
• What are the values, norms and cultural expectations that civil society represents and advocates (**values**)?
• What are the contributions of civil society in terms of voice, policy-making, service provision or equity (**impact**)?

As Table 2.3 shows, the four dimensions have central references to economy, polity, culture and society at large. For example, the structural dimension refers to aspects of civil society relative to the basic institutional infrastructure of society. The space dimension relates to the legal and regulatory system and the rule of law, including the democratic process, freedom of association and the ease of registration, but also to the relevant tax laws, governance issues and accountability requirements. The values dimension addresses the value dispositions, norms and attitudes that underlie civil society. Finally, the impact dimension deals with issues of relative contributions in terms of equity, effectiveness and efficiency, but also, more generally, to questions of achievement and improvements.

Depending upon the unit of analysis, the concrete content of each field will be different, and will also assume different levels of measurement when applied to either the field (or meso) level and to single-case (or micro-level) scenarios.

A Note on Causality

The grounding of the CSD in the four analytic dimensions presented in Table 2.3 does not specify any causal relations among them. While an examination of any causal relationships that might be present would be useful for theoretical and policy purposes alike, the present state of knowledge and the availability of data effectively preclude such analysis. Nonetheless, there is an implicit causality in the sense that the dimensions of structure, space and values have an influence on the impact dimension. Any strict test, however, would require statistical procedures that are beyond the interpretative approach introduced here. Therefore, users are advised to frame causal statements with great caution.

Table 2.3 *Grounding the Civil Society Diamond at the Macro Level*

Structure	Values
Key questions: what is the scale of civil society in terms of institutions, organizations, networks and individuals; what are its component parts; and what resources does it command?	Key questions: what values underlie civil society; what values, norms and attitudes does it represent and propagate; how inclusive and exclusive are they; and what areas of consensus and dissent emerge?
Central reference: infrastructure	Central reference: value system
Legal/Political Space	*Impact*
Key questions: what is the legal and political space within the larger regulatory environment in which civil society operates; and what laws and policies enable or inhibit its development?	Key questions: what is the contribution of civil society to specific social, economic and political problems?
Central reference: governance	Central reference: development

Going Beyond One Dimension

With structure, space, values and impact as the key dimensions with which to measure civil society, different indictors can be used to describe each in more detail. While the range of indicators for each dimension will be introduced in Table 2.5, it is important to emphasize that, generally, several indicators are feasible within each dimension and across different units of analysis. The following example may illustrate this basic and significant feature of the CSD.

For the structure dimension there are various size or scale indicators (for example, paid and unpaid work per 1000 employed; membership in civil society organizations) and revenue/resource indicators (for example, share of philanthropic giving of CSO revenue). Similarly, the space dimension could be represented by a measure of the extent to which the fiscal and regulatory environment encourages the development of civil society (the 'degree of enablement'), or by a measure of the level of accountability required of, and met by, civil society organizations. The impact dimension could include an efficiency indicator (for example, how civil society organizations are able to deal with specific tasks, such as allocation, production and distribution – an economic measure – or policy issues, as would be the case in lobbying efforts around some piece of legislation), an effectiveness indicator (for example, how they solve perceived problems), or some general developmental and equity indicators. Finally, for the values dimension, one indicator could measure democratic inclusion or respect for human rights; but others are also possible, such as the level of overall tolerance within society as a whole or for particular segments of the population.

Clearly, the complexity of civil society invites (perhaps even necessitates) multiple indicators, each emphasizing some aspect or another. Yet, none, it would seem, is able to capture the essence of civil society. Measuring the size of civil society with the help of paid employment, for example, does not offer any indication of the extent to which people participate as volunteers or members. Each indicator, while undoubtedly relevant and important, turns out to be deficient in other aspects, leaving out other information that seems equally important. Yet, when indicators are put next to each other, their joint descriptive power increases. Looking at paid employment, volunteering and memberships in civil society organizations jointly adds information. When considering their relative scale, this introduces the possibility of quantitative and qualitative comparisons.

How, then, can we preserve the multidimensionality of civil society *and* achieve a user-friendly indicator system at the same time? One approach would be to develop a composite indicator that combines the various component parts into one single index. For example, using a statistical formula to establish a common metric, the United Nations Development Programme's (UNDP's) Human Development Index combines three indicators: longevity, educational attainment and standard of living. While the single index approach has many advantages (it is easily communicated and understood), it can also be reductionist and 'paint over' important detail. For example, not all facets of civil society may develop in the same direction: economic growth may come at the expense of social and political functions. A composite index would be unlikely to capture such countervailing trends, even though they may be vital for the future of civil society.

The opposite approach would be to list as many indicators as are available or required. While this would, at least in principle, provide a more comprehensive portrait of civil society, it would come at a price: how would we know what indicators are more important than others, and how could we interpret the data and the connections among them? For the sake of wanting to be comprehensive, we could easily end up adding layers upon layers of increased complexity, which would ultimately lead to an unworkable measurement system. In other words, what is needed is a more systematic approach that preserves the multidimensionality of civil society in a parsimonious way. As the quality and availability of data improve, the use of multiple indicator models and other factor-analytic approaches becomes more feasible.

Indeed, the idea of preserving the multidimensionality of civil society in a relatively simple measurement system is at the core of the CSD. The basic approach is to map and measure different facets of civil society along the four major dimensions or 'groundings' mentioned above: structure, space, impact and values. Within each dimension, a range of single and multiple indicators offers choice and a variety of options for users. Across the four dimensions, users can examine the different 'positions' of civil society relative to each other. Therefore, the CSD includes four sets of indicators: structural, legal–political, impact-related and value-related indicators.

Indicators and Standards

Having a menu of options gives civil society representatives, researchers and policy-makers the choice to select the indicators and dimensions that they regard as most useful for their specific purpose. The selection process is part of the structured dialogue that the CSD wants to encourage. Moreover, users can select indicators that fit the context of their culture, country or region. This does not imply, however, that the choice of indicators and measures should be arbitrary and left to the convenience of users alone. Some indicators are better than others and are, therefore, more useful for describing and assessing civil society. Useful indicators are those that show certain qualities: they measure a central rather than peripheral aspect of civil society; they are well established in their measurement properties in terms of validity and reliability; they lend themselves to comparisons (cross-cultural, cross-national, across fields, over time); and they enjoy good data availability. By contrast, other indicators are less established and accepted, more context specific and may have significant problems in terms of data coverage and quality.

The selection and use of indicators that are available internationally allow for comparative analysis across countries and regions. Indeed, some of the benefits of the CSD arise from comparisons across both fields and countries, as well as over time, and a wealth of available indicators can be used for such purposes (see Chapters 5 and 6). By contrast, other indicators may have meaning only in some regions or countries and are generally somewhat culture-bound. In other cases, indicators have high data requirements and may, therefore, be available in only a few countries. How, then, can we reconcile the need for comparative data with the need for user choice and cultural sensitivity? In other words, short of establishing some set of universal standards, how can we achieve comparability of CSD applications in terms of quality and purpose?

Types of Indicators

The approach taken in answering these questions is to distinguish between different types or classes of indicators. Considerations of data quality and data availability next to the needs of those who use the CSD guide the classification, as well as the actual selection of indicators. Specifically, the CSD differentiates between preferred, standard, optional and other indicators (see Tables 2.4 and 2.5) to strike a balance in indicator selection between the rigidity of universal criteria, on the one hand, and the seeming arbitrariness of national or local preferences, on the other.

Preferred indicators are those known for their comparability across countries and fields, with the understanding that any country or field comparisons should include some or all of the measures in the set of indicators selected.

Standard indicators have been proven useful and are used by, and available for, many countries and organizational fields. At the same time, these indicators may not have the degree of potential universality as the preferred indicators above, and may involve higher data requirements.

Optional indicators include field- and region-specific indicators that apply primarily in a particular context – for example, indicators for developed countries or transition countries, or country-specific indicators that may be relevant to one country only. This would also apply to organization-specific indicators of individual groups or organizations.

Other indicators cover specific indicators that users may chose to apply in given circumstances and applications, either as stand-alone measures or in combination with other measures (see Appendix C for other indicators and data sources).

Referring back to the discussion about units of analysis, it becomes clear that the CSD methodology includes an 'indicator menu'. Which indicators become relevant for the purposes of a particular application depends upon the unit of analysis (individual/micro; organizational/meso; society/macro), the dimensions (structure, space, impact, values) and the type of indicator (for example, preferred, standard or optional) involved. This menu is presented in Table 2.4. As can be seen, the various menu options comprise the essential decisions that users will have to make before any actual analysis (see Chapter

Table 2.4 *Indicator Menu for CSD Applications*

Dimension	UNIT OF ANALYSIS		
	Individual case/ or micro level	Organizational field/ Meso level	Society/ Macro level
Structure	Preferred Standard Optional Other	Preferred Standard Optional Other	Preferred Standard Optional Other
Space	Preferred Standard Optional Other	Preferred Standard Optional Other	Preferred Standard Optional Other
Value	Preferred Standard Optional Other	Preferred Standard Optional Other	Preferred Standard Optional Other
Impact	Preferred Standard Optional Other	Preferred Standard Optional Other	Preferred Standard Optional Other

5 for a more detailed discussion on how to select indicators). It is important to keep in mind that once a unit of analysis has been selected, only indicators from the same column are to be chosen throughout. In other words, as shown in Table 2.4, indicator selection moves down the columns, not across rows.

Setting Standards

What applies to the selection of indicators and measures also applies to the setting of standards. Civil society representatives, policy-makers and CSD users, generally, should be able to set their own standards and measure their progress in relation to such standards rather than against some rule imposed from outside. For example, for the structure dimension, policy-makers may decide to increase levels of volunteering in society among the adult population from 30 per cent to 40 per cent over three years. Repeated measures would then show to what degree this particular country or region achieved the objective that policy-makers initially set out. Moreover, the CSD would reveal how increases or decreases in volunteering relate to other changes in civil society by providing the values, space and impact dimensions as context.

Table 2.5 presents the key dimensions for the three units of analysis, in each case offering a choice of indicators. For each dimension and unit of analysis, Table 2.5 includes two to four preferred indicators, several standard indicators and a number of optional ones. This means that for each unit of analysis, 6 to 10 preferred, up to 12 standard and a larger number of optional indicators and variations are available for analysis. In total, the current CSD repertoire summarized in Table 2.5 includes some 50 indicators, with more included in Appendix A. Undoubtedly, over time, this repertoire of available indicators will grow as users gain experience with existing and new indicators. The country case studies in Chapter 6 also offer discussions of indicator selection.

Conclusion

Having introduced the basics in terms of assumptions, definitions, dimensions and indicators, we can now explore the CSD and methodological aspects in more detail. In particular, we are interested in how indicators can be combined within and across the four dimensions, and how the CSD can be used for comparative purposes, as well as for other uses. This is the task to which we now turn in Chapter 3.

Table 2.5 *Central List of CSD Indicators*

Structure: size	Macro	Meso	Micro
Preferred	**Paid employment in CSOs per 1000 employed** Volunteering in CSOs as a percentage of total adult population Membership in CSOs	**Paid employment in CSOs per 1000 employed in the field** Volunteering in CSOs in the field as a percentage of total adult population Membership in CSOs in the field	**Paid employment in CSO relative to average size of CSO in the field** Volunteering in CSOs relative to average size of CSO volunteer force in the field Membership held in CSO relative to average CSO membership size in the field
Standard	*Macro* CSOs' operating expenditures as a percentage of GDP Participation in CSOs	*Meso* CSOs' operating expenditures relative to GDP in the field Participation in CSOs in the field	*Micro* CSO operating expenditures relative to average size of CSO in the field Participation in CSOs in area of operation
Optional	*Macro* Number of CSO establishments per 100,000 population Rate of CSO establishments per year Foundation density	*Meso* Number of CSO establishments in the field per 100,000 population Rate of CSO establishments in the field per year Foundation density in the field	*Micro* Number of memberships in CSO establishments relative to potential membership Economic size of CSO relative to average for-profit firm in the field

Structure: composition			
Preferred	**(Paid) employment in advocacy CSOs relative to employment in service-providing CSOs** Volunteering in advocacy CSOs relative to volunteering in service-providing CSOs	**(Paid) employment ratio of advocacy CSOs/service-providing CSOs relative to for-profit and public-sector employment ratios in the field** Volunteering ratio of advocacy CSOs/service-providing CSOs relative to ratio of paid employment in advocacy CSOs/service-providing CSOs field	**Ratio of (paid) employment in advocacy/service-providing activities in CSO (relative to ratio for field)** Volunteering ratio of advocacy/service-providing activities in CSO relative to ratio of paid employment in advocacy/service-providing activities in CSO

	Macro	*Meso*	*Micro*
Standard	Memberships in advocacy CSOs relative to memberships in service-providing CSOs Expenditures in advocacy CSOs relative to expenditure in service-providing CSOs	Memberships in the field in advocacy CSOs relative to membership in service-providing CSOs Expenditure in the field in advocacy CSOs relative to expenditure in service-providing CSOs	Share of members who volunteer for advocacy versus service delivery activities CSO expenditure in advocacy relative to expenditure in service-providing activities
Optional	Density of CSO umbrella organizations (number per 1000 CSOs)	Density of CSO umbrella organizations in the field (number per 1000 CSOs)	CSO memberships held in umbrella organizations
Structure: revenue			
Preferred	**Index of Philanthropic Giving (time, money, in kind)** Value of volunteer input Indicators of resource dependency: • marketization • public-sector dependency	**Index of Philanthropic Giving (time, money, in kind) in the field** Value of volunteer input in the field Indicators of resource dependency in the field: • marketization • public-sector dependency	**Index of Philanthropic Giving (time, money, in kind) for CSO** Value of volunteer input in CSO Indicators of resource dependency for CSO: • marketization • public-sector dependency
Standard	Individual giving as a percentage of personal income Corporate giving as a percentage of corporate profits Individual CSO donations per capita Volunteer hours in CSOs per capita	Individual giving in the field as a percentage of personal income Corporate giving in the field as a percentage of corporate profits Number of givers to CSOs in the field per capita Number of volunteers in CSOs in the field per capita	Individual giving as a percentage of revenue Corporate giving as a percentage of revenue Number of givers to CSOs relative to members/employees Number of volunteers in CSOs relative to members/employees
Optional	Foundation giving as share of total CSO revenue	Foundation giving as share of total CSO revenue in the field	Foundation giving as share of total CSO revenue

Table 2.5 *continued*

	Macro	Meso	Micro
Values	Corporate giving as share of total CSO revenue Corporate social responsibility programmes as share of corporate profits	Corporate giving as share of total CSO revenue in the field Share of CSO in the field reached by corporate social responsibility programmes	Corporate giving as share of total CSO revenue Government grants as share of CSO revenue
Preferred	**Trust in people by CSO members relative to adult population** Tolerance levels among CSO members relative to adult population Increase in number of CSOs with explicit code of conduct/ethics over previous year	**Trust in people by CSO members in the field relative to adult population** Tolerance levels among CSO members in the field relative to adult population Share of CSOs in the field with explicit code of conduct/ethics	**Trust in people by CSO members relative to adult population** Tolerance levels among CSO members relative to adult population Share of members aware of code of conduct/ethics
Standard	*Macro* Expected corruption/corrupt behaviour among CSO members relative to population levels Confidence in selected institutions among CSO members relative to population levels	*Meso* Expected corruption/corrupt behaviour among CSO members in the field relative to population levels Confidence in selected institutions among CSO members in the field relative to population levels	*Micro* Expected corruption/corrupt behaviour among CSO members relative to population levels Confidence in selected institutions among CSO members relative to population levels
Optional	*Macro* Membership in human rights organizations among CSO members relative to population levels Post-material versus material value dispositions among CSO members relative to population levels Other measures of tolerance, trust and confidence	*Meso* Membership in human rights organizations among CSO members in the field relative to population levels Post-material versus material value dispositions among CSO members or representatives in the field relative to population levels Other measures of tolerance, trust and confidence	*Micro* Membership in human rights organizations among CSO members relative to population levels Post-material versus material value dispositions among CSO members relative to population levels Other measures of tolerance, trust and confidence

Space

	Measure of the degree of enablement of the overall fiscal and regulatory environment in civil society (focus: law):	Measure of the degree of enablement of the overall fiscal and regulatory environment for CSOs in the field (focus: law):	Measure of the degree of enablement of the overall fiscal and regulatory environment for CSO/within CSO:
Preferred	• Johns Hopkins University (JHU) Non-Profit Law Index • USAID Legal Environment Indicator Corruption Perceptions Index (Transparency International)	• JHU Non-Profit Law Index • USAID Legal Environment Indicator Corruption Perceptions Index (Transparency International) as applied or ranked by CSO representatives in the field	• JHU Non-Profit Law Index • USAID Legal Environment Indicator Corruption Perceptions Index (Transparency International) as applied or ranked by representatives of CSO
Standard	*Macro* Tax incentives Freedom of association Civil liberties (Freedom House) Political Freedom Index (PFI) or a variation	*Meso* Tax incentives in the field Freedom of association in the field Civil liberties (Freedom House) as applied or ranked by CSO representatives in the field Extent to which representatives rank democratic forms of representation in the field	*Micro* Tax incentives as applied to case Freedom of association as applied to case Civil liberties (Freedom House) as applied or ranked by representatives of CSO Extent of democratic measures of decision-making in CSO
Optional	*Macro* Freedom of association (qualitative review) by national CSO representatives CSO formation CSO financing CSO fundraising sources permitted under the law Governance (World Bank) Other related measures	*Meso* Freedom of association (qualitative review) CSO representative in the field CSO formation in the field CSO financing in the field CSO fundraising sources permitted under the law in the field – Other related measures	*Micro* Freedom of association (qualitative review) by members of CSO CSO formation CSO financing CSO fundraising sources permitted under the law – Other related measures

Table **2.5** *continued*

Impact

Preferred	**Fulfilled CSO commitment index as ranked by national representatives of CSOs (eg stakeholder survey)** USAID NGO Sustainability Index Media coverage of CSOs in given period as share of total coverage	**Fulfilled CSO commitment index as ranked by representatives of CSOs in the field (eg stakeholder survey)** Perceived impact survey by representatives in the field Media coverage of CSO in field-specific trade press/media (mobilization measure) in given period	**Fulfilled CSO commitment index as ranked by representatives of CSO (eg stakeholder survey)** Perceived impact survey by representatives or members in CSO Media coverage in given period/event
Standard	*Macro* Change in HDI over previous period Change in Gini coefficient over previous period Perceived impact survey by national representatives	*Meso* CSOs' share of total output in the field USAID NGO Sustainability Index as applied to the field Relative efficiency of CSOs in the field as applicable	*Micro* CSO share of total output in relevant field Specific activity measures as applicable to CSO or case Efficiency measures as applicable to CSO or case
Optional	*Macro* Overall levels of subjective well-being in society Other capacity and output measures	*Meso* Overall levels of subjective well-being for members of CSOs in the field Other capacity and output measures	*Micro* Overall levels of subjective well-being among CSO members Other capacity and output measures

Chapter 3

The Civil Society Diamond:
An Unfolding System

*What is to be sought in designs for the display of information
is the clear portrayal of complexity. Not the complication
of the simple; rather, the task of the designer is
to give visual access to the subtle
and the difficult – that is, the
revelation of the complex.*

E R Tufte (1999)

The Civil Society Diamond (CSD) brings together information about different dimensions of civil society to facilitate a structured dialogue among civil society representatives, policy-makers and researchers.[1] Or, in the terminology introduced in Chapter 2, the CSD combines indicators or sets of indicators for each of the civil society dimensions (structure, space, impact and values). The CSD does not achieve this by collapsing the various indicators into one single measure, number or score. Instead, the CSD combines indicators by projecting them in a common 'property space' in mathematical terms. In more common parlance, the CSD is primarily a visual display of different dimensions and their respective values in a common space, using the same or comparable metrics.

The type of visual representation that the CSD uses is the coordination system, a widely employed method to display the relation between different indicators. In a coordination system, 'axes' represent the different dimensions, with their respective values indicated by measurement points. The axes originate from a joint zero point, are typically bounded, and their values increase in equal steps with growing distance from the zero point. In many instances (though not necessarily), the shape of the combined property space or graph will resemble a rhombus or diamond form, hence the name Civil Society Diamond. This is displayed in a somewhat stylized form in figure 3.1a, which also introduces some of the basic terms used to refer to coordinate systems.

The simplified graph in Figure 3.1b shows that the 'property space' of the coordinate system preserves the various dimensions and indicators, while at the same time contextualizing them in the diamond structure. In other words,

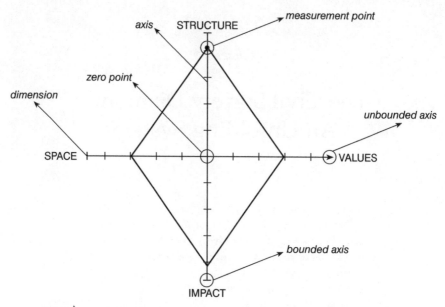

Figure 3.1a *Simple Representation of the Civil Society Diamond (CSD)*

the CSD presents information about the structural characteristics of civil society next to data about the values dimension, the legal–regulatory space in which civil society operates, and the impact that civil society has. The presentation of indicators in each dimension within the same property space or measurement system reveals important information and allows for a richer interpretation than any single number approach could achieve.

As suggested in the discussion of units of analysis in Chapter 2, similar graphs can be generated to show the location of civil society in terms of the four dimensions at the national, regional, local and even international level, given adequate data availability. In any case, the measures for the indicators of the structure, space, impact and values dimensions must all be in the same, or comparable, metric: they must use the same or very similar system and units of measurement. In most cases, this can be achieved by transforming raw data into percentages or some other measurement of relative share or proportionality.

Thus, instead of reporting the number of volunteers (the 'raw data'), users would relate this number to the total adult population, or express it in relation to paid employment in civil society organizations. Unless data is in comparable metrics, the quality and interpretative use of the CSD will be very limited. In this context, it is important to refer back the indicators listed in Table 2.5 of Chapter 2 and the indicator bank or repertoire presented in more detail in Appendix A. These indicators are typically defined and constructed as the same, or of similar, metrics – usually as a percentage or share measure.

Figure 3.1b uses hypothetical data to illustrate the CSD. The structure dimension is represented by the indicator 'membership in civil society

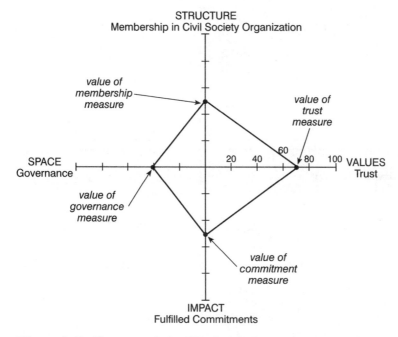

Figure 3.1b *Illustration of the CSD (1 indicator per dimension – 'line' version)*

organizations' and is measured as a percentage of total employment in the economy. The values dimension uses the indicator 'trust', measured as the percentage of civil society organization (CSO) members who report high levels of generalized trust in other members of society. The indicator for space uses a ranking system for the degree to which the legal environment enables the sound governance of CSOs. This ranking system has been projected into a measurement range of 0 to 100, bringing it to the same metric as the percentage measures for the structure and values indicators. A similar approach is taken for the impact indicator. It is based on a (hypothetical) expert assessment of the extent to which civil society representatives have been able to implement agreed-upon policy changes. This fulfilled commitment ranking, used in international relations and policy analysis, is then transformed into a measurement space ranging from 0 to 100.

In a next step, the *values* for each dimension are plotted along the respective axes (marked '•') and are visually combined to yield the diamond-like shape displayed in Figure 3.1b. A cursory interpretation of Figure 3.1b would, first of all, suggest a country with a medium-sized civil society in terms of membership and relatively high levels of trust. It would also show a legal environment that does not rank very high in terms of 'governance', and a medium level of achieved commitments on behalf of civil society leaders in meeting set policy targets.

Of course, the data and the meaning of selected indicators in Figure 3.1b are hypothetical; but some of the wider implications of the CSD are apparent.

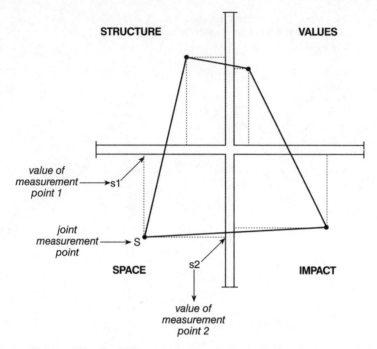

Figure 3.2a *Simple Representation of the CSD (2 indicators per dimension –*
'plane' version)

For example, it would be possible to project the average values of other comparable countries onto the CSD property space, which would enhance the base of CSD interpretations. Moreover, the various 'diamonds' generated can be set against each other – for example, regional shapes can be compared to the national configuration to identify differences and commonalities within a given country. However, the different uses and applications of the CSD do not end here, as the rest of this chapter will show.

Combining, Displaying and Interpreting Indicators

The CSD methodology is based upon the notion of an 'unfolding system.' Clearly, the diamond analysis in Figure 3.1b can be carried out with more than one indicator for each of the four dimensions. For example, one can focus on the structure dimension and examine how various size measures and revenue indicators relate to each other. In fact, users can determine the level of complexity and detail according to their purpose, provided that data is available to carry out the analysis. For example, because many important policies focus upon the question of resources, users may decide to examine the relationship between different revenue patterns and the scale of civil society organizations in different fields. In any case, by making it possible to

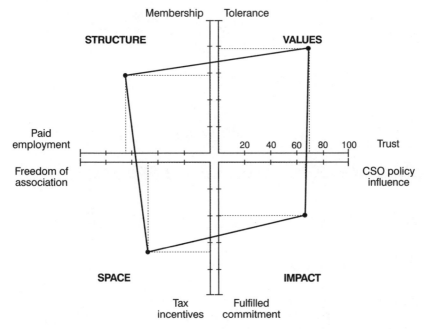

Figure 3.2b *Illustration of the CSD (2 indicators per dimension – 'plane' version)*

'unpack' civil society along various dimensions and, indeed, by inviting us to do so, the diamond becomes a fertile tool for assessing the health and trends of civil society at different levels of detail.

Figure 3.2a presents an example of a CSD with two indicators per dimension. Once we move beyond one indicator, each dimension has two measurement points (or more, as is demonstrated below). These measurements are shown both separately (for example, **s1** and **s2** in the space quadrant of Figure 3.2a), as well as jointly (point **S**, where the vectors of the two indicators intersect). The joint measurement points in each quadrant would be combined to yield a somewhat more complex 'shape' for the CSD. No longer a simple diamond, the 'push and pull' behind multiple measurements within each dimension reveals relationships among separate indicators and allows for a richer interpretation when compared to single indicator models.

An application of a CSD with two indicators per dimension is shown in Figure 3.2b. For the structure dimension, paid employment and membership in CSOs are the two indicators selected; scoring systems for freedom of association and tax incentives make up the indicators for the space dimension; CSO policy influence and a fulfilled policy commitment index provide the indicators for the impact dimension; and for the values dimension, the indicators are levels of trust and tolerance among CSO members. As before, the same graph can be generated at the national, regional, local and even international level, given adequate data availability. Similarly, the various

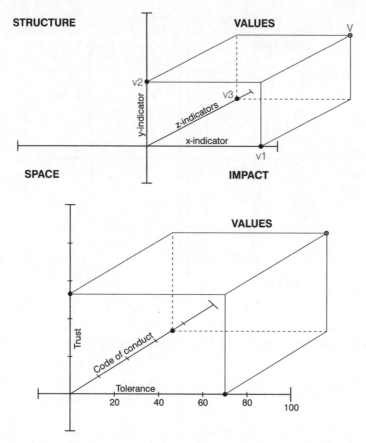

Figure 3.3a–b *Simple Representation (a) and Illustration (b) of the CSD (3 indicators per dimension – 'cube' version)*

'diamonds' can be compared with each other, even though the interpretation may be more complex as specific dimensions may pull in different directions. Note that indicators other than the ones selected above are also possible, and users can mine a rich repertoire of social and economic indicator models for this purpose (see Appendix A).

Yet, the CSD is not limited to two indicators per dimension. Indeed, the notion of the CSD as an unfolding system is further illustrated in Figures 3.3a and 3.3b. Figure 3.3a shows the three-indicator model for the values dimension only, indicating the resulting cube structure. In other words, whereas one indicator per dimension yields a line (see Figure 3.1b), and two indicators per dimension yield a plane (see Figure 3.2b), three indicators result in a cube or box-like structure. Figure 3.3b illustrates a three-indicator model using three hypothetical measures. The indicator 'trust in civil society' is measured along the Y-axis; the indicator 'level of political tolerance' is measured along the X-axis; and 'the share of civil society organizations with a code of conduct' indicator is measured along the Z-axis. This yields three

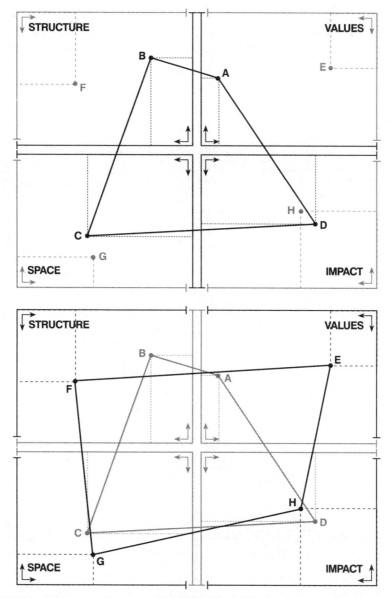

Figures 3.4a–b *Simple Representation of the CSD (4 indicators per dimension – 'two-plane' version)*

measurements (**v1, v2** and **v3**) that jointly produce the cube structure and the combined measurement point **V** shown in Figure 3.3a.

Figures 3.4a–3.4c add one additional indicator per dimension. Because of the increased complexity of working with four indicators, one can present the graphical representation in various ways, two of which are presented below. One option is presented in Figure 3.4a, which plots four values for each

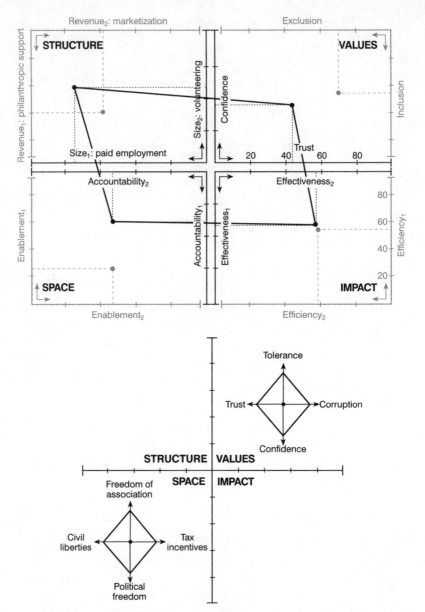

Figure 3.4c–d *Illustrations of the CSD (4 indicators per dimension –*
'two-plane' and 'diamond-in-diamond' version)

dimension but connects only four of the eight measurement points
(A–B–C–D) for producing the overall diamond shape. This leaves the other
four measurement points (E–F–G–H) in the 'background' as additional
information that might be usefully brought in when interpreting the CSD.
Appropriately, the background indicators are printed in grey to illustrate the

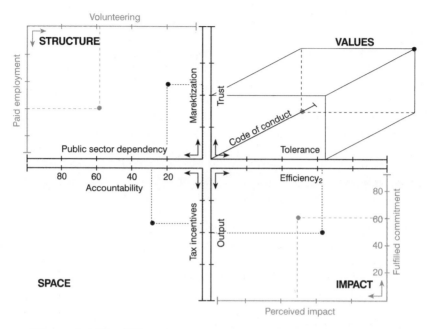

Figure 3.5 *The CSD with Varying Number of Indicators per Dimension*

contrast. Of course, users could highlight the E–F–G–H combination instead, as shown in Figure 3.4b, holding measurement points A–B–C–D as additional background information.

A four-indicator model is useful in situations when two distinct sets of characteristics (sub-dimensions) are placed in contrast to each other. An illustration is presented in Figure 3.4c. For the structure dimension, one set of indicators measures characteristics of the sub-dimension 'size': paid employment in civil society organizations and volunteering. The other indicator set reports on two aspects of the sub-dimension 'revenue by sources' (an indicator for philanthropic support and an indicator measuring the share of fee income as a percentage of total revenue).

An alternative way of presenting the four-indicator model is the diamond structure itself. In this case, as is shown in Figure 3.4d for values and space only, each dimension would represent a diamond within a diamond. While such an approach adds to the overall richness of the interpretation, the increased complexity of the four-indicator model makes it less intuitive in its interpretation. Of course, no overall diamond structure is possible at this level.

Finally, Figure 3.5 shows that combinations of one, two, three and four indicators are feasible within the same CSD application. Depending upon the desired level of detail and data availability, users can decide to focus more on some dimensions rather than others. In Figure 3.5, the structure and impact dimensions have four indicators each, whereas three indicators measure the values dimension and two indicators measure aspects of space.

Comparisons

The possibility of using the CSD for comparative purposes constitutes one of its major advantages. It is important to keep two possible presentations and interpretations of the CSD in mind. If we profile actual indicators and their relative values or rankings using a common metric, the interpretation of the information presented in Figure 3.1b would be as follows: a country with a medium-sized civil society in terms of paid employment, relatively high levels of trust, small to medium levels of legal space and medium levels of fulfilled commitments. This would represent the use of the CSD as a *status report.*

If, however, the data mapped into the CSD represents degrees of achievement or progress relative to a set of specific goals that would equal 100 at each of the four dimensions, we would come up with a very different reading. This is displayed in Figure 3.6, where a country or region has made significant progress in the area of values (differences between '•' and '•' along each axis) and structure, but less so in terms of space and impact. In other words, this interpretation of the diamond in Figure 3.6 is similar to a *progress report*, whereas the version in Figure 3.1b is more like a status report. In a similar way, users may decide to compare the state of civil society in their country or region to regional, national or international averages, as well as to field- and area-specific standards.

Finally, while the CSD can be used to track developments over time, it can also compare one particular case (country, region or field) to another. This

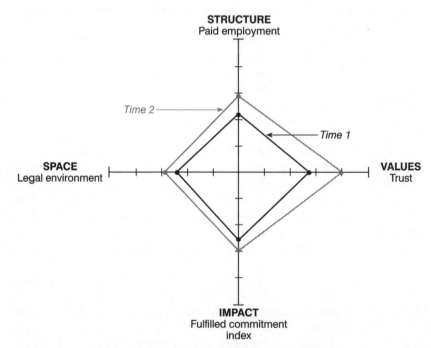

Figure 3.6 *Progress Report (1 indicator per dimension)*

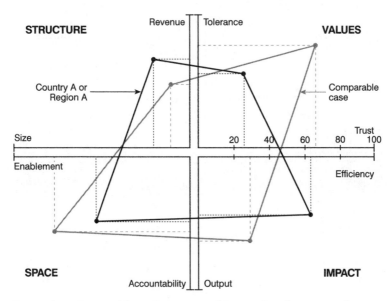

Figure 3.7 *Comparable or Cross-sectional Report (2 indicators per dimension and 2 cases)*

comparison may involve, for example, two countries, a region within a country relative to the country as a whole, or a particular field of civil society in contrast to civil society at large. Figure 3.7 illustrates the comparative, cross-sectional use of the CSD. In this case we see how country A differs from the average values of the group of countries in the same region – for example, Thailand in the context of Southeast Asia, or Mexico among the North American Free Trade Agreement (NAFTA) countries.

For *progress report applications*, the individual indicators would reflect actual improvements toward set targets. If all targets were fully met, the score for particular indicators would be 100; in cases where partial achievements have been made the score would range between a number greater than zero and less than 100. In terms of fulfillment measures, this set of over time comparisons is useful in cases where benchmarking is possible and where status measures have initially been agreed upon. An example is presented in Figure 3.8 for two indicators and three time periods.

In a standard-setting application, at least three measurement points come into analytic focus, a number that expands significantly as the number of indicators per dimension increases. For example, a standard-setting CSD analysis with four indicators for each dimension would involve 36 comparisons. Figure 3.9 illustrates the comparisons with two indicators, X and Y.

Specifically, the difference between value $Y1$ and the standard SY represents the degree of improvement required to reach the set target, and the difference between $Y2$ and $Y1$ relative to difference $Y1–SY$ represents the actual achievement made. The same reasoning would apply to the X indicator.

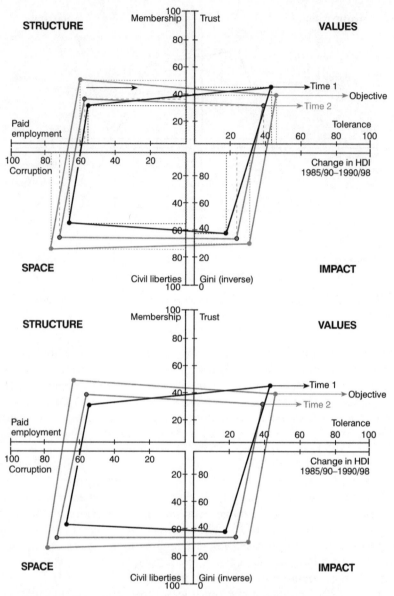

Figures 3.8a–b *Standard-Setting Report (2 indicators per dimension)*

As can be seen in Figure 3.9, the *Y* indicator reports a significant improvement, whereas values for *X* show a decline relative to time-1 levels.

A different way of examining changes over time or comparing different regions or countries across multiple dimensions is the 'vector or radar diagram,' a variation of the unfolding coordinate system presented so far. An example of this approach is presented in Figure 3.10, where the grey line indicates the values for time 1 and the black line the values for time 2.

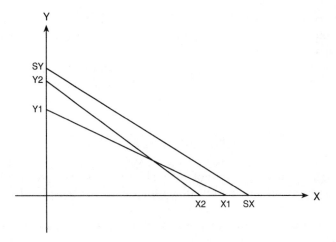

Figure 3.9 *Comparisons Involved in Standard-setting Applications of the CSD (2 indicators)*

In summary, depending upon the unit of analysis, the CSD can be used for different purposes:

- report and analysis of the current status of civil society and its component parts (eg Figure 3.1b);
- comparative report and analysis of the current status of civil society and its component parts relative to other countries, regions or fields (eg Figure 3.7);

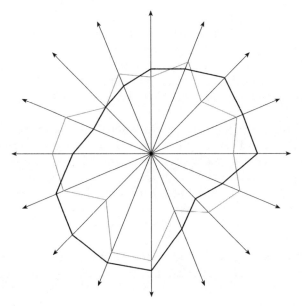

Figure 3.10 *Simple Representation of the CSD Using a Radar Diagram*

- comparative report and analysis of the development of civil society and its component parts relative to set goals (see Figure 3.8); and, as a combination,
- comparative report and analysis of the development of civil society and its component parts relative to other countries, regions or fields over time, and in relation to set goals.

Summary Measures

Even though a primary purpose of the CSD is to preserve core facets of civil society and to avoid single indicator approaches for the reasons stated in Chapter 2, it is possible to collapse the various CSD dimensions into one common figure or score. Depending upon the purpose of the CSD application and the number of indicators involved, there are different ways of doing so (see Figure 3.11).

Let us first look at a simple case: a status report application with one indicator per dimension. In this instance, assuming that indicators are projected onto a common metric – typically, from 0 to 100 – in each dimension, they are simply added up to a combined total and expressed as a share of the theoretically highest score. For example, if a country has a score of 40 in structure, 60 in space, 30 in impact and 70 in values, the combined score would be 200 or 50 per cent of the possible total score of 400.

When the number of indicators is higher than one, several options are available and users can decide which one suits their purpose best:

Additive scoring procedures for multiple indicators are simply an extension of the single case scenario presented above. Instead of adding one indicator per dimension, we would add two or more, depending upon the number in each dimension, and change the theoretically possible total sum accordingly. In a two-indicator model for each dimension, for example, with each indicator ranging from 0 to 100, the sum of all eight indicators would be expressed as a percentage of the total of 800 possible points.

Average scoring procedures are a variation of the above in the sense that the values of multiple indicators in each dimension would be averaged before being added to yield a total score. For example, assuming that the three indicators for the values dimension are 50, 60 and 70, respectively, the average score for this dimension would be 60. This number would be added to the average values for the other dimensions and related to the theoretically possible score: 400.

Multiplicable scoring is somewhat more complicated. In a two-indicator model, the score for each dimension would equal the product of the two indicator values. For example, if the two values for the indicators in one dimension are 30 and 40, respectively, their product would be 1200 or 12 per

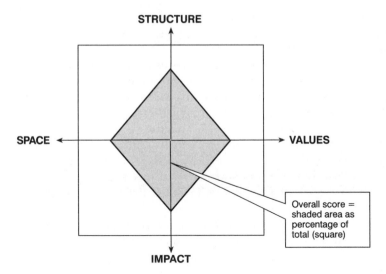

Figure 3.11 *Common Score for the CSD*

cent of a possible total of 10,000 (100 x 100). The scores for the other dimensions would be calculated accordingly and added to yield the overall score. The shaded area in Figure 3.11 graphically illustrates this scoring method, using a generic model. The shaded areas in each dimension are added and related to the overall area circumcised by the square and expressed as a percentage. Of course, countries, regions, fields or cases could then be rank-ordered accordingly, depending upon the unit of analysis.

In a three-indicator model, the score per dimension would be the product of three values. If the values were 30, 80 and 60, their product would be 144,000. This number would then be expressed relative to the total of 100^3. Because of the non-linearity of these calculations, joint scores based on products appear lower than those achieved through simple additions and average scoring methods.

Comparative scoring, either over time or across cases, is essentially an extension of any of the three methods introduced above. In simple terms, comparative scoring is a repeat application of either additive, average or multiplicable scoring, with the difference that each score is related to each other. For example, assuming a one indicator per dimension, ranging from 0 to 100, an over time comparison would be calculated as follows:

$$S_{\text{Time 1}} = (\text{STRUCTURE}_{\text{Time 1}} + \text{SPACE}_{\text{Time 1}} + \text{IMPACT}_{\text{Time 1}} + \text{VALUES}_{\text{Time 1}})/400$$

$$S_{\text{Time 2}} = (\text{STRUCTURE}_{\text{Time 2}} + \text{SPACE}_{\text{Time 2}} + \text{IMPACT}_{\text{Time 2}} + \text{VALUES}_{\text{Time 2}})/400$$

with the overall change obtained by $(S_{\text{Time } 2}/S_{\text{Time } 1}) \times 100$, with time 1 data as the base of the time series. Of course, other ways of expressing over time changes are also possible.

As shown in Figure 3.7, CSD comparisons can also be applied to countries or regions. In such cases, comparative scoring can be used to summarize differences among the compared units. Here, a country (or some other specified unit) is set in the context of similar cases – for example, a member country of the European Union (EU) relative to other EU members. The country-specific scores would be represented as differences from an EU-wide average, either through some simpler percentage score comparisons or with the help of z-score transformations for other than share data.

Note that comparative scoring requires that data is available for all indicators across the various countries in question. The actual calculations for comparative scores across several cases and involving multiple indicators are naturally somewhat more complex, but still relatively simple. In essence, the user has to calculate the common score for each time period or case and then compare each score, either in terms of percentage change or some other means of measuring differences over time.

All scoring systems suggested so far rest on two crucial assumptions. First, all dimensions carry the same weight; and second, common scores are, in fact, a valid way of representing civil society and its components. Because both assumptions involve complex judgements, users are advised to employ scoring methods with great caution, particular in cross-national and cross-cultural contexts.

Conclusion

We began this book by pointing out the need for a measurement and analysis system for civil society. Such a system will undoubtedly take many years to perfect and many measurement issues and mathematical, as well as statistical, implications remain to be worked out. Nonetheless, the approach of an unfolding system presented here, resting on the idea of multiple indicators and graphical representations, could be the first step towards a fuller and institutionalized reporting method for civil society. In the following chapters, we take a look at a series of examples to suggest potential uses of CSD applications across a wide range of countries and fields.

Chapter 4

The Civil Society Diamond:
First Applications

Introduction

The previous two chapters introduced the methodological background and development of the Civil Society Diamond (CSD) approach. This chapter builds upon the technical discussion and offers sample applications. These applications provide an illustration of how the CSD will operate as an assessment or profiling tool. The examples illustrate multiple uses of the civil society diamond:

1   an 'unfolding' series showing the detailed and complex levels of CSD applications as the number of indicators increases;
2   a 'purpose' series that depicts how the CSD can be applied to single and multiple comparisons over time and across different countries, fields or regions; and
3   a 'unit of analysis' series, which presents CSD applications at the macro, meso and micro levels.

It is important to note that examples presented in this chapter remain *illustrative* of the potential and range of CSD use and applications.[1] Throughout, it will become clear that the availability of different types of indicators for different units of analysis and across different time periods greatly enhances the utility of CSD applications. Some of the indicators used in the following sample applications are discussed in more detail in the following chapters, and more information on each indicator can be found in Appendix A, which presents the full menu of CSD indicators used in this book.

The unfolding series

The notion of the CSD as an unfolding system is analogous to that of a telescope. After initially focusing on one facet of civil society, others facets are brought into play by shifting the 'telescope' so that patterns will emerge to help understand the overall configuration. We use three countries as examples for the unfolding series. This series follows Figure 3.1a to Figure 3.4c in Chapter 3 and illustrates the use of the CSD with varying numbers of indicators per dimension:

First, a developed country, the US, illustrates the complete 'folding-out' of the CSD:

- a 'line' version of the CSD with 1 indicator per dimension (Example 4.1a);
- a 'plane' version with 2 indicators per dimension (Example 4.1b);
- a 'cube' version with 3 indicators per dimension (Example 4.1c); and
- a 'two-plane' version with 4 indicators per dimension (Example 4.1d).

Next, two developing countries, South Africa and Brazil, illustrate:

- a 'combo' version with varying indicators per dimension (Example 4.1e); and
- a 'plane' version with 2 different indicators per dimension (Example 4.1f).

The purpose series

The purpose series uses several examples to illustrate different purposes of the CSD:

- an 'over time' version with 1 indicator per dimension for Brazil (Example 4.2a);
- an 'over time' version with 2 indicators per dimension for France (Example 4.2b);
- a 'standard-setting' version with 1 indicator per dimension for Brazil (Example 4.2c);
- a 'comparative' version with 2 indicators per dimension for the US and Germany (two developed countries) (Examples 4.2d–1 and 4.2d–2); and
- a 'comparative' version with 1 indicator per dimension for the UK and South Korea (developed and developing countries) (Example 4.2e).

For a 'cross-sectional' example, see Example 4.3c in the 'unit of analysis' series.

The unit of analysis series

The final series applies the CSD methodology across the three different units of analysis to illustrate its use at the national, regional and field level:

- two 'macro-level' versions with 2 indicators per dimension for Japan and Hungary (Examples 4.3a–b);
- a 'meso-level, over time, cross-sectional' version using East and West Germany (Example 4.3c); and
- an 'over time, micro-level' version with 1 indicator per dimension using a (hypothetical) international organization in the field of human rights (Example 4.3d).

We will present each example in turn, with the understanding that the emphasis of the various cases lies *less* in the in-depth interpretation of the results and *more* in the illustration of the wide range of uses of the CSD approach. However, readers are invited to explore the various examples presented in this chapter, to interpret resulting patterns and configurations, and to reflect upon what other aspects or facets of civil society could be taken into account.

The 'Unfolding' Series

Example 4.1a is a macro-level application of civil society in the US using one indicator per dimension. Example 4.1a uses the following indicators.

Paid employment for the structure dimension uses 1995 from the Johns Hopkins Comparative Non-profit Sector Project (JHCNSP) (Salamon et al, 1999a). Paid employment is defined as the non-profit share of total paid employment, based on full-time equivalent data. Users may also wish to disaggregate paid employment by sector at this unit of analysis, as the data reported by Salamon et al (1999a; 1999b) includes large-scale service providers such as hospitals and universities, which may be of less interest for some CSD applications that focus on the voice function of non-profit organizations. In either case, paid employment is a solid measure of the economic weight of organizations operating in civil society.

Trust among CSO members for the values dimension uses the 1990–1993 World Values Survey (WVS).[2] This measure combines generalized trust in society *only among* those people who report belonging to (are members of) voluntary organizations and activities. The trust question during the 1990–1993 WVS was: 'Generally speaking, would you say that most people can be trusted or that you can't be too careful in dealing with people?' (World Values Study Group, 1994). Trust was chosen because it is a way of describing the potential of individuals to associate voluntarily in order to advance common interests.[3]

The membership question during the 1990–1993 WVS was: 'Please look carefully at the following list of voluntary organizations and activities and say which, if any, you belong to' (World Values Study Group, 1994). The organizations and activities included in this measure were social welfare services for elderly, handicapped or deprived people; religious or church organizations; education, art, music or cultural activities; trade unions; local community action on issues such as poverty, employment, housing and racial equality; developing world growth or human rights; conservation, the environment and ecology; professional associations; youth work; sports or recreation; women's groups; peace movements; animal rights; voluntary organizations concerned with health; and other groups. Measuring trust *among members* of civil society organizations, rather than for the population at large, gives us a more nuanced and relevant look at the values of civil society participants.

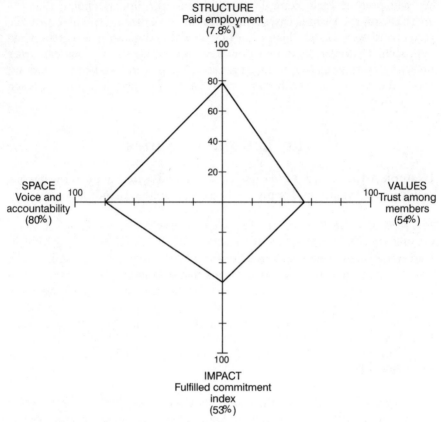

STRUCTURE
Paid employment
(7.8%)*

SPACE
Voice and
accountability
(80%)

VALUES
Trust among
members
(54%)

IMPACT
Fulfilled commitment
index
(53%)

Note: * multiplied by 10 for scale
Source: see Notes (p211)

Example 4.1a *United States (a 'line' version with 1 indicator per dimension)*

Fulfilled Commitment Index (FCI) for the impact dimension uses data from the year 2000 from Social Watch. The FCI is a standards-based rating of countries based on either 'progress' or 'regression' in commitments made by governments at the World Summit on Social Development and the Fourth World Conference on Women in Beijing (Social Watch, 2000). As a result, this indicator serves as an example for the kind of measure needed for assessing the impact of civil society organizations in policy-making. Social Watch does not use a scoring system as such; all percentage conversions are based on our own calculations (for details, see the indicator methodology assessments in Appendix A).

Voice and accountability for the space dimension uses 1997–1998 data from the World Bank's Worldwide Governance Research Indicators Dataset (Kaufmann et al, 1999a; 1999b; World Bank, 1999). Voice and accountability is a subset of the governance dataset and measures the extent to which citizens can participate in the selection of governments (political process, civil liberties and political rights).

Example 4.1a displays a diamond-shaped structure, and all measurement points are within a relatively narrow range of 27 points (53 to 80). It shows a medium-sized economic weight of civil society organizations in terms of paid employment, with moderate levels of trust and fulfilled commitment, and a high level of voice and accountability.

Example 4.1b is a macro-level CSD application of the US using two indicators per dimension. Specifically, Example 4.1b adds the following indicators to those presented in Example 4.1a.

Membership in civil society organizations is added to the structure dimension using 1990–1993 data from the WVS. Membership was chosen because – as a behavioural measure – it is an important predictor of volunteering and other participation patterns (see 'trust among members' in Example 4.1a for the relevant WVS question; World Values Study Group, 1994).

Tolerance among members was added to the values dimension using 1990–1993 data from the WVS. The tolerance question from the 1990–1993 WVS was: 'On this list are various groups of people. Could you please sort out any that you would not like to have as neighbours.' We chose the following groups of people to measure tolerance in society: people of a different race; left-wing and right-wing extremists; Muslims; Jews; Hindus; immigrants/foreign workers; people who have AIDS; and homosexuals (World Values Study Group, 1994). Depending upon the purpose of the CSD, users may either wish to include other groups or exclude some of the groups in their application. Like trust, tolerance is also measured *among members* of civil society organizations rather than the population at large.

Civil liberties was added to the space dimension using 1990–1991 data from the *Annual Survey of Political Rights and Civil Liberties* by Freedom House (2001). Civil liberties are defined in the CSD as the freedom to develop views, institutions and personal autonomy apart from the state. They are measured using a standards-based rating of a country's civil liberties based on freedom of expression and belief; associational and organizational rights; rule of law and human rights; and personal autonomy and economic rights. The disadvantage of using the Freedom House rating is that the civil liberties dimension is not disaggregated, which is perhaps something that could be included in future applications. Future CSD applications could also take a measure of civil liberties that accounts for the diverse political and cultural factors that affect the interpretation of human rights.

Change in the Human Development Index (HDI) was added to the impact dimension using 1990 and 1998 data from the United Nations Development Programme's (UNDP's) *Human Development* reports (UNDP, 2000). The main limitation is that the HDI does not directly measure the impact of civil society and civil society organizations (CSOs). However, change in the HDI is used in

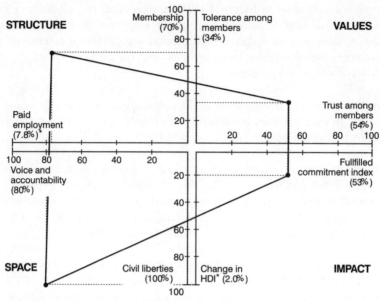

Example 4.1b *United States (a 'plane' version with 2 indicators per dimension)*

this context because it is a widely available and accepted indicator of well-being in society.

Example 4.1b shows, in the structure dimension, that the large level of paid employment (7.8 per cent, multiplied by 10 for scale) is complemented by a relatively high membership rate of 70 per cent (or two out of three adults). In terms of the space dimension, the high score for voice and accountability and civil liberties contrasts markedly with the low rate of tolerance among members and medium levels of trust among members in the values dimension. An enabling legal environment and a medium-sized civil society in structural terms seem to coexist in a society with modest tolerance and trust levels. In terms of the impact dimension, the Fulfilled Commitment Index of 53 per cent suggests that of all the policy commitments made by the US federal government in the social policy field at two UN conferences, slightly more than half have been implemented. This somewhat mediocre legislative achievement can be seen in the context of a small increase in human development – albeit from an already high level – over the previous decade as measured by the UNDP's Human Development Index (note that the increase shown in Example 4.2b is magnified tenfold for purposes of scale).

   Could it be that some aspects of the US value system are related to the lack of legislative progress? What is the role of the legal system for civil society in this regard, and how can high membership rates and low levels of tolerance coexist? What do these findings, when taken together, suggest about the strength and weaknesses of civil society in the US, and what are the policy options and implications? These are some of the questions that come to mind and that indicate how the CSD can encourage a structured dialogue among different stakeholders.

Example 4.1c is a macro-level CSD application of the US using three indicators per dimension. Compared to Example 4.1b, which used two indicators per dimension, Example 4.1c adds complexity; but importantly, a three-indicator model also adds depth to the analysis of civil society. Specifically, Example 4.1c adds the following indicators.

Volunteering was added to the structure dimension using 1991 data from Independent Sector's annual *Giving and Volunteering Survey*. The question used in Independent Sector's survey was: 'Listed on this card are examples of the many different areas in which people do volunteer activity. By volunteer activity, I mean not just belonging to a service organization, but actually working in some way to help others not for monetary pay. In which, if any, of the areas listed on this card have you done some volunteer work in the past 12 months?' (Independent Sector, 1994). The volunteering indicator is measured as the number (head count) of volunteers relative to the US adult population.

Confidence among CSO members was added to the values dimension using 1990–1993 data from the WVS. The 1990–1993 survey question was: 'I am going to name a number of organizations. For each one, could you tell me how much confidence you have in them: is it a great deal of confidence, quite a lot of confidence, not very much confidence or none at all?' The following types of institutions were included: the legal system, major companies, the social security system and the political system (World Values Study Group, 1994). For the purpose of illustration in this example, the two answer categories 'a great deal' and 'quite a lot' define confidence. Confidence is also measured among members of civil society organizations.

The Political Freedom Index (PFI) was added to the space dimension using data from Desai's (1994) attempt to measure individual political freedom cross-nationally (see, also, UNDP, 1992). The PFI is a simple average score of five clusters: integrity of self; rule of law; political participation; freedom of expression; and equality before the law. While composite indices such as the PFI and the HDI above may blur finer distinctions, their main advantage is that they are easily communicated and understood. The PFI was only published in 1992 and is used here for illustrative purposes. However, for future applications of the CSD, users might consider developing a similar standards system with contextualized scores based on the history and background of the country.

Subjective well-being among members was added to the impact dimension using data from the 1990–1993 WVS. The 1990–1993 survey question was: 'Taking all things together, would you say you are very happy; quite happy; not very

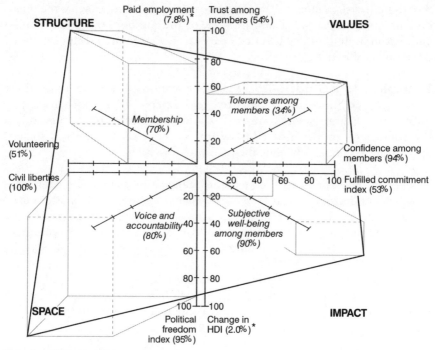

Note: * multiplied by 10 for scale
Source: see Notes (p211)

Example 4.1c *United States (a 'cube' version with 3 indicators per dimension)*

happy; not at all happy; don't know?' (World Values Study Group, 1994). We define well-being in this example as 'very happy' and 'quite happy'.

Despite its added complexity, Example 4.1c sheds additional light on all dimensions. The volunteering rate confirms the high participation rate; and the overall high sense of well-being in the impact dimension suggests a general sense of contentment amongst the population, despite a somewhat lacklustre social policy performance over the last decade. Interestingly, in the values dimension, the medium levels of interpersonal trust are met with higher levels of confidence in central social institutions. Nonetheless, the contrast between trust and confidence, on the one hand, and low levels of tolerance, on the other, invite further exportation. Indeed, the current debate about loss of social capital and trust seem closely related to these findings (see Putnam, 2000).

Example 4.1d is a macro-level CSD application of the US using four indicators per dimension. Accordingly, Example 4.1d presents the location of civil society in terms of 4 dimensions and 16 indicators, allowing for a highly detailed analysis.

Example 4.1d presents a more complex but also rich view of civil society in the US. The following indicators are added to this application.

Operating expenditures was added to the structure dimension using 1990 data from the JHCNSP. Operating expenditures add another sub-dimension to structure, revealing medium-high levels of expenditures by CSOs relative to GDP. As data becomes available, operational expenditures by civil society organizations should be matched with another indicator from the sub-dimension 'revenue', rather than from the sub-dimension 'size' (see Figure 3.4c in Chapter 3). Operating expenditures, which are measured relative to GDP, are defined as the costs of the general operations of the organization, including wage and salary disbursements; purchases of goods other than capital equipment; material and services; fees; and charges paid (Salamon and Anheier, 1996).

Membership in human rights organizations was added to the values dimension using 1990–1993 data from the WVS. The membership question for this wave of the WVS was: 'Please look carefully at the following list of voluntary organizations and activities and say which, if any, you belong to.' We used membership in the following organizations to form this indicator: local community action on issues such as poverty, employment, housing and racial equality; developing world growth or human rights; and peace movements (World Values Study Group, 1994). Note that for purposes of scale and presentation, the data is multiplied by a factor of ten.

Corruption is added to the space dimension using 1996 data from Transparency International's (TI) Corruption Perceptions Index. TI defines corruption as the misuse of public power for private benefit – for example, bribing of public officials, kickbacks in public procurement or embezzlement of public funds (Transparency International, 1999–2000). For the CSD, corruption is used to measure the enabling environment provided by the overall fiscal and regulatory environment (0 per cent represents total corruption and 100 per cent represents transparency).

The Gini Index of Income Inequality was added to the impact dimension using 1994 data from the World Bank's *World Development Indicators* (World Bank, 2000). As a widely available and accepted indicator of inequality in society, the Gini index could be used to test whether income becomes more equal or unequal in the distribution of resources from civil society.

Example 4.1d allows users to highlight different combinations among indicators within and across dimensions. In the example shown, A–B–C–D and E–F–G–H focus on particular relationships, although users can examine other combinations, as well (see Figures 3.4a–c in Chapter 3). In the impact dimension, a relatively high degree of income inequality and a small increase in the HDI coexist alongside a medium level of fulfilled commitment and high levels of subjective well-being among members of civil society organizations. Together, this data suggests stagnant social progress amidst general contentment, and – in the context of an enabling legal environment (space) – mixed (perhaps even somewhat contradictory) value patterns. Regarding

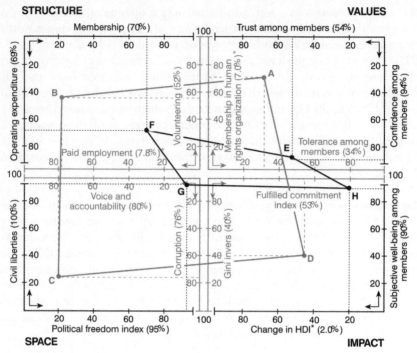

Example 4.1d *United States (a 'two-plane' version with 4 indicators per dimension)*

Note: * multiplied by 10 for scale
Source: see Notes (p212)

membership in human rights organizations, compared to the following Organization for Economic Cooperation and Development (OECD) countries, the US falls roughly in the middle: 17.5 per cent in The Netherlands; 11.7 per cent in Sweden; 9.2 per cent in Canada; 9 per cent in Denmark; 8.7 per cent in Belgium; 7.7 per cent in Finland; 7.7 per cent in Norway; 5.6 per cent in France; 5.1 per cent in Ireland; 4.9 per cent in Northern Ireland; 4.9 per cent in the UK; 3.9 per cent in Austria; 3.1 per cent in Italy; and 2.2 per cent in Spain. Therefore, we can say that in this example, the US has a medium level of membership in human rights organizations. We also see medium levels of trust among members in the values dimension, but low levels of tolerance and very high levels of confidence in major social institutions.

Clearly, much more could be said about the emerging patterns in Examples 4.1a–d. Using the US as a case study, the unfolding series demonstrated how the CSD invites users to analyse and interpret, even to speculate, about the nature of civil society. With this in mind, let us turn to a very different country: South Africa.

Example 4.1e is a macro-level, 'combo' CSD application of South Africa using two and three indicators per dimension. Specifically, Example 4.1e uses the following indicators.

Public-sector dependency and marketization illustrate the structure dimension using 1998 data from a membership survey by the South African Nongovernmental Organisation Council (SANGOCO) (Volkhart, 2001).

Trust, tolerance and confidence among members illustrate the values dimension using 1995–1997 data from the WVS. The membership question in the 1995–1997 survey was: 'Now I am going to read off a list of voluntary organizations; for each one, could you tell me whether you are an active member, an inactive member or not a member of that type of organization?' For this indicator, we use active and inactive membership in the following organizations: church or religious; sport or recreation; art, music or educational; labour union; environmental; professional; charitable; any other voluntary organization. The trust question in the 1995–1997 WVS was: 'Generally speaking, would you say that most people can be trusted or that you can't be too careful in dealing with people?' The tolerance question was: 'On this list are various groups of people. Could you please sort out any whom you would not like to have as neighbours.' We chose the following groups of people to measure tolerance in society: people of a different race; political extremists; Muslims; immigrants/foreign workers; people who have AIDS; and homosexuals. Finally, the confidence question was: 'I am going to name a number of organizations. For each one, can you tell me how much confidence you have in them: is it a great deal of confidence, quite a lot of confidence, not very much confidence or none at all?' We chose the following central social institutions: legal system, the government [in your country], major companies and the Green/ecology movement (World Values Study Group, 1999).

Corruption and civil liberties illustrate the space dimension. Corruption data is from Transparency International's 1996 Corruption Perceptions Index (Transparency International, 1999–2000) and civil liberties data is from Freedom House's 1995–1996 survey (Freedom House, 2001).

The Gini Index of Income Inequality and subjective well-being among members illustrate the impact dimension. Gini data is from the World Bank's *World Development Indicators* (World Bank, 2000) and subjective well-being data is from the 1995–1997 WVS: 'Taking all things together, would you say you are very happy, quite happy, not very happy or not at all happy' (World Values Study Group, 1999). We define well-being in this example as 'very happy' and 'quite happy'.

Example 4.1e shows the location of civil society depicted in terms of four dimensions with two indicators in the structure, space and impact dimensions and three indicators in the values dimension. More indicators can be added as data becomes available, or users can use the combo template to focus more on some dimensions rather than on others. This example uses the sub-dimension 'revenue' in the structure dimension to examine resource dependency. In the values dimension, we see low levels of trust and tolerance among members next to high levels of confidence among members in central

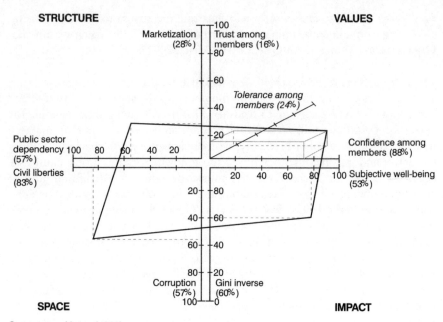

Source: see Notes (p212)

Example 4.1e *South Africa (a 'combo' version with varying indicators per dimension)*

social institutions. This high level of confidence is matched by a high level of well-being among members in the impact dimension, but also a high level of inequality. In space, relatively high levels of civil liberties are met with medium levels of corruption.

Example 4.1f is macro-level CSD application of civil society in Brazil using two indicators per dimension. Specifically, Example 4.1f uses the following indicators.

Paid employment and membership illustrate the structure dimension. The paid employment indicator uses 1995 data from the JHCNSP (Salamon et al, 1999a). Membership figures are from the 1995–1997 WVS (World Values Study Group, 1999). The membership question is the same as that used in Example 4.1e. However, we use only active membership for all indicators in Example 4.1f (and all Brazil examples), and provide two versions of the indicator: one with church or religious organizations and one without.

Trust and tolerance among members illustrate the values dimension using 1995–1997 data from the WVS (World Values Study Group, 1999). See Example 4.1e for the relevant survey questions.

Subjective well-being among members and the Fulfilled Commitment Index illustrate the impact dimension. See Example 4.1e for the relevant WVS survey question.

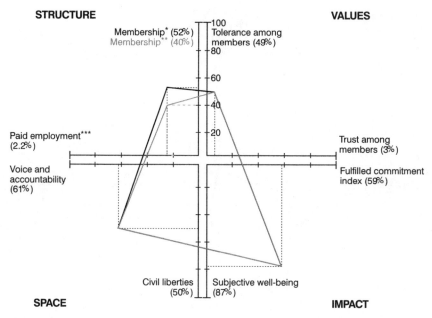

Note: * Including 'church or religious organizations'; ** excluding 'church or religious organizations'; *** multiplied by 10 for scale
Source: see Notes (p212)

Example 4.1f *Brazil (a 'plane' version with 2 indicators per dimension)*

The Fulfilled Commitment Index uses data from the year 2000 from Social Watch (2000).

Civil liberties and voice and accountability illustrate the space dimension using 1995–1996 Freedom House data (Freedom House, 2001) and 1997–1998 World Bank data (World Bank, 1999; Kaufmann et al, 1999a; 1999b), respectively. See Example 4.1b for an explanation of the civil liberties indicator and Example 4.1a for an explanation of voice and accountability.

This example is similar to Example 4.1b (a 'plane' version). It shows a small civil society in terms of membership and paid employment, where religion makes a 12 per cent difference in membership rates. In the values dimension, we see moderate levels of tolerance among members, but very low levels of trust despite high levels of well-being in the impact dimension. Finally, the space dimension reveals a moderate enabling environment in legal terms.

The 'Purpose' Series

Example 4.2a is an over time, macro-level application of civil society in Brazil using one indicator per dimension. Example 4.2a uses the following indicators.

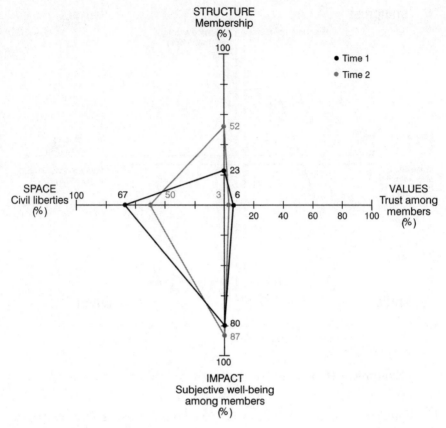

Source: see Notes (p212)

Example 4.2a *Brazil (an 'over time' version with 1 indicator per dimension)*

Membership illustrates the structure dimension using the 1990–1993 and 1995–1997 data from the WVS (World Values Study Group, 1999, active members only). See Example 4.1e for the survey question.

Trust among members illustrates the values dimension using 1990–1993 and 1995–1997 data from the WVS (World Values Study Group, 1999, active members only). See Example 4.1e for the survey question.

Subjective well-being among members illustrates the impact dimension using 1990–1993 and 1995–1997 data from the WVS (World Values Study Group, 1999, active members only). See Example 4.1e for the survey question.

Civil liberties illustrates the space dimension using 1990–1991 and 1995–1996 data from Freedom House (2001). See Example 4.1b for an explanation of the civil liberties indicator.

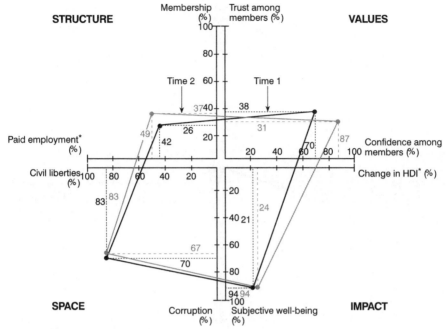

Note: * multiplied by 10 for scale
Source: see Notes (p212)

Example 4.2b *France (an 'over time' version with 2 indicators per dimension)*

Example 4.2b is an over time, macro-level CSD application of civil society in France with two indicators per dimension. Time 1 represents a past date and time 2 represents the present. Specifically, we use the following data sources and indicators for Example 4.2b.

Membership and paid employment illustrate the structure dimension using data from the 1981–1984 and 1990–1993 WVS (World Values Study Group, 1994), and the 1990 and 1995 JHCNSP (Salamon et al, 1999b), respectively.

Trust and confidence among members illustrate the values dimension using 1981–1984 and 1990–1993 data from the WVS (World Values Study Group, 1994).

Change in HDI and subjective well-being illustrate the impact dimension using 1985–1990 and 1990–1998 data from the UNDP (UNDP, 2000) and 1981–1984 and 1990–1993 data from the WVS (World Values Study Group, 1994), respectively.

Civil liberties and corruption illustrate the space dimension using 1989–1990 and 1995–1996 data from Freedom House (2001) and 1996 and 2000 data from Transparency International (1999–2000), respectively. See Examples 4.1a–d for more detailed explanations of the indicators used in this example.

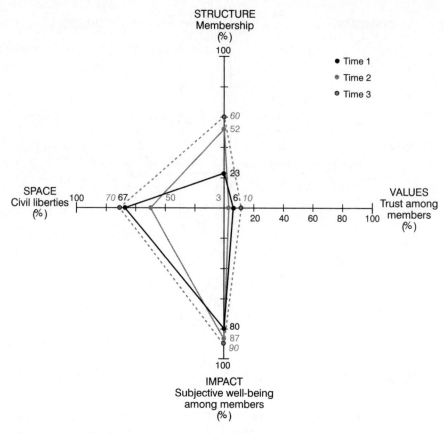

Source: see Notes (p212)

Example 4.2c *Brazil (a 'standard-setting' version with 1 indicator per dimension)*

From time 1 to time 2 we see an improvement in the structure dimension in both membership and paid employment. In the space dimension, we see an enabling legal environment, despite a small decrease in corruption. The values dimension shows a mixed pattern, with a decrease in trust among members from time 1 to time 2, but an increase in confidence among members (in major social institutions). The mixed pattern continues in the impact dimension with high levels of well-being among members alongside a small (albeit increased) level of change in the HDI.

Example 4.2c is a standard-setting, macro-level CSD application of civil society in Brazil using one indicator per dimension. Time 1 represents a past date (in this case, 1990); time 2 ideally represents the present (in this case, we have data for 1995–1998); and time 3 represents a future goal. The same indicators as in Example 4.2a apply.

In Example 4.2c, goals (represented by time 3) are set based on the information provided in Example 4.2a. We expect to see a further increase in membership and subjective well-being, and hope to improve civil liberties and, perhaps, encourage an increase in trust among members.

Example 4.2d–1 is a comparative version of the US and Germany with two indicators per dimension. Specifically, the following indicators are used for example 4.2d.

Paid Employment and membership illustrate the structure dimension using 1995 JHCNPS data (Salamon et al, 1999b) and 1995–1997 WVS data (World Values Study Group, 1999, active members only), respectively. See Example 4.1a for more information on the paid employment indicator and Example 4.1e for the membership survey question.

Trust and tolerance among members illustrate the values dimension using 1995–1997 WVS data (World Values Study Group, 1999, active members only). See Example 4.1e for the relevant survey questions.

The Fulfilled Commitment Index and subjective well-being illustrate the impact dimension using data from the year 2000 from Social Watch (2000) and 1995–1997 WVS data (World Values Study Group, 1999, active members only), respectively. See Example 4.1a for more information on the Fulfilled Commitment Index and Example 4.1e for the subjective well-being survey question.

Finally, *corruption and civil liberties* illustrate the space dimension. Corruption data is from Transparency International's 1996 Corruption Perceptions Index (Transparency International, 1999–2000) and civil liberties data is from Freedom House's 1995–1996 survey (Freedom House, 2001). See Example 4.1d for more information on the corruption indicator and Example 4.1b for more information on civil liberties.

Here we see that the US has a much larger civil society in terms of paid employment and membership in the structure dimension. In the values dimension, the US has a slightly higher – but moderate – level of trust among members, but twice the level of tolerance among members. Both countries reveal an enabling legal environment in the space dimension; in the impact dimension, we see high levels of well-being among members next to a mediocre level of fulfilled commitment.

Example 4.2d–2 presents the same data using a radar diagram. The configuration for Germany is contained within the one for the US, suggesting a larger civil society in the US as measured by the six indicators used.

Example 4.2e is a cross-sectional CSD application comparing the UK and South Korea with one indicator per dimension. Specifically, the following indicators are used to illustrate this example.

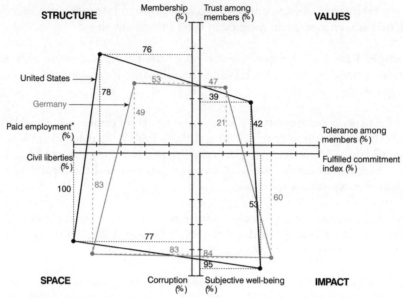

Note: * multiplied by 10 for scale
Source: see Notes (p212)

Example 4.2d-1 *United States and Germany (a 'comparative' version with 2 indicators per dimension) (two-plane version)*

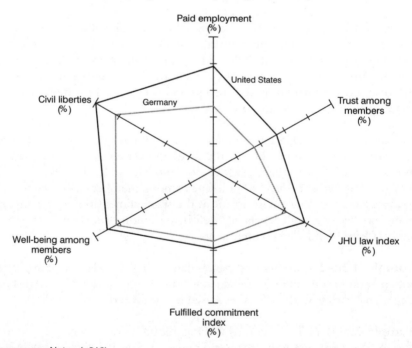

Source: see Notes (p212)

Example 4.2d-2 *United States and Germany (a 'comparative' version with 2 indicators per dimension) (radar version)*

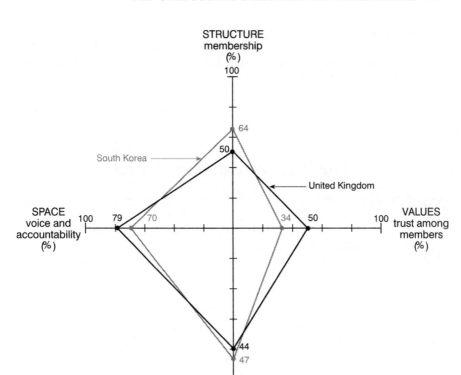

Note: * multiplied by 10 for scale
Source: see Notes (p212)

Example 4.2e *South Korea and the UK (a 'comparative' version with 1 indicator per dimension)*

Membership illustrates the structure dimension using 1990–1993 WVS data (World Values Study Group, 1999, active and inactive members). For the relevant survey question, see Example 4.1e.

Trust among members illustrates the values dimension using 1990–1993 WVS data (World Values Study Group, 1999, active and inactive members). For the relevant survey question, see Example 4.1e.

Change in HDI illustrates the impact dimension using 1990–1998 data from the UNDP's *Human Development* reports (UNDP, 2000). See Example 4.1b for more information on this indicator.

Finally, *voice and accountability* illustrates the space dimension using 1997–1998 data from the World Bank's Worldwide Governance Research Indicators Dataset (Kaufmann et al, 1999a; 1999b; World Bank, 1999). See Example 4.1a for more information on this indicator.

Example 4.2e compares a developed and developing country. The two diamonds that emerge do not necessarily reveal a healthier civil society in the UK compared to South Korea. In fact, we see only marginally higher values and legal enablement in the UK (represented by trust among members and voice and accountability, respectively). We also see significantly higher levels of membership and a moderately higher level of change in human development in South Korea.

The 'Unit of Analysis' Series

Macro level

Examples 4.3a–b are similar to Example 4.1b. We use a 'plane' version of the CSD (two indicators per dimension) to illustrate the macro-level units of analysis. Specifically, Examples 4.3a–b use the following indicators.

Paid employment and membership illustrate the structure dimension using 1995 data from the JHCNSP (Salamon et al, 1999a) and 1995–1997 data from the WVS (World Values Study Group, 1999), respectively. The membership question in the 1995–1997 WVS survey was: 'I am going to read off a list of voluntary organizations; for each one, can you tell me whether you are an active member, an inactive member or not a member of that type of organization?' For this indicator we use active and inactive membership in the following organizations: church or religious; sport or recreation; art, music or educational; labour union; environmental; professional; charitable; any other voluntary organization.

Trust and confidence among members illustrate the values dimension using 1995–1997 data from the WVS. The trust question in the 1995–1997 WVS was: 'Generally speaking, would you say that most people can be trusted or that you can't be too careful in dealing with people?' The confidence question was: 'I am going to name a number of organizations. For each one, can you tell me how much confidence you have in them: is it a great deal of confidence, quite a lot of confidence, not very much confidence or none at all?' We chose the following central social institutions: legal system, the government [in your country], major companies and the Green/ecology movement.

The Fulfilled Commitment Index and subjective well-being among members illustrate the impact dimension. FCI data is from Social Watch (2000) and subjective well-being data is from the 1995–1997 WVS: 'Taking all things together, would you say you are very happy, quite happy, not very happy or not at all happy' (World Values Study Group, 1999). We define well-being in this example as 'very happy' and 'quite happy'.

Civil liberties and voice and accountability illustrate the space dimension. Civil liberties data is from Freedom House's 1995–1996 survey (2001), and voice and

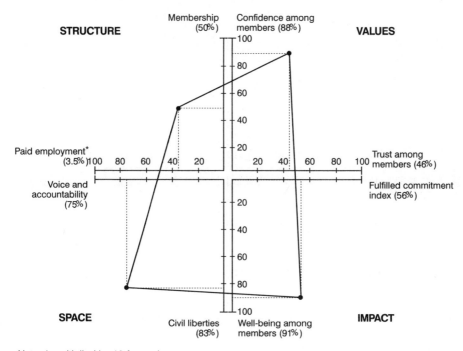

Note: * multiplied by 10 for scale
Source: see Notes (p212)

Example 4.3a *Japan (a 'macro' version with 2 indicators per dimension)*

accountability data is from the World Bank's Worldwide Governance Research Indicators Dataset (Kaufmann et al, 1999a; 1999b; World Bank, 1999).

Example 4.3a is a 'plane' macro version of Japan with two indicators per dimension. It shows, in the structure dimension, a medium membership rate and a relatively small level of paid employment (3.5 per cent, multiplied by 10 for scale) compared to other OECD countries. In terms of the impact dimension, the Fulfilled Commitment Index of 56 per cent suggests that of all policy commitments made by the Japanese government in the social policy field at two UN conferences, slightly more than half have been implemented (similar to the US in Examples 4.1a–d). However, the impact dimension also reveals a very high level of well-being among members (91 per cent), which is matched by a high level of confidence among members in the values dimension. Finally, the fairly strong legal enabling environment in the space dimension contrasts with a mediocre level of trust among members in the values dimension.

Example 4.3b is another example of a 'plane' macro version of civil society with two indicators per dimension. Here we see in Hungary a mediocre membership rate and a small level of paid employment. The values dimension reveals a high level of confidence among members, but a low level of trust among members. In impact we see a medium level of fulfilled commitments

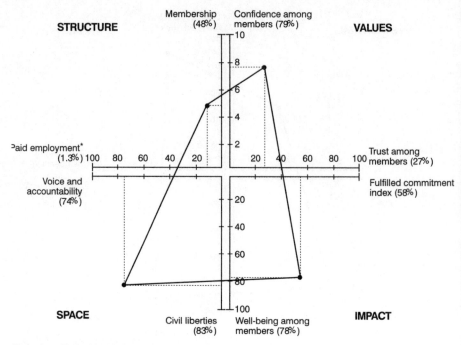

Note: * multiplied by 10 for scale
Source: see Notes (p212)

Example 4.3b *Hungary (a 'macro' version with 2 indicators per dimension)*

and a relatively high sense of well-being among members. Finally, the space dimension reveals a fairly strong legal enabling environment.

Meso level

Example 4.3c is an over time, cross-sectional, meso-level CSD application of East and West Germany with one indicator per dimension. Time 1 represents a past date (in this case, 1989–1993 data), and time 2 ideally represents the present (in this case, we have data for 1995–1998). In this example, we have disaggregated data (East and West Germany) for all dimensions in time 1, but only for the structure, values and impact dimensions in time 2. Specifically, Example 4.3c uses the following indicators.

Paid employment illustrates the structure dimension with 1990 and 1995 data from the JHCNSP. See Example 4.1a for more details of this indicator. *Trust among members* illustrates the values dimension using 1990–1993 and 1995–1997 data from the WVS (World Values Study Group, 1999, active and inactive members). See Example 4.1e for more details of this indicator. *The Gini Index of Income Inequality* illustrates the impact dimension using 1990 and 1993 data (WIDER-UNU, 2000). See Example 4.1d for more information.

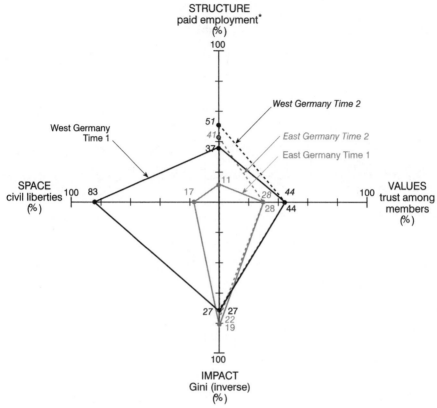

Note: * multiplied by 10 for scale
Source: see Notes (p212)

Example 4.3c *East and West Germany (a 'meso, over time, cross-sectional' with 1 indicator per dimension)*

Civil liberties illustrates the space dimension using 1988–1989 data from Freedom House (2001). See Example 4.1b for more information.

Example 4.3c explores the over time and cross-sectional use of the CSD by taking a meso-level look at Germany divided into two regions: East and West. In time 1 we see that West Germany (represented by the dark solid line) has a much larger diamond than East Germany (represented by the light-grey solid line) in every dimension except impact. In time 2, we cannot complete the diamond because we do not have data disaggregated by regions for civil liberties. However, we see significant improvement in paid employment compared to time 1, especially in East Germany (1.1 per cent to 4.1 per cent, multiplied by 10 for scale). Yet, we see relatively little movement from time 1 to time 2 for both countries in the values and impact dimensions.

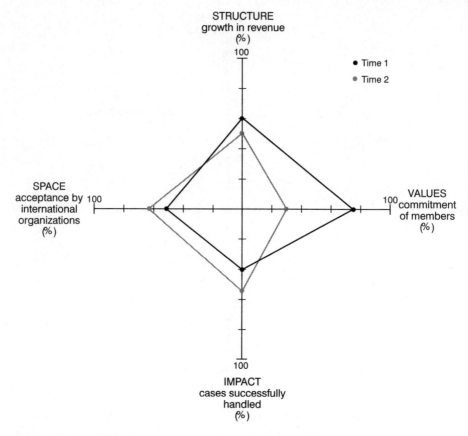

Example 4.3d *Membership Organization in the Human Rights Field (a 'micro, over time' hypothetical version with 1 indicator per dimension)*

Micro level

Finally, **Example 4.3d** offers a hypothetical example of an organizational case study – in this instance, a membership organization in the human rights field. The purpose of this CSD application is to track changes in the organization along the four dimensions. In the structure dimension, growth in annual revenue was selected as the indicator; for the values dimension, the indicator measures how committed members are to the goals of the organization; for the space dimension, the indicator measures the degree of acceptance of the organization by international governmental agencies in the field of human rights; and in the impact dimension, the number of successfully handled human rights cases serves as an indicator of achievement. The hypothetical values for each indicator are plotted in Example 4.3d for each year, yielding two diamonds, one for 1999 and one for 2001.

The resulting pattern in Example 4.3d clearly suggests an organization undergoing significant changes. Even though revenue growth declined somewhat between 1999 and 2001, the organization did, in fact, deal with more cases successfully, making it more efficient overall. At the same time, however, commitment levels among members plummeted, and acceptance among international agencies increased. At this point, users would have to ask critical questions: what is the relationship between greater acceptance and loss of commitment? What is behind the greater efficiency in purely economic terms? Could it be that the organization, while becoming more successful in meeting its goals, is losing its base in civil society, as is suggested by the decline in member commitment?

Conclusion

This chapter deals with CSD applications across a broad range of counties that vary in economic development, political system, culture, religion and ethnicity. The purpose of these applications is less to test the methodology in any rigorous sense of the term, and to interpret each case in detail, and more to demonstrate the variety of the use and applicability of the approach across different circumstances and units of analysis. Yet, how do we know what indicators to select and what data to use? So far, we have sidestepped such questions. Indeed, without the right indicators and without sufficient data to measure them, the CSD is likely to remain little more than an intellectual exercise. The following chapter, therefore, will address indicator selection and data issues, two closely related and equally important aspects in developing the civil society diamond.

Chapter 5

Indicators, Data, Process

Although a variety of indicators and different data sources have already been
either mentioned or introduced in the previous chapters of this book, the
issue of indicator selection and data availability has not been systematically
addressed so far. Indeed, in developing and presenting the Civil Society
Diamond (CSD) in Chapters 3 and 4, two implicit assumptions have been
made throughout. The first is that indicators appropriate and adequate for
CSD purposes can either be identified or otherwise developed; and, second,
that data for these selected indicators is actually available in sufficient quality
and quantity.

In this chapter, however, we will make these assumptions explicit and
address both indicator and data availability. Obviously, any CSD application
requires data, either quantitative information – for example, measures of
membership size or revenue structure – or qualitative information – for
example, impact assessments or measures of legal aspects. Naturally, the more
comprehensive and systematically available that data is for a wide range of
indicators across the various dimensions, the more valid and useful CSD
applications ultimately become.

Therefore, a discussion of indicator assessment and data availability,
coverage and quality is an important aspect of developing a system such as
the CSD. In this respect, the purpose of this chapter is twofold. First, it
presents some background on what indicators are, and how they relate to the
various dimensions and sub-dimensions. This also includes a discussion of
how to assess and select indicators. Second, this chapter will address data
issues in general, while data issues for each of the four dimensions are covered
separately. Finally, the chapter concludes by describing the process of CSD
applications and by taking a brief look at the potential of the internet and
information technology.

Indicators

Indicators are the building blocks of the CSD and as such are the key to the
overall integrity and quality of any CSD application. Therefore, much thought
and care has been taken to guide the selection of indicators, and users are
advised to begin this process by revisiting the initial list of key indicators

presented in Table 2.4 of Chapter 2 and the more extensive indicator repertoire in Appendix A. Of course, as we suggest below, the search for indicators should not stop there. Indeed, the ultimate aim is to establish and build an indicator bank for each type and unit of analysis over time.

As shown in the previous chapters, indicators measure one of the four CSD dimensions: structure, space, impact and values. Indicators and dimensions differ in their level of abstraction and specificity. In general, the four dimensions are more abstract and multifaceted, whereas indicators are more concrete and typically address one aspect or facet only (see Figure 5.1). For example, the dimension structure includes the three sub-dimensions of size (or scale), revenue and composition. Each sub-dimension, in turn, includes different aspects: size covers employment, volunteering, membership, the number of civil society organizations (CSOs) or growth in expenditure; composition indicators cover the 12 major groups of the International Classification of Non-profit Organizations (ICNPO) (see Salamon and Anheier, 1997); and revenue includes membership dues, contributions, grants, public-sector payments, etc. These are the required indicators for CSD applications: they are less abstract than the dimensions and sub-dimensions, and can be measured.

A great variety of indicators is available for each dimension and, at least potentially, a rich repertoire of different indicators exists for most countries and fields. However, as already pointed out in Chapter 2, not all indicators are alike. Some are complex and demanding in their use; others are intuitive and require less effort in terms of collection and preparation. Others are specific to a particular culture, country, field or type of organization, while still others are useful for comparative purposes and apply across a range of circumstances. Some indicators are available regularly and at levels of high

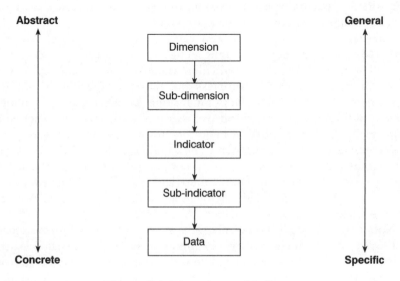

Figure 5.1 *Dimensions and Indicators*

data quality, while others may be questionable in terms of their validity and are available at irregular intervals only.

Thus, indicators vary in a number of ways. To establish a sense of priority and preference among them, we introduced a ranked classification of indicators in Chapter 2. For each dimension, indicators are grouped into four classes: preferred, standard, optional and a residual group entitled 'other'. Accordingly, Table 2.4 in Chapter 2 listed the indicator menu for each dimension by unit of analysis, and in Chapter 4 we used indicators from different categories to present the various country and field illustrations. What are the criteria to guide the selection of indicators and their subsequent classification into one of the four categories? Specifically, indicators are assessed with the help of several criteria: analytic soundness, measurability, significance, integrative capacity and availability.

The first requirement is that the indicator is *analytically sound* – that is, clearly defined and understood, and with a minimal level of ambiguity about its meaning. For example, the definition of a values indicator should clearly differentiate between what is meant by interpersonal trust, on the hand, and confidence in institutions, on the other. Likewise, indicators of legal enablement should not only focus on measuring tax incentives for non-profit organizations, but should also cover aspects of registration, governance, accountability and transparency.

As the last example suggests, in many instances, the indicators themselves frequently consist of separate sub-components or sub-indicators. If this is the case, users may wish to establish an explicit hierarchy of indicators, as is presented in Figure 5.2 for the structure dimension. This figure clearly shows that some of the indicators for structure in Table 2.5 of Chapter 2 are, in fact, sub-indicators of more abstract and general indicators, which in turn represent the various sub-dimensions and dimensions. For example, there are several indicators for specific types of revenue, which together measure the more abstract, composite notion of revenue structure.

Another example of an indicator can be found in Verba et al (1995, pp345–48) on the concept of political engagement as a sub-dimension in values. The unit of analysis is individual (micro), and the concept covers aspects of values, interests, awareness and activities. Specifically, political engagement consists of four sub-dimensions: political interest, political efficacy, political information and partisanship. In a next step, each sub-component is further specified by indicators or variables, which in turn come to be represented by survey questions. These questions then provide the actual data for measuring political engagement. For purposes of analysis, this data is typically broken down by population groups and related to levels of education, income and other aspects, such as membership, volunteering or political variables related to the concept of political engagement.

Note that Figure 5.3 shows only some aspects of the full measurement model. A similar hierarchy would branch the sub-dimension social participation and, one step down, additional hierarchies would emerge from more refined measurements of specific dimensions relating to political interest, efficacy and partisanship. The central point is that the construction

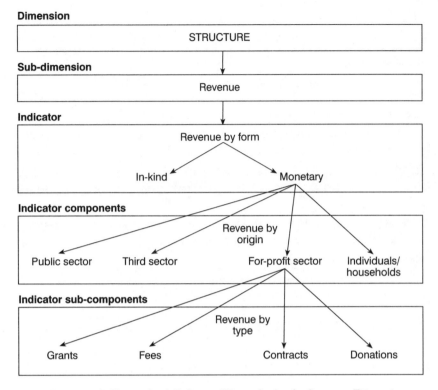

Figure 5.2 *Example of Indicator Hierarchy for the Structure Dimension*

of such indicator hierarchies offers a good insurance policy for testing the analytic soundness of indicators and measures used. Standard social science dictionaries and data descriptors (used to search data in data archives) are useful tools in this regard.

CSD indicators should not only be analytically sound, they should also be *measurable* in the sense that they could be observed in actual situations. For example, the indicator 'impact of civil society organizations on environmental policy-making' may be analytically sound, but, ultimately, is impossible to measure as specified. Clear manifestations of when, how and where such impact could be observed would be required. In other words, indicators need specific units of observation that can be identified and measured in concrete circumstances. In the case of impact on environmental policy, this would include a range of observation units such as government documents and policy drafts, media coverage, CSO statements and activities, funding allocations and flows, and impact assessments by other stakeholders and experts.

> Indicator selection is an integral part of the CSD...indeed, it is part of the very dialogue that the CSD wants to encourage.

This step is illustrated in Figure 5.4 for the indicator 'CSO impact on environmental policy'. The four major types of units are documents covering

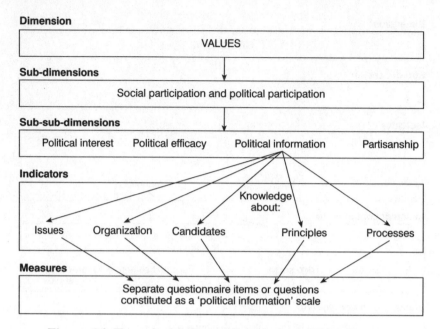

Figure 5.3 *Example of Indicator Hierarchy for the Values Dimension*

the process of policy formulation and implementation; the change in public awareness achieved through CSO campaigns during the policy process; the reports of print and other media about the policy and the attribution of influence and impact on different stakeholders; and the policy impact assessment by other stakeholders and experts. For each of these units, measurement would focus on capturing the policy change that can be attributed to CSO relative to the influence that other stakeholders had.

Moreover, for each unit of observation, a variety of measures with different metrics is involved. For example, the actual policy change achieved by CSOs could be measured by looking at changes in funding allocation in implementing the policy. Are these changes in the direction and magnitude encouraged by CSOs, and to what extent? A population survey of environmental attitudes could yield data on change in public awareness about the relevant policy issues and the extent to which CSOs are seen as change agents in bringing about desired policy outcomes.

The criterion of measurability also implies that reasonable requirements are met in terms of data quality. Of particular interest in this respect are the notions of validity and reliability.[1] Validity refers to the extent to which an indicator actually measures the concept that it is supposed to measure. For example, if interpersonal trust among people in society is the concept behind the indicator, validity addresses the extent to which a question in a telephone survey (of the type 'do you think that most people can be trusted or not?') does, in fact, cover the meaning intended. Or (referring back to the example about environmental policy) if only changes in public spending had been taken into account when measuring the impact of CSOs, the

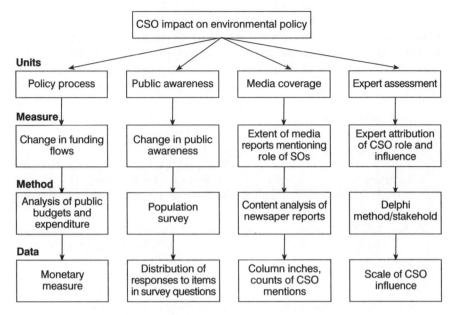

Figure 5.4 *Unit of Observation for the Impact Dimension*

resulting measure, taken alone, would have been partially invalid as other aspects, such as changes in public awareness or expert opinions, remain unspecified.

Reliability refers to the technical quality of indicator measurement. Measures should be objective, communicable and independent of data collectors and interested parties in their actual meaning. For example, indicators of effectiveness should not only measure effectiveness – and not efficiency or equity (a validity problem) – they should also do so with acceptable degrees of accuracy, precision and stability (a reliability issue). In the environmental policy example above, the accuracy with which public budgets and expenditure flows are measured, classified and prepared for analysis would be a question of reliability.

Both validity and reliability cannot be assessed *prima facie* but require statistical assessments that go beyond the purpose of this book (see van der Vijver and Leung, 1997). The important point is that users are well advised to consult expert opinion on the measurement quality of selected indicators in their particular country or region.

The criteria of analytic soundness and measurability apply to all types of indicators. The following criteria, however, refer only to preferred, standard and optional indicators. In other words, significance is not a requirement for 'other' indicator type that users might select for CSD applications.

The criterion of *significance* means that the indicator should pick up the central aspects of the concept that it is trying to measure (see Salamon and Anheier, 1997; Deutsch, 1963). The indicator should be a clear expression of the essence of the dimension or concept measured, and point to what is most relevant. By implication, the indicator should not be concerned with non-essential aspects of the phenomenon. In other words, the criterion of significance emphasizes the principle of parsimony of measurement. For example, a measure of civil rights should measure central rights only, and not include other legal rights that a person may enjoy in a country's legal system or its judicial process.

While the criteria of analytic soundness, measurability and significance are a joint requirement for all but 'other' types of indicators, the final set of criteria apply to preferred and standard indicators only.

Preferred and standard indicators should also be *integrated* within the overall conceptual and operational framework of the CSD; selected indicators should relate to each other and allow users to make connections among them. This criterion applies within, as well as across, dimensions. For example, size indicators in the structure dimension, such as paid employment, membership and volunteering, each take up a distinct facet of CSO scale. At the same time, they relate to each other. Similarly, if size indicators are of particular importance for a CSD application, users may wish to select space or impact indicators that 'speak to' aspects of scale – for example, that are relevant to them. The indicator hierarchies displayed in Figures 5.2 and 5.3 are a method for the systematic detection of how specific indicators relate to other dimensions.

Preferred and standard indicators must, in addition, satisfy the criterion of a general cross-national availability. These indicators must be *available* and *accessible* at low cost and at regular intervals across a wide range of countries, regions and fields. For example, governance measures; operating expenditures of CSOs as a percentage of GNP; membership in civil society organizations; or measures of trust, confidence, civil rights and transparency are available for many countries. This is not to say that such data is available for all or even most countries; as we have argued throughout, the lack of comparable information about even the most basic contours of civil society is an ongoing problem in this field.

Finally, preferred indicators are those additionally characterized for their international comparability. In terms of meaning, they are applicable across a broad range of national and regional experiences and settings. In other words, they carry some degree of *universality*. Clearly, the number of such indicators may be small; but the understanding is that country or field comparisons should primarily focus on this set of indicators. Ideally, preferred indicators should be easy in their application and interpretation – that is, have a high degree of intuitiveness about them in order to encourage dialogue and debate among users.

Table 5.1 shows the relationship between the various criteria for selection and the status of individual indicators. All indicators should be analytically sound and measurable in the sense that they meet basic requirements of data quality; and all except those in the category 'other' should be significant in capturing the essence of the dimension or sub-dimension. In addition, preferred and standard indicators would have to fulfil the requirement of being integrated within the overall CSD architecture. Finally, preferred

Table 5.1 *Indicators and Indicator Selection Criteria*

Criteria/Indictors	Preferred	Standard	Optional	Other
Analytically sound	Yes	Yes	Yes	Yes
Measurable	Yes	Yes	Yes	Yes
Significant	Yes	Yes	Yes	No
Integrated	Yes	Yes	No	No
Available cross-nationally	Yes	Yes	No	No
Some degree of universal comparability with intuitive meaning and ease of use	Yes	No	No	No

indicators would carry some universal element, combined with ease of use and meaning. This criterion would not be as essential for standard indicators. By implication, optional indicators do not need to be potentially universal in meaning or widely available cross-nationally.

How can indicators be assessed and classified in terms of their conceptual and measurement qualities? While comprehensive and sophisticated social science methodologies have been developed in response to this question, and can be consulted in this regard by users familiar with this literature, we propose a simpler interim solution. This involves examining each potential indicator with the help of an 'indicator methodology assessment' in order to ensure their relevance to each dimension (structure, space, impact and values), and, most importantly, their ability to provide relevant information for measuring aspects of civil society. The form used for such an indicator assessment exercise is displayed in Table 5.2. Appendix A presents a variation of this form for over 60 indicators.

> Indicator assessments are a crucial part of any CSD application.

Data

Not surprisingly, countries, fields and organizations vary in the extent to which data and information are available for the various dimensions and indicators that make up the CSD. Unfortunately, around the world, the data situation for civil society in terms of coverage and quality is less than satisfactory. Data availability is generally better for developed countries than for developing countries; better for service-providing organizations than for voice and advocacy organizations; better for larger formal organizations than for smaller informal movements; and better for the well-to-do members of society than for those marginalized and living in poverty.

> ...data is the essential input for any CSD use...

The development of the CSD does not change this data situation; but, at the very least, it creates a demand for more and better data on civil society over time. Therefore, a major part of the effort behind the CSD is to encourage the development of a *basic information infrastructure on civil society*

Table 5.2 *Indicator Methodology Assessment*

Name (of indicator):
Brief definition:
Indicator dimension and sub-dimension:
Technical definition (unit of measurement):
Type of indicator (preferred, standard, optional)
Unit of analysis (macro, meso, micro)
Unit of observation:
Methodological description and underlying definitions

Measurement and methodological aspects:	
Potential usefulness:	
Potential limitations:	
Likely modifications:	
Links to other measures:	

Assessment of data quality and availability

Method of data collection:	
Data provider:	
Access to data:	
Frequency of data collection:	

Comments and justification of indicator classification

around the world – an effort that would not only aim at the national level but also includes data on regions and specific fields.

A systematic and full assessment of available data sources is a first and crucial step towards the building of such an information infrastructure. Indeed, examining the range and quality of data available for analysis is an essential preparatory task of any CSD application. Fortunately, there are numerous sources that can be explored for the purpose of information and data gathering on aspects of civil society (see Appendix C for a list of data sources):

- statistical offices at international, national, regional, local and municipal levels; many statistical offices maintain data sources that can be either directly or indirectly relevant to civil society purposes;
- social science data collections and archives, including public opinion surveys (eg membership, volunteering, social participation, individual

values and attitudes), and organizational surveys (size, purpose, structure, revenue etc);

- specialized data collections by international, national and regional organizations, think-tanks and web-based data providers; this includes field-specific data collections and surveys on areas such as social movements; culture and arts; education; health and social services; environment; economic and social development; housing; and international aspects;
- special research projects on membership, volunteering and CSOs; and
- information collected by CSOs and representatives themselves.

In the field of civil society, however, many of the sources are scattered and not readily available (see Chapter 1). Therefore, in the balance of this chapter, we will point to all of these data sources to suggest to users the full range of options available to them. However, particularly for CSD applications at national, regional and local levels, users are advised to examine the full range of these data sources before embarking on the actual analysis. As a rule of thumb, experience suggests that more data and more information are normally available than is published or otherwise disseminated (see Salamon and Anheier, 1996).

> Rich data sources exist in most countries, including in developing regions; these can be mined for CSD purposes.

We will now take a brief look at the data availability for each of the four CSD dimensions, beginning with structure, which is, in some ways, the dimension with the best data availability in terms of coverage and quality. Appendix A provides more background information on these indicators and indicator systems mentioned below.

Structure

Fortunately, there are several major social science efforts currently underway that provide basic information for at least some of the CSD dimensions across a wider range of countries. Most prominent among them are the Union of International Associations (UIA), the World Values Survey (WVS), and the Johns Hopkins Comparative Non-profit Sector Project (JHCNSP).

The UIA has collected information on several types of international associations since the early 20th century. It is the world's largest source of data on international organizations and includes data on activities; staff and volunteers; founding date; board membership; management; expenditures; relations with other organizations; and range of operations across countries and regions, among others. The UIA can be contacted at www.uia.org.

The WVS developed from the European Values Survey in 1980 and takes place every five years, supplementing the more frequent general social surveys that take place annually in many countries. Typically, these population surveys provide data on membership in a range of voluntary associations, volunteering and related items, such as social and political participation, in addition to information on the socio-economic and demographic background of members. Population surveys available for countries or regions are generally found in social science data archives and can be accessed via the internet (see the section on 'Values').

Next to these ongoing efforts to collect data on international organizations is the Johns Hopkins Comparative Non-profit Sector Project. This project now covers over 40 countries worldwide and is a major source of basic economic data on the non-profit sector – a term that overlaps with the organizational aspects of what is defined as civil society for the purposes of the CSD (see Chapter 2). The JHCNSP follows a systematic approach in applying a complex methodology in collecting and analysing data on the basic contours of non-profit organizations. Specifically, the approach includes a common definition, classification system, measurement tools and survey forms, and elaborate data-reporting systems.[2]

Clearly, CSD applications will be most useful in countries that are part of this project, particularly when combined with the UIA and WVS data and other more country-specific efforts. The latter include data collected by institutions such as the Independent Sector in the US (www.independent sector.org); the Charities Aid Foundation (www.cafonline.org) and the Institute for Volunteering Research (www.ivr.org.uk/institute.htm) in the UK; Non-profit Japan (www.igc.org/ohdakefoundation); Maecenata in Germany (www.maecenata.de); and many national statistical offices, as well as university-based and policy-oriented efforts in developed and developing countries.

Special care has to be applied to the definitions employed in these efforts and to the assumptions that they might entail. For example, some of the major data items for non-profit organizations covered by the JHCNSP are:

- paid employment: number of employees (full time, part time), wages and salaries and structure of employment;
- expenditures: operating expenditures, capital expenditures and other expenditures;
- unpaid employment/volunteers: number of volunteers and frequency and amount of volunteering;
- public-sector revenue/payments: grants, contracts, statutory transfers, third-party payments and contributions in kind;
- private giving to non-profit organizations: foundation giving, corporate giving and individual giving; and
- private fees and payments: fees and services charges, dues, sales and investment/endowment income.

While the Johns Hopkins project primarily covers economic variables relating to non-profit organizations, the World Values Survey – and similar regional surveys – report data on:

- membership (number of members, number of memberships held, membership by country); and

- volunteering by socio-demographic characteristics and related social participation measures.

The Union of International Association's database offers information on:

- number of international organizations (with paid employment and without employment, number of membership associations, number of endowment-based foundations, number of organizations by legal form, etc);
- profile of chair person or chief executive officer; and
- membership profile by country.

Of course, there are also other international efforts that collect basic information on the scale and revenue structure of civil society organizations. The Commonwealth Foundation in the UK carried out an initial mapping of civil society in the majority of Commonwealth countries (www.common wealthfoundation.com); the National Centre for Volunteering Research conducted a study of volunteering within several European countries (Gaskin and Smith, 1997) to be repeated in 2002; and the University of Sussex conducted a Ford Foundation-supported effort to examine the basic contours of civil society around the world (www.ids.ac.uk/ids/civsoc/home.html).

Many countries have national and regional data collections that provide some of the data needed for the CSD. These would be available either at statistical offices or umbrella organizations such as the National Council of Voluntary Organizations in the UK, the Centre on Philanthropy in Canada or Independent Sector in the US. Other sources of information on civil society organizations are employment surveys, social security statistics, government finance and budget data, and a host of other data collected by statistical offices (time-budget surveys, special industry or field studies). The Johns Hopkins Comparative Non-profit Sector Project has developed the most systematic and comprehensive system for assessing available data sources for the purpose of the structure dimension.

Space

In terms of the space dimension, several indicator approaches are available for either the legal aspects of civil society or the larger political and regulatory system in which civil society operates. This includes:

- the legal assessments carried out by the International Centre for Non-profit Law and the World Bank (ICNL and World Bank, 1997);
- The USAID Legal Environment Indicator (USAID, 2000), particularly for Central and Eastern Europe (see also USAID NGO Sustainability Index in the section on 'Impact'). This expert ranking scheme covers seven legal features of non-governmental organizations (NGOs). After initial assessments, a working group meets to review rankings and score sheets, and to compare them with the expert's overview statement, other countries' rankings and prior years' scores.

- The legal scoring system developed as part of the JHCNSP (Salamon and Toepler, 2000) for some 15 to 20 countries worldwide with 24 legal features. This has an emphasis on developed market economies (see, also, Appendix A for a more detailed description).
- The World Bank's governance project (Kaufmann et al 1999a; 1999b; World Bank, 1999) collects a wide range of information on a country's political and administrative system. The governance indicator covers, on a country-by-country basis, the following aspects and reports them both separately and combined: voice and accountability; political stability and lack of violence; government effectiveness; regulatory framework; rule of law; and corruption.
- The Harvard Centre for International Development–World Bank DataMart project includes datasets on political institutions, risk indicators and a mapping of political conflict and civil society (www.paradocs.pols. columbia.edu/datavine/ and www.data.fas.harvard.edu/cfia/pnscs/). This includes data on a country basis on conflict civility; conflict carrying capacity; civil coercion; classification of civil society event categories; and other political and social conflict characteristics.

Other indicator systems include:

- The Corruption Index developed by Transparency International (Lambsdorff, 1999a; 1999b) to measure the degree of corruption in society in approximately 100 countries worldwide. This index is based on a complex set of different surveys, sampling frames and various methodologies, and combines assessments from 2000 to 2003 to reduce abrupt variation in scoring.
- The Political Freedom Index by Desai (1994; see also UNDP, 1992) covers five areas: integrity of self; rule of law; political participation; freedom of expression; and equality before the law. A similar indicator produced by Freedom House uses freedom of expression; associational and organizational rights; rule of law and civil rights; and personal autonomy and economic rights.

Values

In the values dimension, CSD applications can benefit from a growing number of general and specific public-opinion and social-attitude surveys. Many of these surveys are conducted at the national and regional level – for example, the UK Social Attitude Survey; the General Social Survey in the US; the Eurobarometer survey in the European Union and Central and Eastern Europe; the Latinobarómeter in Latin America; and electoral surveys that now cover most democratic countries. In addition, there is a wide range of more special surveys that can be explored for the purpose of measuring people's value, norms and attitudes. Many such surveys are available for public use from social science data archives that operate in over 30 developed and developing countries. These archives form a worldwide network, the

International Federation of Data Organizations (IFDO-net), and can be accessed through the website of the Central Archives at the University of Cologne, Germany, under www.za.uni-koeln.de (see Appendix C for a list of data sources).

The data collected as part of the World Value Survey, the European Value Survey, Eurobarometer, and Latinobarómeter and other efforts offers the most systematic approach to measure values, norms and attitudes cross-nationally. At the level of individual respondents, the data covers:

• interpersonal trust;
• confidence in different social institutions;
• political opinions;
• social and political participation;
• degrees of tolerance and discrimination;
• aspects of religion and belief systems;
• membership in different types of voluntary organizations; and
• volunteering in different types of voluntary organizations.

It also comprises other aspects of people's values, norms and attitudes that can be examined in the context of socio-economic and demographic characteristics.

The University of California, San Diego, data bank (2001a) is an important source of information in values-related data. This site includes a searchable catalogue to over 440 data sites with downloadable data, nearly 100 data libraries worldwide, and various other sources, including the Lijphart Election Archive (University of California, San Diego, 2001b).

Impact

Data availability is perhaps most critical for the impact dimension. Nonetheless, a number of options are available: progress charts and indicators; sustainability assessments; organizational performance measures; stakeholder surveys using the Delphi method or some other more qualitative approach; and output and capacity measures.

The first is a variation of the Fulfilled Commitment Index (FCI) as applied to civil society. The FCI is a progress chart developed by Social Watch (2000) to illustrate the progress of countries with respect to 13 commitments assumed by governments at the 1995 World Summit on Social Development and the 1997 Fourth World Conference on Women in Beijing. It is used illustratively in the CSD examples in Chapter 4, but could be employed as a model to measure CSO commitments at either the policy level or within particular fields or organizations.

For example, if CSO representatives commit to improving primary education, several agreed-upon indicators are chosen to monitor progress toward the set goal. A table for each commitment will show the value of the indicator(s) for the year x, the value for the last year available, the value that should be reached by the year x+8, and the goal to be reached by the year x+10. Ratings would then indicate the actual progress made, which can then be converted to percentages for the CSD.

Next, several countries, particularly those in Central and Eastern Europe, can use information based on the USAID NGO Sustainability Index to gauge the extent to which civil society, generally, and policy measures, specifically, 'make a difference' (USAID, 2000). This indicator system, largely grounded in qualitative expert assessments, covers six additional dimensions to the legal environment mentioned above. These are:

- organizational capacity of NGOs;
- financial viability of NGOs;
- visibility and impact of advocacy activities;
- public image that NGOs enjoy;
- quality of service provided by NGOs; and
- quality of NGO infrastructure.

Taken together, these dimensions provide a basic description of what a sustainable NGO sector should look like. Individually, these dimensions provide a reasonable measure of impact over time, and a basis for identifying both needs and opportunities in a strategic planning process (see Appendix B.1 for more detail). While the system has been applied primarily to the countries of Central and Eastern Europe, it can, in principle, be used in other parts of the world. It complements the Johns Hopkins Non-profit Law Index in the space dimension.

Organizational Performance Measures

The measurement and assessment of organizational performance and impact constitutes a vast field of social science research. Unfortunately, it is also a field that offers somewhat inconclusive advice to applied research efforts such as the CSD, in large part because of the very diversity of organizations and tasks involved. For civil society organizations, the problem is complicated by the absence of a fully tested and accepted repertoire of performance and assessment measures. Many available measures derive from public-sector management and business applications. Nonetheless, recent years have seen significant development in the field, particularly work carried out by Forbes (1998), Paton (1998), Herman and Renz (1997), Osborne (1998), Murray (2000) and, especially, Kendall and Knapp (2000).

Kendall and Knapp (2000, p114) follow the production of welfare framework (POW) that has been developed by the Personal Social Service Research Unit to assess the performance and impact of social service providers. With modifications, the POW can be extended to apply to advocacy organizations and informal organizations as well. The main elements of the POW are:

- resource inputs (eg staff, volunteers, finance);
- costs associated with resource inputs, as indicated in budgets and similar accounts, including opportunity costs;
- non-resource inputs that are not priced (eg motivations, attitudes and values of staff or volunteers);
- intermediate outputs (eg volumes of output, capacity provided, etc); and
- final outcomes in terms of organizational goals and missions (welfare increase; quality of life, including externalities associated with the organization's activities).

While a full presentation of POW is beyond the confines of this chapter, Figures 5.4 and 5.5 offer an overview of the basic approach taken by Kendall and Knapp (2000, pp115–117) in measuring the impact of voluntary associations in the field of service provision. Figure 5.4 offers a conceptual framework on how the input–output outcomes chain relates to crucial notions, such as:

- economy – ie the relationship between 'costed' and 'uncosted' resource inputs (resource savings);
- efficiency – ie the economic cost relationship between inputs and intermediate outputs;

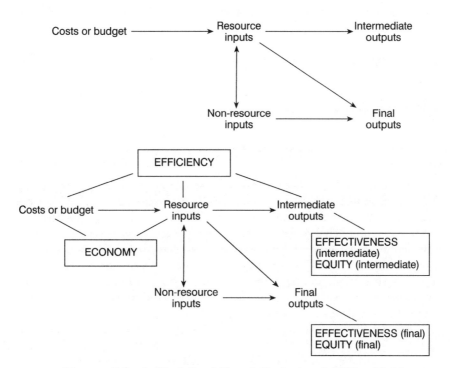

Figures 5.5a–b *Kendall and Knapp's Production of Welfare Model*

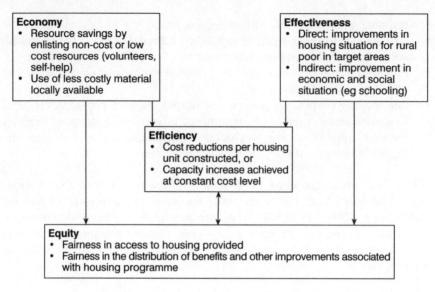

Figure 5.6 *Relations among Evaluation Criteria*

- effectiveness – ie the relationship between inputs and organizational objectives; and
- equity – ie the fairness and net welfare contribution achieved by the organization.

Some of the major domains and indicator sets used in the POW framework are presented in Appendix B.2. Figure 5.5 shows the relationship among the concepts in the case of a housing association providing low-cost housing to rural poor in developing countries.

Stakeholder Surveys

Next to sustainability indices and organizational assessment approaches are indicators that measure the assumed strengths and weaknesses of civil society. Such measures can be generated through 'stakeholder surveys' that are conducted among civil society representatives. Such surveys can also include representatives of government and business that might be relevant in the context of a particular CSD application. Ideally, indicators for the impact and other dimensions should be based on existing 'hard' data sources. However, this objective can hardly be met in the majority of countries around the world, as this data simply does not exist.[3]

Complementing existing data with data from stakeholder surveys is particularly important as the CSD seeks to foster the links between the research community, on the one hand, and civil society representatives, on the other. Surveys cover civil society stakeholders: representatives of CSOs, government and business officials working closely with civil society, as well as researchers and journalists. Of course, information obtained from the stakeholder survey carries substantive and methodological challenges that need to be taken into account. This includes concerns about the social desirability of answers, the response rate, as well as the potential effect of re-inforcing rather than challenging existing myths concerning the state of civil society. In order to correct for biases introduced by subjective opinions and selection effects, it is useful to combine the results of the stakeholder survey with both secondary and primary data.

The Delphi method is one prominent way of carrying out stakeholder surveys of perceived impact. A Delphi is a method for structuring a group communication process. The aim is to address a complex problem and to reach, if possible, some form of consensus, or to establish some demarcation around areas of dissent. In this case, the result would be the establishment of some agreed-upon scale or ranking to measure the impact of civil society. The Delphi method documents the basis and extent of the consensus or dissent achieved, and shows the process by which it was established over dissenting opinions, if any. There are many different versions of the Delphi method and it typically involves several steps:

Selection of Delphi participants
The selection of Delphi participants has to follow certain rules, which are largely dictated by the issue at hand. Some issues or topics require broad selection criteria in an effort to include all of the major stakeholders; others focus on particular expertise and experience. In the case of a macro-level application, participants would include representatives of major civil society organizations, policy-makers, social movements, experts and other relevant groups. For field-level applications, specialists for the particular area under question should be represented. Clearly, the composition of participants has a significant impact on Delphi results. Depending upon the purpose, the selection process can emphasize the likelihood of reaching consensus among participants or the probability that areas of disagreement emerge during the process.

Decision on the form of communication
The process of soliciting opinion and reaching consensus or dissent must be fair and efficient. In some settings, mail questionnaires or web-based communication work fine; in others, a telephone interview may be sufficient, while in still other instances, personal interviews and roundtable discussions are more appropriate. The use of information technology is particularly helpful to enable long-distance communication among stakeholders. For first-time applications of the CSD, we recommend face-to-face interactions in a workshop setting.

Development of a questionnaire or interview schedule
Typically, the questionnaire includes:

- *an opening part* that introduces background information on the purpose, organization, participants and use of the Delphi (here: impact of civil society);
- *key questions* relating to the impact of civil society/CSOs;
  (The formulation of questions must make it clear to the respondents what the options are in terms of their assessments and opinions, and the questions must also ask for the reasons or experiences that lead Delphi participants to express one opinion rather than another. The key questions would include specific rankings of the extent to which particular policy objectives have been achieved; of the impact CSOs had in dealing with particular problems; or of the degree to which agreed-upon changes in governance or performance have been obtained. In soliciting these rankings from participants, each scale should have at least ten steps to accommodate the needs of the CSD in terms of measurement. Participants can then plot their response (ranking) in the CSD, using either a pencil-and-paper method or some computer-assisted approach. Average scores (mean rank) and the range of disagreement (standard variation, span) can easily be calculated and plotted in the CSD.)
- *background questions* that solicit information on the respondent as such (ie experience with civil society/CSOs; educational, professional, religious and political background; as well as other information that might be useful in putting answers into perspective); and
- *a closing part* that reminds respondents about the next step in the Delphi procedure and the CSD, if any.

Analysis of initial returns
With initial answers in place, users should examine the range of responses given to the key questions, trying to identify similar opinions, grouping them under one, two or three 'opinion clusters'. These clusters represent summaries of the emerging lines of consensus and divergence in the opinions held by the Delphi participants. In this context, it is important to develop rating and ranking systems for different aspects of civil society impact.

Revision of questionnaire
With these opinion clusters in mind, users revise the initial questionnaire on how civil society impact is to be measured and assessed.

Second (and third, etc) Delphi round and analysis
The revised questionnaire is then made available to participants with a new set of instructions. With the second round of questionnaires completed, users analyse the information, particularly the ratings and rankings of civil society impact. Some Delphi methods require additional rounds. Importantly, once a Delphi method has been established, repeated use is usually much less time consuming and labour intensive. The same ranking system can be employed using the same or similar experts. This makes the Delphi method and its related scaling or rank methods particularly attractive to regular CSD applications.

Output and Capacity Measures

Finally, in situations where more direct impact measures are unavailable, capacity and output measures can be used as proxy indicators. However, the major problem with capacity measures, in particular, is that they overlap significantly with the structure dimension, and users are advised to resort to such indicators only as a second-best solution. The usefulness of capacity and output indicators lies primarily in efficiency measures that can be generated with their help, and which contrast with government and business figures. For example, users may wish to calculate the expenditure of non-profit primary schools per student relative to that of government-run establishments. The Johns Hopkins Comparative Non-profit Sector Project compiled an initial inventory of output and capacity measures for a number of selected fields. For illustrative purposes, Appendix B.3 offers a set of examples. These measures can be incorporated within the organizational impact assessment approach developed by Kendall and Knapp (2000) above.

Process: Using the CSD

CSD applications generally follow nine separate steps. Of course, at each part of the sequence, users can go back and change some decisions, as well as correct for any mistakes or misunderstandings that may have been implemented in earlier steps. For these reasons, it is best to think of the following sequence less as a strict procedure and more as a set of guidelines for best practice. Figure 5.7 offers a summary presentation of the nine steps involved.

Step 1: identify the purpose of the CSD application

Is the purpose to describe civil society or some of its component parts, either as a status report, to track progress or to put civil society in context? Or is the

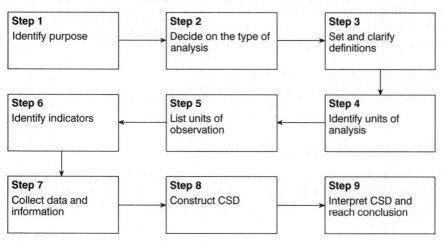

Figure 5.7 *Steps in CSD Application*

purpose an analytic one in which a particular fact or trend, relationship, problem or theoretical issue is to be examined? Or are policy considerations involved in the sense that policy issues are to be discussed with the help of the CSD, and possible scenarios are to be explored? Of course, applications can have multiple objectives; but there is a certain hierarchy: description is usually the first task, followed by conceptual analysis and, finally, analysis for policy purposes.

Step 2: decide on the type of CSD analysis to be performed

Should the CSD analysis be over time, comparative, status or progress report, etc? This will guide the selection of indicators and will also point to the type of data to be collected. If the CSD is to be applied over time, the relevant time periods need to be selected; if a civil society or some of its component parts are to be put in comparative context, users have to decide on what other cases to include. If the purpose of the CSD is to set standards or to track progress, agreement must be reached on what the standards are and what level of progress performance is to be measured.

Step 3: set and clarify definitions

Make clear what aspects of civil society are the focus of the CSD application. This involves establishing a borderline for the inclusion and exclusion of some element or another, and dealing with grey areas that may require closer scrutiny and qualitative judgement. We recommend that users establish clear guidelines on how to apply the operational definition of civil society, civil society organizations and other central concepts in relation to available indicators.

Step 4: identify the unit of analysis

Identify the level at which the CSD is to be applied. Referring back to Figure 2.1 in Chapter 2, users have to decide if the CSD will be constructed at the macro level (generally, country or region), meso level (fields, industries) or the micro level (case study, scenario). This decision will determine what kind of indicators to select (see step 5).

Step 5: list the units of observation

List the types of entities covered, such as organizations, individuals or events, and match them to the appropriate unit of analysis.

Step 6: identify and select indicators

Identify and select indicators by first listing the key characteristics or variables of interest. Following this, select indicators accordingly for each of the four dimensions. The stage of indicator selection is one of the most critical steps in applying the CSD. Users are advised to examine a wide range of potential indicators and to use multiple indicators for each dimension. If necessary,

Table 5.3 *Indicator–Data Matrix*

Indicator	Data for Year 1	Data for Year 2	Data for Year 3
Dimension A			
Indicator 1	data	data	data
Indicator 2	etc	etc	etc
Indicator 3	...	...	...
Indicator 4	...	...	...
Dimension B			
Indicator 1	...	...	...
Indicator 2			
etc	...	...	...

develop indicator hierarchies showing the relationship between dimensions, sub-dimensions and indicators, as shown in Chapter 4.

Step 7: collect data and information accordingly for each indicator

In many cases, this will involve available as well as newly assembled data, particularly in the impact field, where stakeholder surveys are likely to provide crucial information. It is best to develop a database of indicators for easy reference and retrieval. It is useful to construct and fill in a data matrix table, with the indicators in the rows and the required data in the columns, organized by year or some other relevant time period, as suggested in Table 5.3.

Step 8: construct the CSD

Construct the CSD either by using a 'pencil-and-paper' approach or, preferably, with appropriate software packages. Users may wish to explore a link between the indicator database and the software package capable of generating the actual coordinate system and graphics.

Step 9: interpret the CSD

Incorporate additional measures as needed, reach a conclusion and decide on actions to be taken, if any. This can involve a more structured debate among major stakeholders, the posting of the CSD on a dedicated website for comments and suggestions, or simply an individual or group exercise in data analysis and interpretation using flipcharts and other methods that invite debate and active participation. Of course, the development of appropriate dissemination strategies, if any, depends upon the purpose of the CSD application and the nature of the audience involved.

Initially, most of these steps will be rather time consuming, and users are likely to encounter many methodological and practical difficulties. Upon repeated application, however, the use of the CSD will become easier and less cumbersome. Users will undoubtedly gain experience in conducting the structured dialogue about civil society that the CSD wants to encourage, and the database available for CSD application is likely to broaden in coverage and improve in quality over time.

Use of Information Technology

The significance of the internet and information technology (IT) for CSD applications has become apparent at several points in this chapter. Increasingly, information about many aspects relevant to measuring civil society and its component parts is available on the internet. In many instances, such information can be downloaded free of charge and can become part of the database needed for continued and expanding use of the CSD among civil society representatives, researchers and other stakeholders (see data sources in Appendix C). The use of IT goes beyond employing the internet as a source of information, and uses it to construct and conduct CSD applications themselves. The use of dedicated web sites, user groups and networks among stakeholders in holding debates about particular CSD methodologies and results is just one of many examples that come to mind and are worth exploring. Thus, IT can facilitate the data collection, preparation, storage, updating and sharing of CSD input.

Conclusion

Fortunately, the availability of even a minimal set of data makes CSD applications possible and useful. Nonetheless, in most countries additional and sustained efforts will be needed to collect and draw in additional information to fill in major data gaps. While the internet and increased IT access and use are helpful in this respect, much of the task remains to be done.

Chapter 6

Applying the Civil Society Diamond:
Case Studies

The usefulness of the system suggested here is, ultimately, judged by the insights that it generates for civil society practitioners, policy-makers and researchers. Several countries participated in a pilot phase, conducted by CIVICUS, to test the Civil Society Diamond (CSD) approach and its assumptions, and to explore what can be learned from its applications across a range of different circumstances that differ in political context, level of economic development, objectives and data availability.[1] In this chapter, we will selectively summarize the experiences of some of these country studies to offer readers a sense of what the CSD 'feels like' in action. Given the pilot nature of the various case studies, none could apply the full range of options developed in the previous chapters; but when taken together, they present a picture of what is possible upon first CSD use, and with minimum data and little experience in its application.[2]

Although we will offer these summaries in alphabetical order, they include two developed market economies (Canada and New Zealand); three former communist countries from Central and Eastern Europe (Belarus, Estonia and Ukraine); two countries where a recent history of social and ethnic conflict and divisiveness has given way to conscious efforts at building and rebuilding civil society (Croatia and South Africa); and two developing countries of very different cultural and political circumstance (Mexico and Pakistan). Of course, we cannot offer a full account of each case study, how participants worked through the steps outlined in the previous chapter, or the decisions they had to make about data coverage and analysis. What we can do, however, is to highlight aspects of the approach taken and focus on some of the main findings.

Belarus[3]

The objectives of the study are to increase the knowledge and understanding of civil society by assessing its current status in Belarus, and to promote dialogue in order to strengthen civil society towards developing a common vision and agenda of fostering social change.

Methodology

The Belarus Support Centre for Associations and Foundations (SCAF) coordinated the study. SCAF used an innovative approach by creating a web page where interested parties with relevant expertise in civil society could participate at any stage of the project's development. The project was conducted in three stages:

1 review of existing data;
2 distribution of targeted experts/stakeholder survey through group meetings; and
3 a national workshop to discuss the findings.

The project made use of a range of existing data and added a stakeholder survey of 158 experts from civil society, researchers, journalists, and government and parliament. The four CSD dimensions were measured along ten sub-sectors: ethnicity; culture; women; business; social characteristics; education; human rights; ecology; youth; and international characteristics.

Structure

While substantial growth in the number of civil society organizations (CSOs) took place between 1994 and 2001, much of this growth was limited to the capital and regional centres, and bypassed rural areas and small towns. What is more, a negative assessment of the activities of umbrella organizations and resource centres emerged from the stakeholder survey, which forced participants to review the nature of cooperation and divisions within civil society. Frequently, lack of transparency prevents collaboration. Western funding remains the major source of revenue, with government funding being limited to those loyal to government funding or in non-political fields. There is virtually no support from the private sector.

Space

The great majority of stakeholders and government experts believe that existing legislation does not promote the establishment of non-governmental organizations (NGOs). Four out of ten believe that NGO status is often used by commercial organizations to avoid paying taxes, and nine out of ten favour legislative reform. Together, these findings suggest serious deficiencies in the legal environment of civil society in Belarus, which is reinforced by current practices: civil society respondents indicated low access to, and minimal influence on, the legislature. Government agencies generally have a negative opinion and attitude about civil society representatives, although a survey of both government officials and NGO experts suggests positive attitudes by government officials.

Values

The stakeholder survey revealed that accountability and transparency are not greatly valued among CSOs, and a majority of survey respondents agree that there is a need to develop better oversight methods and stricter legal requirements on the financial behaviour of non-profit organizations. These issues are also reflected at the interpersonal level. Belarus shows comparatively low scores in general trust levels, and confidence levels in institutions appear contradictory.

Impact

Perhaps because of the mixed track record of civil society institutions in the country, impact measures are inconclusive and suggest a serious need for policy reform, both at the political level and within civil society. For example, while stakeholders believe that their impact on broader society is rather strong, their influence on government policy is weak. 65 per cent believe that they represent the interests of their constituents (not a very good measure of real impact); 39 per cent are seldom invited to participate in relevant meetings; and 34 per cent believe that they don't cooperate with government in implementing policies. 85 per cent of respondents believe that they are effective in advancing the common good; but this is not confirmed by secondary data. Opinions by experts hold that only 20 to 30 per cent of NGOs are effective in implementing their mission and activities. This assessment has to be seen in the context that stakeholders are concerned about the lack of favourable media coverage.

These assessments were reached against the simple CSD represented in Figure 6.1, and it is useful to keep in mind the contradictory nature of some of the results. Initially, the high score on the space dimension, given the political environment, surprised SCAF. The high score of 68 in the values dimension is contradicted by secondary data in the sense that stakeholders had different 'readings' from what the available data suggested.

Results

This study added value to civil society in the following ways: existing studies had limited focus, lacked a holistic approach and only targeted specific groups; results were not widely accessible and did not encourage dialogue at local, national or international levels. In addition to bringing civil society stakeholders (who have never before collaborated) together, the CSD allowed them to discuss, analyse, quantify and measure civil society in a systematic way. The project also allowed them to identify specific areas or action to strengthen civil society; to develop more effective umbrella organizations; to achieve a more even distribution of organizations throughout the country; and to improve cooperation and unity among CSOs.

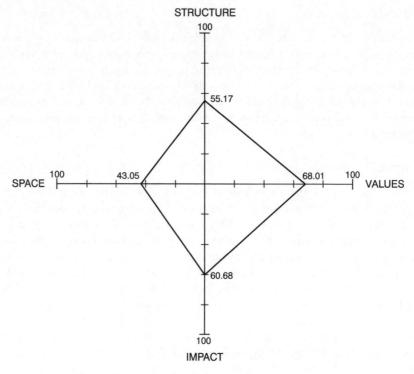

Figure 6.1 *Civil Society Status Diamond for Belarus*

Canada[4]

The purpose of this study, conducted by the Canadian Centre for Philanthropy, was to explore the strengths and weaknesses of civil society in Canada, with a focus on government–non-profit relations.

Methodology

The study was implemented in two stages:

1   a review of existing data; followed by
2   a targeted opinion survey.

The review of existing data includes national surveys and quantitative and qualitative studies of civil society. In order to develop the questionnaire, the Canadian Centre for Philanthropy interviewed 16 key informants, representing civil society practitioners and researchers. These interviews were conducted in order to select indicators relevant to assessing Canada's civil society. 50 per cent of the indicators are 'universal indicators' and are being used by all countries participating in the project. The remaining indicators are specific to Canada. The Centre surveyed 200 key civil society informants representing 15 civil society sub-sectors, academics/researchers, businesses and governments across Canada. Most were top executives of civil society organizations (CEOs, presidents or executive directors). The Centre also contacted senior government and private-sector officials, and researchers/academics who interact with CSOs. Of the 200 contacted across Canada, 104 (52 per cent) replied. The responses flowed into the development of the CSD presented in simplified form in Figure 6.2.

Structure

The results of the structure area suggest widespread and robust participation in civil society, but also high expectations on behalf of the population and CSO members. Approximately 31 per cent of Canadians performed some kind of organized volunteer work in 1997. 41 per cent of Canadians believe that political participation is essential and 43 per cent believe that it is very important. 89 per cent of survey respondents agree or strongly agree that CSOs need an active membership base. 84 per cent 'agree' or 'strongly agree' that CSO membership should cut across a range of constituencies. More than half (57 per cent) of survey respondents believe that umbrella organizations seldom or only sometimes have the capacity to represent the interests of members. Indeed, results indicate that collaboration among CSOs and with umbrella organizations remains weak.

Space

Results about the legal and political environment of CSOs in Canada are mixed and point to a need for reform. Only 45 per cent of survey respondents believe the existing tax system encourages individuals and businesses to donate to CSOs. Only 32 per cent of respondents agree that the existing tax system encourages the development of CSOs. By contrast, the majority of respondents (59 per cent) agree that the existing regulations make it difficult to register CSOs as charities. 67 per cent believe existing tax laws and regulations make it difficult for CSOs to engage in advocacy activities. Although there are initiatives in place in legislature to foster working relationships between government and CSOs, the majority (68 per cent) of respondents disagree with the statement that governments have established appropriate mechanisms and channels to link CSOs with government departments and agencies. The majority (78 per cent) of respondents disagree with the statement that governments have established appropriate mechanisms and channels to link CSOs with political representatives.

62 per cent of survey respondents disagree with the statement that CSOs have the capacity (the human resources, knowledge, etc) to interact with political representatives and government departments and agencies. With regard to the change in public support for CSOs, 64 per cent of key informants indicate that public support has either increased or remained the same.

Values

Assessments in the value area were more positive. CSOs are frequently active in the following issues: environment and sustainable development (58 per cent); human rights (65 per cent); gender equity (57 per cent); social justice (66 per cent); and cultural diversity (49 per cent). 67 per cent of respondents agree that CSOs make information about their activities available to constituents and stakeholders. 62 per cent of respondents agree that CSOs make their financial statements publicly available. 47 per cent agree that CSOs have adopted codes of conduct. 68 per cent agree that CSOs involve constituents and stakeholders in planning, designing, implementing and evaluating activities. 54 per cent agree that CSOs involve volunteers (other than board members) in planning, designing, implementing and evaluating activities. 69 per cent agree that CSOs have created participatory mechanisms to facilitate achieving their stated missions.

Impact

Government has not reached out to CSOs in ways that are judged adequate by CSO representatives. 63 per cent note that CSOs are 'seldom' or 'only sometimes' successful in putting the interests of their constituents on the policy agenda. 63 per cent believe that CSOs are 'not frequently' successful in submitting policy options to decision-makers during the policy process. 71 per cent say that CSOs are 'seldom' or 'only sometimes' capable of influencing governments to undertake policy decisions that foster social and community well-being. 90 per cent feel that governments 'seldom' or 'only sometimes' cooperate with CSOs when implementing social policies and programmes.

By contrast, the impact of CSOs themselves is judged more favourably: 59 per cent of respondents say that CSOs are 'very frequently' or 'frequently' able to deliver programmes and services demanded by their constituents. 69 per cent believe that CSOs 'very frequently' or 'frequently' have the capacity to identify new needs and demands arising from their constituents. 63 per cent feel that CSOs 'very frequently' or 'frequently' have the ability to find 'innovative' solutions and ideas to meet the needs of their constituents. 94 per cent agree that CSOs enhance the capacity of their constituents to participate in improving social and community well-being. 95 per cent believe that CSOs foster attitudes that lead to higher levels of civic engagement. 78 per cent 'strongly agree' or 'agree' that CSOs are capable of adding more value to programmes and services than the state or the private sector.

Results

As implied above, much research has been conducted on Canadian civil society. However, the CSD study has yielded additional insights. Three of the more important conclusions of the study are:

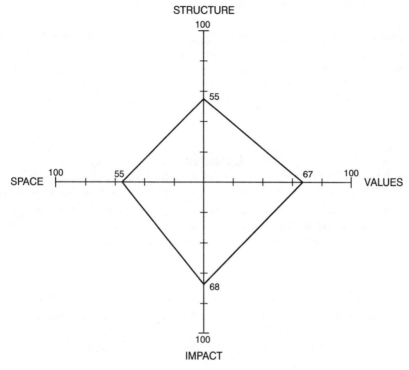

Figure 6.2 *Civil Society Status Diamond for Canada*

1   CSOs need to find timely and effective solutions to challenges, as specified
     by the four dimensions, or risk the lost of credibility within the
     community;
2   The Canadian government needs to take clear steps to establish a stronger
     working relationship with CSOs if it continues to view CSOs as playing a
     role in improving the quality of life of Canadians;
3   The private sector needs to become more involved with CSOs and the
     community or it will become isolated from community improvement
     activities.

In addition, the study has outlined specific actions and areas of improvement
that will help to focus the activities of current initiatives, such as the
government's Voluntary Sector Initative (VSI). Canada's VSI works to
strengthen the capacity of the voluntary sector and to enhance the relationship
between the sector and the government. Two research findings may be of
particular relevance to Canada's VSI:

1   Effort should be focused on improving the regulatory environment since
     a significant number of key civil society informants believe that the
     existing tax regime is a burden on the sector and plays a minimal role in
     guiding or supporting the sector.

2   CSOs need to play a more vital role in the policy-making process.

A majority of respondents felt that the government does not involve them when implementing social policies and programmes and that CSOs are unsuccessful in putting constitutent interests on the policy agenda. The government, therefore, needs to do a better job of reaching out to CSOs and involving them significantly in the entire policy-making and implentation process.

Croatia[5]

The objectives of this study are to assess the strengths and the weaknesses of civil society, to have the National Goal and Agenda-Setting Workshop reflect on the findings and identify areas for action, and to provide the media with empirical information on problems facing civil society today.

Methodology

The study was coordinated by the Centre for Development of Non-profit Organizations (CERANEO) and was carried out in two general phases:

1   Existing information and previous research concerning civil society in Croatia were compiled and analysed.
2   A stakeholder survey was conducted among 353 key civil society representatives from a variety of subsectors.

Structure

Croatia has about 20,000 registered CSOs, with approximately half in the field of sports and recreation. While 38 per cent of the population belong to at least one association, the distribution of CSOs shows that the majority of CSOs are located in the four larger towns, with a lack of CSOs in areas with less than 20,000 inhabitants (World Bank, 2000). The existence of umbrella organizations with specific scopes of interest is moderate. These organizations fail to adequately encourage membership and participation, and are unlikely to promote the common interest of the sector that they represent. The smaller organizations are marginalized and only partially participate in the activities of big organizations.

Moreover, survey results indicate that a tradition of cooperation between CSOs and the private sector is lacking. There is also a lack of CSO awareness of mechanisms of interest representation and lobbying; as a result, CSO interests in the public sphere are rather underdeveloped. The survey also indicates that funding of CSOs is improving, although foreign funding continues to play a major role.

Space

The registration of CSOs was seen as unproblematic; however, some pressure seems to exist for CSOs to join or endorse certain political groupings. Tax laws were perceived as a major obstacle to CSO development. There is still a need to introduce considerable tax benefits for individuals and businesses, and some for membership fees. Moreover, cooperation with state and parliament was seen as presenting difficulties. Local authorities and the national government usually do not invite CSOs' involvement in public policy formulation. CSOs cannot access the legislature in order to articulate their points of view. Likewise, businesses rarely support the role of their employees as activists in CSOs, and very few are actively engaged in philanthropy.

Values

CSOs play an active role in promoting harmonious relations between different political, cultural, religious and ethnic groups in society. Their success in achieving these relations received a slightly lower rating. While CSOs do not promote conflicts between members of different cultural and religious groups, they should, however, become more engaged in the process of social integration. However, transparency and financial accountability were seen as problematic, although issues of internal democracy and membership participation were not.

Impact

CSOs only partially succeeded in representing their constituents' interests and putting these interests on the public policy agenda. Representatives of civil society are rarely invited to participate in the generation and discussion of legislation, and laws vital to the interest of CSOs are frequently passed without their involvement. Successful cooperation between CSOs and government in implementing policies is the exception. CSOs have not been successful in monitoring government commitments and policies. What is more, the public image of CSOs is critical, and the little media coverage that they have attracted has, generally, been unfavourable.

The impact assessment was more positive in the area of service delivery, and CSOs felt that they are able to provide services in a manner that is not feasible for the state or for businesses. However, this high score may indicate that CSOs are not sufficiently critical and objective of their capacity achievements.

Results

The most critical challenge for civil society development that emerged from the CSD application is the limited space in which is has to operate, as defined by the legislative, political and social–cultural framework. The negative attitude of the state, restrictive legislation, a lack of social responsibility on the part of the corporate sector and the absence of a culture of volunteering and public

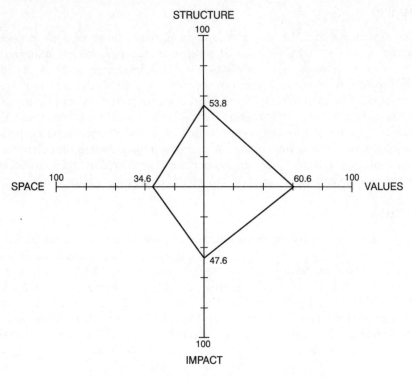

Figure 6.3 *Civil Society Status Diamond for Croatia*

spiritedness are vital problems. In order to enhance their reputation and credibility, as well as of civil society, in general, CSOs need to improve their financial transparency and accountability. Croatia still considers the government responsible for delivering services and solving problems. Therefore, CSOs must legitimize their efforts and initiatives and create a movement for change. In general, the value derived from this exercise is a more focused approach to CSO development and discussion in the future. Stakeholders are now able to identify certain areas of improvement and have measures to track their progress.

Estonia[6]

The objectives of this report are to:

1   Increase knowledge, understanding and awareness of civil society through reflecting upon and assessing the strength, health and impact of the sector.
2   Empower civil society stakeholders through promoting dialogue, alliances and networks.

3   Develop visions of mechanisms in order to achieve stronger civil society through providing an agenda-setting and goal-setting tool to help foster positive behavioural change.

Methodology

There were three stages to the study, which was conducted by the Open Estonia Foundation:

1   collection of existing data, findings, and publications;
2   stakeholder survey;
    (495 questionnaires were sent out and 296 were completed. Surveys were not sent to experts directly; rather, they were sent to nine NGOs in different towns/counties to be distributed in their regions to different areas of activity, such as health, education, religion and culture. In addition, 44 questionnaires were sent to representatives from business, government, non-profit organizations, academia and the media asking them to evaluate the non-profit sector as a whole. Approximately one out of three replied.)
3   a workshop by members of the representative board of the Estonian Non-profit Association's roundtable to review the results of the survey.

Structure

A total of 13,666 non-profit associations and 371 foundations are currently registered. CSOs employ approximately 4 per cent of the working-age population in Estonia. The major subsectors are real estate associations, sport clubs, culture CSOs, professional and trade unions, hobby associations and faith-based CSOs. A relatively large proportion of CSOs are located in the capital city. Over 70 per cent of the CSOs surveyed work primarily at a local level, 19 per cent nationally, and 5 per cent work on an international level.

Space

Only a minority of respondents view the registration process as complicated; but nearly half feel that the tax system is unfavourable to donors. The basic problem, however, seems to be that respondents lack information and knowledge about laws, which suggests a serious information deficit in Estonian society.

Impact

61 per cent believe that they have an impact beyond their membership base; but, at the same time, they fear that the general public remains uninformed because CSOs lack adequate outreach and dissemination. Media coverage is weak, and most coverage is on the negative side. Local and regional coverage are more positive. There is mistrust between the state and CSOs, with no formal channels of communication in place. More than one third say that

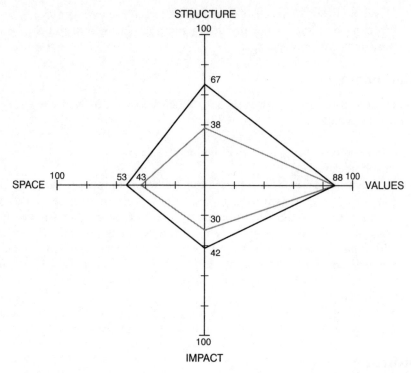

Note: The larger diamond shows scores from the original survey, and the smaller diamond comprises 'revised scores' based on the workshop and roundtable after reviewing initial findings.

Figure 6.4 *Civil Society Status Diamond for Estonia*

they are not invited to participate in policy processes at the government level; but national CSOs tend to be more actively involved. 53 per cent do not actively seek contact with political parties. However, among larger CSOs, 28 per cent do actively seek political cooperation. 58 per cent believe that their work is not valued as much as the public or business sector.

Values

Respondents and participants of the workshops drew a generally positive picture of their own involvement in Estonian society and the values that they express and enact. In fact, Figure 6.4 suggests great unanimity in this field, in contrast to differences between respondents and workshop participants in the other three dimensions. Workshop participants, when reviewing the results, were more critical of the structure, space, and impact dimensions and readjusted the values accordingly, as represented in Figure 6.4.

In a next step, a 'vision diamond' was considered (see Figure 6.5) to show what the sector should look in two years. As can be seen, the 'vision diamond' offers a very optimistic future, perhaps due to the influence of the parallel debate about the Estonian Civil Society Development Concept (EKAK) and

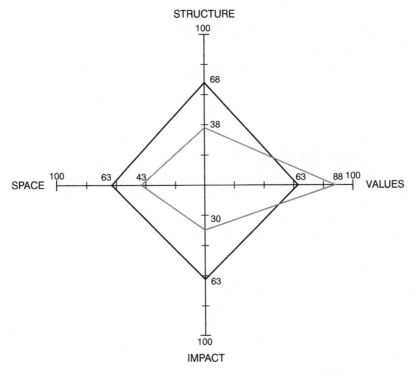

Figure 6.5 *Civil Society Vision Diamond for Estonia*

its subsequent presentation to the Estonian parliament in 2001. EKAK advocates the support and promotion of non-profit activities and their legitimacy in public policy.

Results

The CSD study has produced new insights into Estonia's civil society sector, particularly with regard to its values and impact dimensions. As Figure 6.5 shows, workshop participants adjusted the values dimension to reflect what they felt to be a more realistic 'goal' for this dimension in the future. Workshop participants argued that:

> the very high score for values in the status diamond is an expression not of the realities, but of the ambitions and dreams of the young non-profit sector in Estonia. If these high expectations fail to be fulfilled, the support for those values is bound to decrease. Both future disappointments and the realism fostered by practice would accordingly moderate the present ambitions that are reflected by answers to the values questions. Eventually, CSOs will come to look at their values more realistically and evaluate them from the point of view of practice.

Indeed, all parties involved agreed that the most important contribution of the CSD study is the creation of new ideas for further research.

Mexico[7]

The objectives of this study are to:

1 Contribute to the debate about civil society in Mexico, while learning from the experiences of other countries that are undergoing a similar political transition.
2 Facilitate critical discussion among Mexican CSOs aimed at improving the ways in which they operate.
3 Analyse possible paths for strengthening CSOs and for solidifying their relationships with government and the business sector.

Methodology

This study was coordinated by the Mexican Centre for Philanthropy (CEMEFI). The study was conducted according to the following steps:

1 Identify and review existing literature and data on civil society.
2 Consult key informants regarding indicators and questionnaire.
3 Administer the questionnaire via telephone by an independent consulting company.
4 Interview experts from academia, government, business and the media.

Structure

The key question about structure focused on the size of the non-profit sector in Mexico, which was judged as small by some experts but larger by others. This led the study to examine the validity of different size indicators in the Mexican context. The study also recognized the difficulty of cooperation and collaboration among CSOs. This, according to Olvera (2001), may be due to a culture of plurality or 'space for conflict'. The geographical distribution of organizations was seen as a crucial problem and as somewhat paradoxical: as the number of CSOs increases, their distribution continues to be more inconsistent with the social deficiencies of the poorest states in Mexico.

Space

This dimension received a low ranking by survey respondents. There seems to be a mistrust of CSOs by government due to the history of oppression and struggle under decades of authoritarianism. The Mexican government can also be selective in choosing which civil society sectors to support. However, efforts to promote dialogue and to influence legislation among CSOs with government are underway. The legal environment for CSOs has been modified during the last ten years but remains confusing and incomplete.

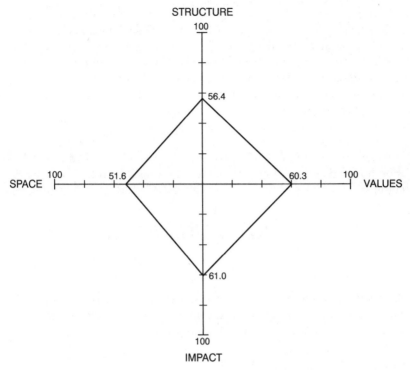

Figure 6.6 *Civil Society Status Diamond for Mexico*

Clear regulation and operation legislation exist for certain CSOs, such as unions, but not for others. Tax policies are inconsistent.

Values

Do the values that the CSOs promote exist within their own organization? Respondents believe that they have weakly enshrined norms of internal democracy, accountability and financial transparency. Financial transparency received the lowest rating.

Impact

CSOs believe that they have been successful in positive portrayals in the media. However, general observation of media pieces on civil society suggests that this belief may be overrated. Most negatively rated is policy impact. However, policy impact may be made through less 'transparent' means, especially through personal relationships between CSO leaders and government officials.

Results

The value derived from this study is that it identifies areas of weakness and areas for improvement; brought key actors together; and outlined the structure of civil society. Specifically, Mexican CSOs face challenges similar to those of other developing nations: economic crisis, state abandonment of many social tasks and the constant deterioration of living conditions within large sectors of the population. At the same time, CSOs must also develop long-term strategies and revenues for capacity and sustainability, while addressing immediate short-term needs. The report poignantly states that CSOs should not face this tension alone; the more important and strategic approach, rather, is to involve the government and private sectors in order to make a more meaningful impact. The CSD project, by pointing out the need for collaboration and cooperation between the three sectors, is a step in the right direction.

New Zealand[8]

The two objectives of the study are to:

1   Assess the status and health of civil society in New Zealand.
2   Develop policy lessons to increase understanding of civil society in the country as a whole and for specific sub-groups.

Methodology

100 questionnaires were sent to a broad cross-section of civil society stakeholders and 47 responses were received and analysed. The responses were consistent with the stakeholder range being sought. Ages ranged from 31 to 76 years, with a good gender balance. Under-sampling occurred with regard to the Maori population, who make up 15 per cent of the New Zealand population, while our responses included only 6 per cent by Maori.

Structure

The total number of community organizations (incorporated societies, charitable trusts and unincorporated associations) is unknown; but in 2001, there were 21,443 registered incorporated societies and 11,582 charitable trusts. This does not take into account the many incorporated societies that are not on the register but may still be active. Voluntary activity is widespread, with almost 50 per cent of the population engaged in some form of voluntary activity or unpaid help. CSO cooperation with the business sector is generally rare. Contacts with political parties, however, are more frequent and positive. CSOs are positively portrayed in the media; but they have a hard time attracting consistent coverage.

Space

Policies governing CSOs are in place; however, they are in need of modernization and are not uniform across government agencies. They also do

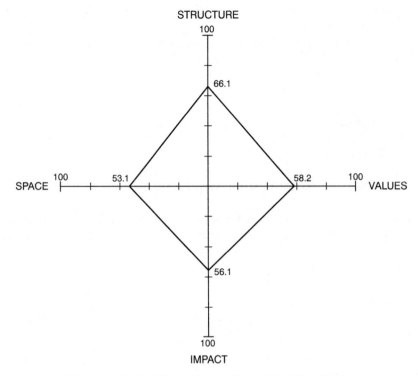

Figure 6.7 *Civil Society Status Diamond for New Zealand*

not recognize indigenous organizations because they are seen as kin-based. Respondents feel tax laws do not encourage private donations.

Values

The third *New Zealand Study of Values* (1999) shows that people will get involved with basic community issues, but have little confidence in politicians. At the same time, accountability and transparency do not seem to be a critical issue within civil society and the public sector.

Impact

CSOs believe that they successfully represent the interests of members, that they have a positive public profile, and that they improve the lives of the people with whom they work.

Results

Results confirm and reiterate the following challenges:

- lack of community-based research capacity;
- role and place of Maori organizations within civil society;

- capacity of civil society organizations, individually and collectively, to have an impact on public policy;
- need for improved relationships and understanding between civil society and government;
- role and functions of umbrella organizations within civil society and in relation to government;
- need for the education of public officials on civil society and the education of civil society organizations on public policy-making.

The project helped to:

- Collate the wide range of existing or planned work.
- Provide a framework for organizing research and analysis.
- Enhance the understanding of issues of collective well-being and place them alongside the growing data on individual, family and environmental status. As such, it clarified how society organizes itself collectively outside the arena of formal state action, and identified areas requiring improvement, while discussing possible solutions.

Pakistan[9]

The nine objectives of the Pakistani study are among the most ambitious when compared to the other countries in this chapter:

1 Take stock of the existing literature on civil society, interpret it afresh and identify areas that merit separate research.
2 Enhance conceptual understanding about civil society and build a consensus of opinion.
3 Enhance understanding about the state of civil society and identify strengths and weaknesses.
4 Bring to light areas of mutual concern and foster a sense of unity among CSOs.
5 Increase collaboration at sector and inter-sector levels.
6 Facilitate linkages between civil society, government and business.
7 Identify impediments to the growth of civil society.
8 Help create an enabling legal, fiscal and socio-cultural environment.
9 Set specific agendas and goals for civil society enhancement.

Methodology

The study was coordinated by the NGO resource centre in association with the Aga Khan Foundation. The following three steps were taken to conduct the study:

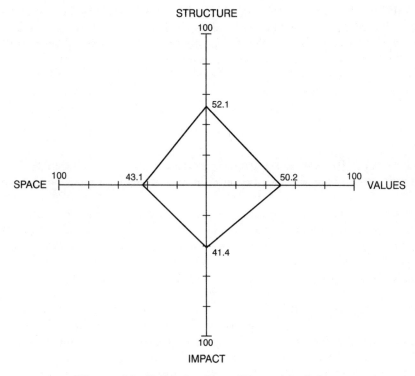

Figure 6.8 *Civil Society Status Diamond for Pakistan*

1   Review secondary data sources: books, research papers, dissertations, newspaper articles and features, interviews; and write an overview report.
2   Conduct consultative focus group sessions with select groups of stakeholders to discuss the overview report and select indicators.
3   Develop a questionnaire to gauge the perceptions about civil society organizations.

The stakeholder survey began in June 2001 and was conducted primarily through electronic mail. Almost 300 questionnaires were sent out to 'knowledge bearers' of civil society, with a total of 106 respondents.

Structure

The ranking of 52 out of 100 by the stakeholder survey suggests moderate 'health' (see Figure 6.8). However, individual sub-dimensions, such as membership base, regional distribution, building alliances and coalitions, and cooperation with the private sector, reflect shortcomings. Survey respondents agree that CSOs are not spread in a balanced way across the regions of the country. Pakistani NGOs are predominately urban, while the population is 65 per cent rural. Over half of registered CSOs are engaged in the educational field. It is also estimated that the sector employs less than 2 per cent of the country's labour force. However, Pakistan has a well-developed *Zakat* and *Ushr* system, as part of the five pillars of Islam. In terms of funding, community-based organizations rely mostly on local resources. Dependence upon foreign donors is an issue for larger CSOs, which has a bearing on their sustainability and credibility. There appears to be a need for CSOs to increase their membership base and improve alliances and networking through the establishment of effective and representative umbrella organizations.

Space

Civil society in Pakistan faces legal, political and socio-cultural challenges. The relatively low score of 43 per cent on this dimension may be due to government interference and lack of cooperation with the state and businesses. However, CSO registration and tax incentives indicate a relatively supportive environment. Certain socio-cultural norms and attitudes, perhaps due to history or state repression, are a detriment to strengthening civil society.

The state has an inconsistent attitude toward NGOs. For example, the report indicates that while the state views NGOs as playing a vital role in providing services, it also perceives them as a competitor for donor funding, political allegiances and influences. However, government is increasingly looking to CSOs for suggestions on policy and it also elected a few CSO leaders to the federal cabinet. CSOs also receive pressure from religious organizations, where strong cultural norms for volunteering prevail. The space dimension points towards the need for improved linkages with the government and the corporate sector. Although the fiscal framework is 'enabling,' the legal framework needs revision. Severe societal pressures persist.

Values

The values score of 50 per cent reflects a mixed record – which suggests a dichotomy between the values of modern CSOs and those of more traditional society. There are, however, differences among the various sub-dimensions. Financial transparency among CSOs and their role in promoting values such as tolerance, human rights and gender equity are indicators that have low scores. While charities lack formal structures and internal democracy and accountability, they provide invaluable relief to the needy. Respondents do not see CSOs as being active in promoting harmonious relationships between different political, cultural, religious and ethnic groups. At the same time, CSOs also see themselves as successful in promoting good relations across different groups in society. Public spiritedness and volunteerism are values that underpin civil society in Pakistan. The majority of CSOs appear to have no well-defined and effective governance structure in place. However, with effective self-regulation, the first steps towards internal democracy and accountability could be taken.

Impact

A score of 41.4 implies that civil society's impact with regard to problem solving and public policy process is not significant. Further analysis reveals that this low score can be attributed to CSOs' inability to influence public policy-making and monitoring. Primary data indicates that respondents generally disagree that CSOs are invited to the policy formulation process, have an effect upon policy or represent constitutents' interest in policy. This is despite the fact that civil society's influence is growing within government as a result of being able to successfully fill in gaps in government service provision.

Results

The term civil society is rarely used in Pakistan. It is apparent that Pakistan's current social, political and economic transformation will impact upon the development of civil society. The CSD study added value by producing a wealth of information and by engaging stakeholders in developing new ideas and approaches. Although results from the CSD study support some findings from existing studies and contradict others, they ultimately help to identify civil society's strengths and weaknesses and prioritize goals and objectives.

South Africa[10]

The five objectives of this study are to:

1 Increase knowledge and understanding of civil society by reflecting upon and assessing the structure, space, values and impact of civil society.
2 Test and assess the effectiveness of the CSD as an agenda-setting tool.
3 Make some preliminary recommendations on how South African civil society can be strengthened.
4 Share the findings and lessons learned from the research with civil society formations in other countries and regions.
5 Provide opportunities to develop, hone and refine an interactive research approach that has proven, time and again, that such processes are most likely to elicit the data and perceptions that South Africa requires.

Methodology

The study was conducted by the Cooperatives for Research and Education and the Institute for Democracy in South Africa. The following steps were taken to conduct the study:

1 A separate definition of civil society was adopted:

> Civil society is the sphere of organizations and/or associations of organizations located between the family, the state, the government

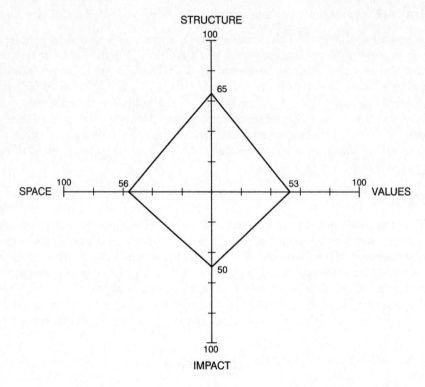

Figure 6.9 *Civil Society Status Diamond for South Africa*

of the day and the prevailing economic system, in which people with common interests associate voluntarily. Amongst these organizations, they may have common, competing or conflicting values and interests.

South African researchers and practitioners disagreed with several aspects of the definition provided in this book (see Chapter 2). Specifically:

Many disagreed with the inclusion of what they saw as 'the market parameter,' arguing that the free market assumptions underlying this are not accepted by many South Africans. Recent experiences have also indicated that civil society can emerge or exist in other forms of economies. Many pointed out that contrary to the belief that civil society 'shared civic rules,' the South African case demonstrated the opposite. Many CSO leaders felt it necessary to disobey unjust laws and to fight against illegitimate authorities. Furthermore, many practitioners disputed that CSOs always share 'common interests' between them.

2   Initial workshops were conducted for researchers, academics and national CSOs to discuss indicators, methodology and questionnaires.

3   Survey questionnaires and interviews were administered in person at workshops or by telephone to a total of 213 civil society leaders in all nine provinces. The total sample had a 50:50 gender distribution. The survey data was analysed by IDASA's public opinion service.

4   The first phase of provincial workshops took place. Between late May and early June 2001, nine workshops were conducted, one in each of South Africa's provinces. CSO leaders from all sectors were invited to attend in order to obtain a representative sample. CORE sent out a total of 404 invitations on the basis of a complex sampling exercise. 167 accepted the invitations, and 139 actually attended. Part of the survey questionnaire was faxed or e-mailed to participants in advance so that they could collect the required data in their offices. The balance of the questionnaire was administered at the workshops.

5   Additional steps included the review of current literature, the monitoring of media coverage over 15 months and key informant interviews.

Structure

There is no accurate, definitive data available on the actual numbers of CSOs currently operating in South Africa. Estimates have ranged from about 17,000 to 54,000 to 140,000. Umbrella organizations exist but do not speak with one voice. When asked to respond to the view that 'CSOs should cooperate more with the private sector', 45 per cent agreed and 33 per cent strongly agreed. 12 per cent neither agreed nor disagreed, and only 7 per cent either disagreed or strongly disagreed.

Space

There is a non-profit organization (NPO) act to establish an administrative and regulatory framework; to encourage NPOs to maintain adequate standards of governance, transparency and accountability, and to improve these standards; to create an environment within which the public may have access to information concerning registered NPOs; and to promote a spirit of cooperation and shared responsibility within government and donors, and amongst other interested persons in their dealings with NPOs. When presented with the statement that 'civil society does not have sufficient access to government', a total of 57 per cent said that they neither agreed nor disagreed. 20 per cent agreed and 17 per cent disagreed. 49 per cent of respondents agreed with the statement that 'civil society does not receive sufficient support from the business community'. In response to the statement that 'the regulatory and legislative environment is sufficiently empowering to CSOs', 29 per cent agreed; 3 per cent strongly agreed; 12 per cent neither agreed nor disagreed; 41 per cent disagreed; and 14 per cent strongly disagreed.

Table 6.1 *Civil Society Status Diamond Score Values and Regional Score Values for South Africa*

	Structure	Value	Impact	Space
Diamond	65	53	50	56
Lowest provincial score	50	30	30	30
Highest provincial score	90	70	70	70

Values

A large percentage of CSOs value democratic rights, human rights, justice, freedom and equity, whereas a considerably smaller percentage value diversity, inclusion, tolerance and non-partisanship. Respondents indicated that 41 per cent make their annual reports available to the public on request, and 24 per cent proactively disseminate them to a distribution list. This data suggests that CSOs are reasonably accountable to the public with regard to the internal workings of their organizations, although there is room for improvement – for example, in preparing and disseminating reports and through public report-back meetings, especially in the rural areas. Organizations appear to be more ready to release information about annual accounts than they are about specific budgets and sources of funding.

Impact

More than 70 per cent believe that CSOs are not successfully representing citizens' interests. However, when asked whether their participation in the policy-making process had brought about any policy change during the past five years, the response pattern was more even: 27 per cent said no; 16 per cent said yes, just once; 28 per cent said yes, a few times; 13 per cent said yes, many times; and 17 per cent said that they did not know. Strong sentiment (73 per cent) amongst CSOs that they should be doing more to critically analyse government policy implies that they are not very successful in putting their interests on the agenda, partly because they are not trying hard enough.

When asked to react to the statement that 'civil society has sufficient influence over government', only 20 per cent agreed, while 50 per cent disagreed. In reaction to the statement that 'civil society has sufficient influence over parliament', even fewer agreed (14 per cent), while 50 per cent disagreed and 20 per cent strongly disagreed. CSOs appear to feel that while they have been invited to make inputs on policy issues, their impact is very limited. 'Civil society receives sufficient support from the media' elicited this reaction: 30 per cent agreed and 37 per cent disagreed. When asked to describe the reaction of the media to the work that their organization does, 44 per cent said that the media is supportive. Consistently, 70 per cent of CSOs felt that the coverage of their organization had been positive.

Results

The process itself accounts for a large portion of the value derived from 'engaging civil society in the design and implementation of the study and in debating and verifying its conclusions'. By including government and donors in the final workshops, they learned to appreciate civil society's diversity and potential contribution to society at large. Another aspect of the study's value is the inclusion of a wide range of CSOs, and not limiting the study to formal non-profits and NGOs. Furthermore, by combining provincial consultations, the national stakeholder surveys and existing secondary data sources, the team was able to cross-check and verify conclusions. Most importantly, by quantifying the four dimensions of South Africa's civil society, the results of the study have provided a baseline against which progress can be measured.

In developing the vision diamond, the team agreed upon the following guidelines and objectives.

Structure

South African CSOs should cooperate more with each other; make their umbrella bodies more representative and accountable – for example, through provincial and sector structures – and work towards more effective cooperation with the private sector, donors and government. They should diversify their funding base in order to achieve a greater degree of independence and sustainability.

Space

South African CSOs must assist each other, particularly those in the most remote and disadvantaged regions, to benefit from new government provisions for registration and tax exemption. Important information with regard to the legislative and regulatory environment should be filtered down to grassroots organizations so that they are empowered to attain all possible benefits. Individual CSOs should take responsibility and seek out the necessary information and educate themselves about available opportunities, and should keep their own houses in order in order to qualify for such benefits. Both CSOs and government (at all levels) should increase their levels of mutual understanding – of their respective values, processes, structures and capacities. CSOs must be more proactive in obtaining access to government with a view to making well-informed, constructive representations on behalf of their communities, and generally improving participation in democratic processes and structures. In turn, government should listen more willingly and carefully to South African CSO inputs. South African civil society must take more responsibility for its own situation, and should respond to issues on the basis of what it is and what it represents.

Values

CSOs should improve their public and financial accountability through self-discipline, ethical responsibility, internal good governance and internal/external transparency: 'CSOs' accountability to their beneficiaries is non-negotiable.' CSOs should encourage and manage diversity within their organizations and promote tolerance of diversity in society as a whole. They should act in a manner that is consistent with the view that 'All development issues are human rights issues.' Most importantly, they should move away from an entitlement mentality, understanding that 'No one owes us a living!' Also, CSOs should ensure that their programmes are consistent with the values that they promote: 'practice what we preach!' Both within their own organisations and amongst individual citizens and other stakeholders, CSOs should promote philanthropic giving as a means of engaging more people and organizations in working towards the ultimate goal of eradicating poverty. Similarly, they should build upon shared values and goals to encourage voluntarism as a means of empowering communities and organizations to do more for themselves.

Impact

CSOs should improve their capacity to measure their impact and to communicate effectively with others regarding the positive effect that they have had on government policy, and on the lives of the South African people, particularly in terms of poverty eradication. They must plan for such measurement by developing baseline data and by identifying appropriate indicators and the means of quantifying them. They should report on and disseminate the results widely. CSOs can use the media more proactively and effectively, with a focus on community radio, local and provincial media and local languages, as appropriate. The media should, in turn, be educated and encouraged to engage in more in-depth coverage of civil society issues.

Ukraine[11]

The three objectives of this study are to:

1 Increase knowledge, understanding and awareness of civil society by reflecting upon and assessing the strength, health and impact of the sector.
2 Empower civil society stakeholders through promoting dialogue, alliances and networks.
3 Develop visions of mechanisms to achieve stronger civil society by providing an agenda and goal-setting tool to help foster positive behavioural change.

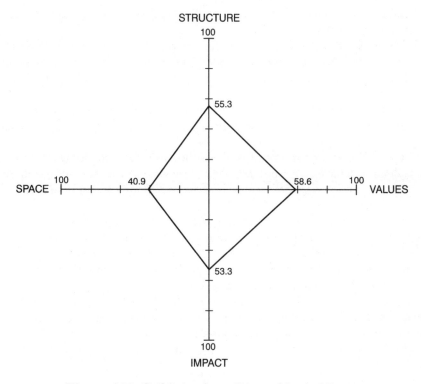

Figure 6.10 *Civil Society Status Diamond for the Ukraine*

Methodology

The study was conducted by the League of Regional Resource Centres. The team conducted focus groups in different regions of the Ukraine and presented an analysis of the data. A global national workshop conducted by CIVICUS provided an excellent opportunity for the Ukrainian team to learn and share insights with their international colleagues. Stakeholder surveys and assessment and agenda-setting workshops all over the country provided basic data on the current situation and helped to set the vision of civil society development in the Ukraine. The team used 58 indicators, both universal and specific to the Ukraine.

Rather than detailing the four CSD areas, the study identified somewhat contradictory findings: relatively low levels of social participation but good scores regarding internal democracy; a positive image in the media, yet limited impact in many areas; a growing non-profit sector but little cooperation; and lack of a working relationship with government. Specifically:

•   It is uncommon for Ukrainian citizens to affiliate with CSOs to solve their common problems and promote their common interests. Public awareness of the role of CSOs is poor, inhibiting CSOs' transformation into actual 'schools of democracy' where the citizens can acquire democratic values and skills.

- The level of civil society's resources strongly depends upon the public's attitude toward civil society, CSOs' professional skills in partnership building, as well as the adoption of an appropriate public communication strategy.
- At the moment, Ukrainian civil society has little impact upon the government in terms of civil rights protection, solving social problems and the improvement of quality of life.
- The foundations for a positive development of civil society exist in the Ukraine, if the existing potential of civic activism of Ukrainians is utilized through raising citizens' awareness about the importance and functions of civil society.

The findings of the CSD study are timely: as the country undergoes a crisis within, and development of, its political, social and economic systems, results from this study highlight critical areas of strength and impact within Ukrainian civil society. The findings on the relative health of civil society against this background impress heavily with their optimistic attitudes and are a source of certain positive sentiments. Although public opinion is still dominated by apathy and mistrust of social institutions, the potential and optimism induced by the research findings may be used as an institutional catalyst for the development of civic initiatives.

Conclusion

The case studies were generally a very fruitful exercise for the countries involved and offered valuable insights into the status of their respective civil societies. For post-communists countries such as Belarus, Estonia and Croatia, with a dearth of information on their countries' civil society, the CSD project allowed them, for the first time, not only to gather descriptive information and statistics, but also to be an active participant in the development, implementation, analysis and discussion of this exercise.

    For more developed countries such as Canada and New Zealand, with a relative wealth of information on their respective civil societies, the CSD project allowed them to gain new insights and ask new questions, particularly regarding the values and impact dimensions. Research in these developed countries has hitherto been fragmented, focusing only on one or two aspects of civil society. The CSD project, therefore, is valued for its comprehensiveness and ability to integrate four dimensions of civil society within one complete picture that can then be compared internationally.

    In addition, the project is valued for bringing various key players and stakeholders together in a national dialogue about the present and future development of civil society. For countries that created a vision diamond, the project allowed them to set specific measurable goals. This allows them to track their progress in a tangible way. For countries that did not create a vision diamond, the project was a valuable initial step in measuring civil society development.

All countries share similar challenges. Specifically, the geographical distribution of CSOs is one recurring challenge among countries. CSOs are concentrated in more urbanized areas and around the country's major cities and capital. Economic and social needs, however, are generally greater in rural areas, particularly in developing countries.

Along the space dimension, legislation and government support tends to be greater for social service organizations and politically neutral organizations than for politically active organizations such as human rights and environmental bodies. There is also a recognition that CSOs need to build stronger ties, cooperation and working relationships with their government and business sectors.

Along the values dimension, transparency – specifically, financial transparency – is a challenge for CSOs in most countries. The values dimension seems to be a sensitive topic for discussion and analysis in many of the case studies. In general, however, countries were appreciative that the project took this dimension into account and recognized that, in the words of South Africa, in order to advocate progressive values in the greater society, CSOs must first 'keep their own houses in order'. The fact that countries recognize accountability and transparency as a challenge to be dealt with is a positive sign.

The impact dimension seems to be weakest for all countries (weak not in terms of the score, but the validity and reliability of the indicators used, particularly the 'service impact' indicators). Most countries did not use the suggested impact indicators outlined in Chapter 5, such as the Fulfilled Commitment Index. Other than for South Africa, who monitored media coverage of civil society over a 15-month period to asses its 'public profile', most countries relied on the stakeholder survey to evaluate impact and made little use of secondary data or observations from outside agencies not involved with civil society. The results, therefore, tend to be rather 'inflated' scores on the impact dimension.

In general, impact indicators were divided into three areas: policy impact, public profile and service impact. Policy impact questions generally asked stakeholders to evaluate their involvement with government policy formation. Although 'service impact' measures remain a vast and 'unperfected' field of research for social science, the impact dimension would be greatly enhanced by adding secondary data or qualitative evaluations rather than relying on stakeholder opinions alone. The Pakistani team states the challenge of impact measures succinctly:

> Finally, it must be added that many civil society initiatives are well-geared toward long-term human development although their results may not be visible in the short-term… Changes in attitudes, levels of awareness and social consciousness are hard to quantify; thus, much of civil society's impact invariably escapes public notice.

Chapter 7

The Way Ahead

Within little more than a decade, the concept of civil society has moved from relative obscurity to centre stage: the aftermath of the events in Central and Eastern Europe in 1989; questions about how to rebuild the social fabric of African societies after humanitarian tragedies and civil wars; concerns about the decline of community and the weakening of social ties in the US; disagreements on how to increase and broaden citizen participation in policy-making in Japan, and how to lower the 'democratic deficit' in the European Union; concerns about how to provide voice to the socially excluded in Latin America; and debates on how to address the impact of globalization on local societies in Asia and the Middle East. All of these are policy issues with the role of civil society figuring large at their centre.

The ultimate aim, however, must be to move regular reporting about civil society into the mainstream of the social sciences and statistical systems in each country and in each international organization, including, prominently, the United Nations (UN), the World Bank, the Organization for Economic Cooperation and Development (OECD) and the Statistical Office of the European Union (EUROSTAT). In the medium and long term, this will require researchers in the field, as well as civil society representatives, to stake out claims both within academia and the policy-making community. In particular, concerted efforts are needed to push for the establishment of what could be called 'civil society focal points' in statistical offices at national and international levels. These focal points would collect, prepare and disseminate the relevant data and serve as stakeholders for the interests of researchers and policy-makers for adequate information on civil society.

> Reporting about civil society has to become part of the mainstream of the statistical system of each country and each international organization.

As Table 7.1 shows for the international level, major functional fields and policy areas have dedicated institutions that are responsible for the collecting, preparation and dissemination of statistical data and information. Such 'institutional guardians' are missing for civil society. Clearly, like the fields of development or social policy, civil society, too, is a cross-cutting field that needs to be part of the remit of most statistical agencies. The medium- to long-term challenge, then, is to identify dedicated lead institutions for civil society statistics, with links to corresponding units in other relevant agencies.

Table 7.1 *Topical Fields and Major Institutions Responsible for Statistics/Data Collection**

Field	Lead Agency
Agriculture	Food and Agriculture Organization (FAO)
	World Food Programme (WFP)
Development	United Nations Development Programme (UNDP)
	World Institute for Development Economics Research (UNU-WIDER)
	World Bank
Economy	Organization for Economic Cooperation and Development (OECD)
	United Nations Statistics Division (UNSD)
Education	United Nations Educational, Scientific and Cultural Organization (UNESCO)
Environment	United Nations Environment Programme (UNEP)
Finance	International Monetary Fund (IMF)
Health	World Health Organization (WHO)
Housing	United Nations Human Settlements Programme (UN-Habitat)
Human Rights	United Nations High Commission for Human Rights (UNHCHR)
Population	United Nations Population Information Network (UN-POPIN)
Social Policy	United Nations Department for Economic and Social Affairs (UN-DESA)
Trade	World Trade Organization (WTO)
	United Nations Commission on Trade and Development (UNCTAD)

Note: *See data sources in Appendix C for a more detailed list.

Such changes, however, take time. In the short term, therefore, more immediate steps need to be taken to address the significant and serious gap in knowledge about civil society and its component parts. The CSD proposed here is one way of dealing with the problems associated with the lack of a systematic information system for civil society.

In addition to the steps involved in particular CSD applications, there are a number of 'infrastructure' tasks involved that go beyond what individual users can achieve. These tasks include, first and foremost, the design and development of an *indicator bank* for a wide range of CSD uses and purposes. The indicators presented in Appendix A are a first step in this direction. This indicator bank must be complemented by a corresponding *data bank* for each indicator, including a full methodological assessment of data coverage and quality. Such an information system would also involve the design and dissemination of user-friendly software programs to assist IT and *internet-based* CSD applications, including a dedicated user website with key information online. These tasks are clearly in the remit of the social sciences. They are called upon to address and improve the data situation in the field of civil society, which continues to be problematic and insufficient for both research and policy-related purposes.

A second important infrastructure task is the development of a user-friendly *toolkit* that shows users how to apply the diamond methodology in different circumstances and for a variety of purposes. This toolkit will also demonstrate in more detail than has been shown here how to set up the information system; set standards; select indicators and measures; analyse and interpret data; and translate results and insights into policies and other measures for improvement.

Finally, and perhaps most importantly, there is a need for an extended test phase of the CSD methodology and approach developed in this book. The pilot case studies presented in Chapter 6, and the extended testing currently planned for 2003–2005 by CIVICUS are important steps into this direction. This involves:

- A toolkit that shows users how to apply the methodology to different circumstances and for a variety of purposes. The toolkit shows users how to set up the system, how to set standards, how to select indicators and measures, how to analyse and interpret the data, and how to translate results and insights into policies and other measures for improvement (Holloway, 2001).
- A regular, high-profile CIVICUS publication that draws on regional, national and international applications and reports on the state and health of civil society across the world from a comparative perspective.
- A website with the key information online, and software for online CSD applications (www.civicus.org).

Only if repeated and varied applications across different circumstances improve the information available on civil society, only if this leads to better understanding of civil society and its component parts, and only if the end result is an improvement in policies can we conclude that the system proposed here has been useful and worthwhile.

As part of an ongoing dialogue with users, civil society leaders and researchers will have to push for a comparative database for the cross-national and cross-regional assessment of civil society. For this purpose, it will be necessary to seek agreement and build consensus about what set of indicators could be sufficiently standardized to allow for comparisons across a maximum number of countries, while remaining flexible enough to accommodate significant regional and cultural differences. Yet, such a consensus can only be reached over time and against the background of ongoing applications of the CSD, and the experiences that have been made in a broad cross-section of countries.

Conclusion

Across the world, civil society has become a major item of the political agenda – in the developed countries of the OECD, in Africa, Latin America and Asia, as well as in transition countries of Central and Eastern Europe. Yet, political agendas change, and the 'seat at the policy table' may be more difficult to maintain for long unless civil society leaders have more and better information to support both their political positions and the policy arguments that they wish to put forward. Information is part of the voice function of civil society and without it – without a supporting pool of current and high-quality data – civil society leaders may find it ever harder to be heard where it matters: in the policy process.

In other words, through its representatives and organizations, civil society must be able to demonstrate repeatedly and decisively that it matters, how, where and for whom. It must be able to examine its current strengths and weaknesses. It must be able to point to policy options and to future challenges. Being able to engage in a systematic, ongoing and structured dialogue is part of this process. The approach proposed and developed in this book represents one initial step toward this goal.

Indicator Repertoire and Assessments

The indicators listed in this appendix are primarily formulated at the macro level. In most instances, however, they can be applied to the meso/field level and the micro/case level following appropriate modifications. Several examples illustrate this possibility.

Structure

Most size and revenue indicators can be calculated at the meso level, and they are certainly applicable for studying specific cases at the micro level. If the data structure allows, field- and case-level analyses can be combined, as, for example, with the *Index of Philanthropic Giving* indicator.

Values

Data for suggested values indicators is typically taken from population surveys (for example, the World Values Survey). If the sample size is large enough, it is possible to break down the data by regions or specific population groups and to calculate the *trust* indicator – for example, at more refined levels.

Space

Measures for legal enablement may vary by type of civil society organization (CSO), such as membership organizations, service providers or grant-making foundations. However, it is possible to modify both the *USAID Legal Environment* and *JHU Law Index* indicators to take account of such variations.

Impact

The *Fulfilled Commitment Index* for CSOs can be applied to specific fields, regions or cases depending upon the actual substantive focus of the policy or programme under consideration. In addition, a broad range of stakeholder surveys and Delphi methods can be used for qualitative assessments at meso and micro levels.

It is, therefore, very important that users of the Civil Society Diamond (CSD) take the following assessments of the various indicators as a starting point for their discussion and not as a 'recipe book' of ready-made solutions. Likewise, it will become apparent that the utility of the CSD is closely linked to the availability of data, or the possibility that data can be generated in a cost-effective way. For this reason, too, it is paramount for CSD users to develop a data strategy for CSD applications in the medium to long term.

STRUCTURE: MACRO INDICATORS

SIZE

INDICATOR NAME PAID EMPLOYMENT

Brief definition	Paid work in civil society organizations (CSOs) per 1000 employed
Dimension	STRUCTURE–SIZE
Unit of measurement	Full-time equivalent (FTE) paid employment in CSOs relative to 1000 FTE labour force

Type of indicator: [X] preferred   [ ] standard   [ ] optional

Unit of analysis: [ ] micro (variation)   [ ] meso (variation)   [X] macro

METHODOLOGICAL DESCRIPTION AND UNDERLYING DEFINITIONS

Measurement and methodological aspects	• Employment in CSOs based on labour statistics or sample surveys of organizations
Potential usefulness	• Basic size measure • Measures the economic weight of civil society in addition to volunteering • Solid indicator of economic importance
Potential limitations	• CSOs may only be partially covered or not identifiable in standard labour surveys • Some degree of universal comparability, but varying survey design, definitions and frequency may limit comparability cross-nationally and across time • Coverage of part-time and full-time employment • Many atypical employment forms (particularly prevalent in CSOs) not captured
Suggested modifications	• Translation into FTE • Incorporation of atypical employment forms where possible • Depending upon the unit of analysis (macro, meso or micro), different denominators apply: total labour force for macro level; and total labour force in field for meso level. For micro level applications, organizational data is needed.
Links to other measures	• Employment in advocacy CSOs relative to service-providing CSOs (composition) • Volunteering (size) • Volunteering in advocacy CSOs relative to service-providing CSOs (composition) • Value of volunteer input (revenue)

ASSESSMENT OF DATA QUALITY AND AVAILABILITY

Method of data collection	• Labour force surveys • Organizational surveys • Industry data (health, education)
Data provider	• National statistical offices • Individual researchers/country-specific
Access to data	• Good – available for some countries • Frequency of data collection • Frequent updates (usually quarterly) for labour force surveys • Full employment census usually every five to ten years • Organizational surveys irregular

COMMENTS

With appropriate modification in the denominator, this indicator can also be employed at the meso and micro levels (see 'Suggested modifications').

INDICATOR NAME VOLUNTEERING

Brief definition	Unpaid workers in CSOs relative to total adult population
Dimension	STRUCTURE–SIZE
Unit of measurement	Number of volunteers (head count) in CSOs as a percentage of adult population

Type of indicator:	☒ preferred	☐ standard	☐ optional
Unit of analysis:	☐ micro (variation)	☐ meso (variation)	☒ macro

METHODOLOGICAL DESCRIPTION AND UNDERLYING DEFINITIONS

Measurement and methodological aspects	• Robust but not refined indicator of social engagement • Composite index of volunteering by sector (depends upon sampling size and how questions are asked) • Assumes cross-national definition of volunteering
Potential usefulness	• Easy to understand • Widely available indicator of social engagement • Measures economic weight of civil society in addition to paid employment
Potential limitations	• Some degree of universal comparability, but varying survey design, definitions and frequency may limit comparability cross-nationally and across time • Does not capture frequency of volunteering and number of hours volunteered • Does not capture extremes • Validity constraint: paid and unpaid work not dichotomous
Suggested modifications	• Modify to capture cultural differences and non-Western applications (for example, countries with large, informal household sectors where unpaid work is not necessarily equivalent to volunteering) • More targeted surveys may be needed to capture extremes
Links to other measures	• Volunteering in advocacy CSOs relative to volunteering in service-providing CSOs (composition) • Participation (size) • Index of Philanthropic Giving (revenue) • Value of volunteer input (revenue) • Paid employment (size)

ASSESSMENT OF DATA QUALITY AND AVAILABILITY

Method of data collection	• Population survey (general random probability population samples) • General household surveys • Other surveys by umbrella organizations
Data provider	• National statistical offices • World Values Survey (rough indicator of volunteering/participation) • Umbrella organizations
Access to data	• Coverage and availability of population census data good for some countries
Frequency of data collection	• Population and household surveys generally conducted annually • Organizational surveys irregular

COMMENTS

With some modification, the indicator can be applied to field-level data, as well as to specific case studies.
See the following for information on volunteering:
Institute for Volunteering Research (for the UK: www.ivr.org.uk/institute.htm); International Year of the Volunteer (www.iyv.org/); Independent Sector (for the US: www.independentsector.org)

INDICATOR NAME MEMBERSHIP IN CSOS

Brief definition	Memberships held by adult population in CSOs
Dimension	STRUCTURE–SIZE
Unit of measurement	Percentage of adult population holding memberships in CSOs

Type of indicator: ☒ preferred ☐ standard ☐ optional

Unit of analysis: ☐ micro (variation) ☐ meso (variation) ☒ macro

METHODOLOGICAL DESCRIPTION AND UNDERLYING DEFINITIONS

Measurement and methodological aspects	• Includes membership in the following types of organizations (based on 1990–1993 WVS): social welfare services for elderly, handicapped or deprived people; religious or church organizations; education, art, music or cultural activities; trade unions; local community action on issues such as poverty, employment, housing and racial equality; developing world growth or human rights; conservation, the environment and ecology; professional associations; youth work; sports or recreation; women's groups; peace movements; animal rights; voluntary organizations concerned with health; and other groups. WVS question: 'Please look carefully at the following list of voluntary organizations and activities and say which, if any, you belong to.' • Representative, national samples used in World Values Survey (covers over 40 societies; 70 per cent of world's population; more in 2000–2001) and similar population surveys • Calculated by Boolean addition of answers to membership categories
Potential usefulness	• Provides standardized cross-national comparison • Easily available indicator of participation in civil society • Behavioural habits (such as membership in organizations) are important predictor of volunteering and contributing patterns
Potential limitations	• Validity constraint: standard wording and terminology of questions may not fit local culture and practice • Membership only indirect measure of participation
Suggested modifications	• Modify to capture cultural differences and non-Western applications • Possibly seek to differentiate active from inactive membership • Note: a refinement of this measure would incorporate multiple memberships held in the population
Links to other measures	• Volunteering (size) • Participation (size) • Membership in advocacy CSOs relative to membership in service-providing CSOs (composition) • Freedom of association (JHU measure and qualitative review) (space)

ASSESSMENT OF DATA QUALITY AND AVAILABILITY

Method of data collection	• World Values Survey (rough indicator of participation) • Standard household/population surveys
Data provider	• World Values Survey • National statistical offices • Social science data archives/centres
Access to data	• Good – published
Frequency of data collection	• Every three to five years; more frequently in most developed countries

COMMENTS

With some modification, the indicator can be applied to field-level data, as well as to specific case studies.

INDICATOR NAME CSO OPERATING EXPENDITURES

Brief definition	Size of CSOs measured by operating expenditures – costs of the general operations of the organization, including wage and salary disbursements, purchases of goods other than capital equipment, material and services, fees and charges paid – relative to the economy measured by GDP
Dimension	STRUCTURE–SIZE
Unit of measurement	CSO operating expenditures as a percentage of GDP
Type of indicator:	☐ preferred ☒ standard ☐ optional
Unit of analysis:	☐ micro (variation) ☐ meso (variation) ☒ macro

METHODOLOGICAL DESCRIPTION AND UNDERLYING DEFINITIONS

Measurement and methodological aspects	• Assumes availability of wage bill and other operating cost items
Potential usefulness	• Basic size measure of economic weight of CSOs
Potential limitations	• Varying survey design, definitions and frequency may limit comparability cross-nationally and across time • Does not include replacement value of volunteer input
Suggested modifications	• Proxy measures needed because informal and irregular work not captured
Links to other measures	• Paid employment (size) • Expenditures in advocacy CSOs relative to expenditure in service-providing CSOs (composition) • Employment in advocacy CSOs relative to expenditure in service-providing CSOs (composition) • Volunteering in advocacy CSOs relative to expenditure in service-providing CSOs (composition) • Public-sector dependency (revenue) • Marketization (revenue) • Giving indicators (revenue)

ASSESSMENT OF DATA QUALITY AND AVAILABILITY

Method of data collection	• National income accounts • Organizational surveys
Data provider	• National statistical offices • CSO annual reports • Individual researchers/country specific
Access to data	• National income accounts good – published for some countries • Organizational surveys irregular
Frequency of data collection	• National income accounts annual • Organizational surveys irregular

COMMENTS

As this measure does not include the replacement value of volunteer input, only the paid aspect of the economic weight enters this indicator. Adding the replacement value to both nominator and denominator yields a 'truer' share of CSO contribution to GDP.

With some modification, the indicator can be applied to field-level data, as well as to specific case studies.

INDICATOR NAME PARTICIPATION

Brief definition	Sum of memberships in CSOs held by adult population relative to population size
Dimension	STRUCTURE–SIZE
Unit of measurement	Number of memberships in CSOs relative to size of adult population

Type of indicator:	☐ preferred	☒ standard	☐ optional
Unit of analysis:	☐ micro (variation)	☐ meso (variation)	☒ macro

METHODOLOGICAL DESCRIPTION AND UNDERLYING DEFINITIONS

Measurement and methodological aspects	• Valuation: assumes that more members implies more participation, but (i) the quality of membership and, therefore, meaningful participation varies; and (ii) the relationship between membership, trust and final outcomes must be verified (Kendall and Knapp, 2000, p127) • Includes membership in the following types of advocacy organizations (based on 1990–1993 WVS): social welfare services for elderly, handicapped or deprived people; religious or church organizations; education, art, music or cultural activities; trade unions; local community action on issues such as poverty, employment, housing and racial equality; developing world growth or human rights; conservation, the environment and ecology; professional associations; youth work; sports or recreation; women's groups; peace movements; animal rights; voluntary organizations concerned with health; and other groups. WVS question: 'Please look carefully at the following list of voluntary organizations and activities and say which, if any, you belong to.' • Representative, national samples used in World Values Survey (covers over 40 societies; 70 per cent of world's population; more in 2000-2001) and similar population surveys • Calculated by adding memberships in sample and estimating numbers for total population, divided by total population size
Potential usefulness	• Easily available indicator of participation in civil society • Provides standardized cross-national comparison • Behavioural habits (such as membership and participation in organizations) are important predictor of volunteering and contributing patterns
Potential limitations	• Validity constraint: standard wording and terminology of questions may not fit local culture and practice
Suggested modifications	• May require separate survey to exclude organizations in which membership is required by law
Links to other measures	• Membership (size) • Membership in advocacy CSOs relative to membership in service-providing CSOs (composition) • Volunteering (size) • Freedom of association (JHU measure and qualitative review) (space)

ASSESSMENT OF DATA QUALITY AND AVAILABILITY

Method of data collection	• World Values Survey (rough indicator of participation) • General household surveys
Data provider	• World Values Survey • National statistical offices • Social science data archives/centres
Access to data	• Good – published
Frequency of data collection	• Every three to five years; more frequently in most developed countries

COMMENTS

With some modification, the indicator can be applied to field-level data, as well as to specific case studies.

INDICATOR NAME NUMBER OF CSO ESTABLISHMENTS PER 100,000 POPULATION

Brief definition	Number of CSO establishments per 100,000 population
Dimension	STRUCTURE–SIZE
Unit of measurement	Number of CSO establishments relative to 100,000 population

Type of indicator:	☐ preferred		☐ standard		☒ optional
Unit of analysis:	☐ micro (variation)		☐ meso (variation)		☒ macro

METHODOLOGICAL DESCRIPTION AND UNDERLYING DEFINITIONS

Measurement and methodological aspects	• Number of establishments of CSOs divided by population size x 100,000
Potential usefulness	• Comparisons (see 'Rate of CSO establishment per year')
Potential limitations	• Should be used in conjunction with other indicators because methods for computing 'numbers of organizations' vary (not always clear whether 'number of organizations' in national statistics counts the separate establishments of complex organizations) (see 'Suggested modifications') • In-country variations can be significant • In general, lack of defined standards and comparability of definitions across countries and over time may reduce reliability of surveys in some countries
Suggested modifications	• Following UN conventions, the separate 'establishments' of complex organizations should be counted separately to the extent possible. Where this is not possible, record the number of separately registered or incorporated entities. • If calculations are based on organizational data, average size indicators may be taken into account
Links to other measures	• Rate of CSO establishments per year (size) • Foundation density (size) • Density of CSO umbrella organizations (number per 1000 CSOs) (composition)

ASSESSMENT OF DATA QUALITY AND AVAILABILITY

Method of data collection	• National statistical offices registers • Organizational surveys • Depends upon provider – varied
Data provider	• National statistical offices/registers • Individual researchers/country specific
Access to data	• Good – published for some countries
Frequency of data collection	• Varied – more current at local levels

COMMENTS

Note: local and regional availability of data may be better than at national levels.
With some modification, the indicator can be applied to field-level data, as well as to specific case studies. An alternative measure is to calculate the number of CSOs per capita rather than per 100,000 population.

INDICATOR NAME RATE OF CSO ESTABLISHMENTS PER YEAR

Brief definition	Number of CSO establishments registered in previous year per 100,000 population
Dimension	STRUCTURE–SIZE
Unit of measurement	Number of CSO establishments registered in previous year per 100,000 population

Type of indicator: ☐ preferred ☐ standard ☒ optional

Unit of analysis: ☐ micro (variation) ☐ meso (variation) ☒ macro

METHODOLOGICAL DESCRIPTION AND UNDERLYING DEFINITIONS

Measurement and methodological aspects	• Number of CSO establishments registered in previous year divided by population size x 100,000
Potential usefulness	• Comparisons (see 'Number of CSO establishments per 100,000 population')
Potential limitations	• Should be used in conjunction with other indicators because methods for computing 'numbers of organizations' vary (not always clear whether 'number of organizations' in national statistics counts the separate establishments of complex organizations) (see 'Suggested modifications') • In-country variations can be significant • In general, lack of defined standards and comparability of definitions across countries and over time may reduce reliability of surveys in some countries
Suggested modifications	• Following UN conventions, the individual 'establishments' of complex organizations should be counted separately to the extent possible. Where this is not possible, record the number of separately registered or incorporated entities. • If calculations are based on organizational data, average size indicators may be taken into account
Links to other measures	• Number of CSOs per 100,000 population (size) • Foundation density (size) • Density of CSO umbrella organizations (number per 1000 CSOs) (composition)

ASSESSMENT OF DATA QUALITY AND AVAILABILITY

Method of data collection	• National statistical offices registers • Organizational surveys • Depends upon provider – varied
Data provider	• National statistical offices/registers • Individual researchers/country specific
Access to data	• Good – published for some countries
Frequency of data collection	• Varied – more current at local levels

COMMENTS

With some modification, the indicator can be applied to field-level data.

INDICATOR NAME FOUNDATION DENSITY

Brief definition	Number of foundations per 100,000 population
Dimension	STRUCTURE–SIZE
Unit of measurement	Number of foundations relative to 100,000 population

Type of indicator: ☐ preferred ☐ standard ☒ optional

Unit of analysis: ☐ micro (variation) ☐ meso (variation) ☒ macro

METHODOLOGICAL DESCRIPTION AND UNDERLYING DEFINITIONS

Measurement and methodological aspects	• Number of foundations divided by population size x 100,000
Potential usefulness	• Measures organized philanthropy
Potential limitations	• Should be used in conjunction with other indicators because methods for computing 'numbers of organizations' vary (not always clear whether number of organizations refers to establishments or entities) • In general, lack of defined standards and comparability of definitions across countries and over time may reduce reliability of surveys in some countries
Suggested modifications	• If calculations are based on organizational data, average size indicators may be taken into account
Links to other measures	• Number of CSOs per 100,000 population (size) • Rate of CSO establishments per year (size) • Density of CSO umbrella organizations (number per 1000 CSOs) (composition)

ASSESSMENT OF DATA QUALITY AND AVAILABILITY

Method of data collection	• National statistical offices registers • Organizational surveys (by umbrella organizations) • Depends upon provider – varied
Data provider	• National statistical offices • Individual researchers/country specific
Access to data	• Good – published for some countries
Frequency of data collection	• Varied

COMMENTS

Similar indicators can be calculated for other types of CSOs, such as advocacy organizations, service providers, etc.
With some modification, the indicator can be applied to field-level data.

COMPOSITION

INDICATOR NAME (PAID) EMPLOYMENT IN ADVOCACY CSOS RELATIVE TO EMPLOYMENT IN SERVICE-PROVIDING CSOS

Brief definition	Employment in advocacy CSOs relative to employment in service-providing CSOs
Dimension	STRUCTURE–COMPOSITION
Unit of measurement	Number of adults in full-time equivalent (FTE) paid employment in advocacy CSOs relative to number of adults in FTE paid employment in service-providing CSOs

Type of indicator: ☒ preferred   ☐ standard   ☐ optional

Unit of analysis: ☐ micro (variation)   ☐ meso (variation)   ☒ macro

METHODOLOGICAL DESCRIPTION AND UNDERLYING DEFINITIONS

Measurement and methodological aspects	• Employment in CSOs based on sample surveys of organizations or labour statistics
Potential usefulness	• Basic composition measure
Potential limitations	• CSOs may only be partially covered in standard surveys • Some degree of universal comparability, but varying survey design, definitions and frequency may limit comparability cross-nationally and across time • Translating part-time and full-time into FTE • Many atypical employment forms (particularly prevalent in CSOs) not captured
Suggested modifications	• Translation into FTE • Incorporation of atypical employment forms where possible • Include volunteering as a variation
Links to other measures	• Paid employment (size) • Volunteering (size) • Volunteering in advocacy CSOs relative to service-providing CSOs (composition)

ASSESSMENT OF DATA QUALITY AND AVAILABILITY

Method of data collection	• Labour force surveys (national statistical offices) • Organizational surveys
Data provider	• National statistical offices • Individual researchers/country specific
Access to data	• Good – published for some countries
Frequency of data collection	• Frequent updates (usually quarterly) for labour force surveys • Full employment census usually every five to ten years • Organizational surveys irregular

COMMENTS

With some modification, the indicator can be applied to field-level data, as well as to specific case studies.

INDICATOR NAME VOLUNTEERING IN ADVOCACY CSOS RELATIVE TO VOLUNTEERING IN SERVICE-PROVIDING CSOS

Brief definition	Unpaid workers in advocacy CSOs relative to unpaid workers in service-providing CSOs
Dimension	STRUCTURE–COMPOSITION
Unit of measurement	Number of unpaid adult workers in advocacy CSOs as percentage of number of unpaid adult workers in service-providing CSOs

Type of indicator: ☒ preferred ☐ standard ☒ optional

Unit of analysis: ☐ micro (variation) ☐ meso (variation) ☒ macro

METHODOLOGICAL DESCRIPTION AND UNDERLYING DEFINITIONS

Measurement and methodological aspects	• Assumes cross-national definition of volunteering • Robust but not refined indicator of social engagement • If World Values Survey as data source: representative, national samples used in WVS (covers 40 societies; 70 per cent of world's population, more for 2000–2001)
Potential usefulness	• Easy to understand • Widely available indicator of social engagement
Potential limitations	• Some degree of universal comparability, but varying survey design, definitions and frequency may limit comparability cross-nationally and across time • Does not capture frequency of volunteering and number of hours volunteered • Does not capture extremes • Validity constraint: paid and unpaid work not dichotomous
Suggested modifications	• Modify to capture cultural differences and non-Western applications (for example, countries with large, informal household sectors where unpaid work is not necessarily equivalent to volunteering) • More targeted surveys may be needed to capture extremes
Links to other measures	• Volunteering (size) • Index of Philanthropic Giving (revenue) • Paid employment (size) • (Paid) employment in advocacy CSOs relative to employment in service-providing CSOs (composition)

ASSESSMENT OF DATA QUALITY AND AVAILABILITY

Method of data collection	• Volunteering (size) • National population surveys (general random-probability population samples)
Data provider	• Country specific • World Values Survey (rough indicator of volunteering/participation)
Access to data	• Coverage and availability of population census data good for some countries
Frequency of data collection	• Typically every two to three years; more frequent at national levels • WVS every three to five years; more frequently in most developed countries

COMMENTS

With some modification, the indicator can be applied to field-level data, as well as to specific case studies.

INDICATOR NAME MEMBERSHIPS IN ADVOCACY CSOS RELATIVE TO MEMBERSHIPS IN SERVICE-PROVIDING CSOS

Brief definition	Share of adult population with memberships in advocacy CSOs relative to share of adult population with memberships in service-providing CSOs
Dimension	STRUCTURE–COMPOSITION
Unit of measurement	Number of adults holding memberships in advocacy CSOs relative to number of adults holding memberships in service-providing CSOs

Type of indicator: ☐ preferred ☒ standard ☐ optional

Unit of analysis: ☐ micro (variation) ☐ meso (variation) ☒ macro

METHODOLOGICAL DESCRIPTION AND UNDERLYING DEFINITIONS

Measurement and methodological aspects	• Includes membership in the following types of advocacy organizations (based on 1990–1993 WVS): trade unions, environment, local community action, women's groups, human rights, animal rights and peace movement • Includes membership in the following types of service-providing organizations (based on 1990–1993 WVS): social welfare services, youth work, health, voluntary • Representative, national samples used in WVS (covers 40 societies; 70 per cent of world's population; coverage improved in 2000–2001)
Potential usefulness	• Provides standardized cross-national comparison • Easily available indicator of participation in civil society • Important predictor of volunteering and contributing patterns
Potential limitations	• Validity constraint: standard wording and terminology of questions may not fit local culture and practice
Suggested modifications	• Modify to capture cultural differences and non-Western applications
Links to other measures	• Participation (size) • Membership (size) • Freedom of Association (JHU measure and qualitative review) (space)

ASSESSMENT OF DATA QUALITY AND AVAILABILITY

Method of data collection	• World Values Survey (rough indicator of participation)
Data provider	• World Values Survey
Access to data	• Good – published
Frequency of data collection	• Every three to five years; more frequent at national levels

COMMENTS

With some modification, the indicator can be applied to field-level data, as well as to specific case studies.

INDICATOR NAME EXPENDITURES IN ADVOCACY CSOS RELATIVE TO EXPENDITURES IN SERVICE-PROVIDING CSOS

Brief definition	Operating expenditures (including wage and salary disbursements; purchases of goods other than capital equipment; material and services; and fees and charges paid) in advocacy CSOs relative to operating expenditures in service-providing CSOs
Dimension	STRUCTURE–COMPOSITION
Unit of measurement	Operating expenditures in advocacy CSOs relative to operating expenditures in service-providing CSOs

Type of indicator: ☐ preferred ☒ standard ☐ optional

Unit of analysis: ☐ micro (variation) ☐ meso (variation) ☒ macro

METHODOLOGICAL DESCRIPTION AND UNDERLYING DEFINITIONS

Measurement and methodological aspects	• Assumes availability of wage bill and other operating cost items • Assumes expenditure data are classified by field
Potential usefulness	• Provides standardized cross-national comparison • Basic composition measure
Potential limitations	• Validity constraint: standard wording and terminology of questions may not fit local culture and practice
Suggested modifications	• Modify to capture cultural differences and non-Western applications
Links to other measures	• CSO operating expenditures (size) • Paid employment (size) • Employment in advocacy CSOs relative to expenditure in service-providing CSOs (composition) • Public-sector dependency (revenue) • Marketization (revenue) • Giving indicators (revenue)

ASSESSMENT OF DATA QUALITY AND AVAILABILITY

Method of data collection	• National income accounts • Organizational surveys
Data provider	• National statistical offices • CSO annual reports • Individual researchers/country specific
Access to data	• National income accounts good – published for some countries • Organizational surveys irregular
Frequency of data collection	• National income accounts, annual data • Organizational surveys irregular

COMMENTS

With some modification, the indicator can be applied to field-level data, as well as to specific case studies.

INDICATOR NAME DENSITY OF CSO UMBRELLA ORGANIZATIONS

Brief definition	Concentration of CSO umbrella organizations per 100,000 CSOs
Dimension	STRUCTURE–COMPOSITION
Unit of measurement	Number of CSO umbrella organizations per 100,000 CSOs

Type of indicator:	☐ preferred		☐ standard		☒ optional
Unit of analysis:	☐ micro (variation)		☐ meso (variation)		☒ macro

METHODOLOGICAL DESCRIPTION AND UNDERLYING DEFINITIONS

Measurement and methodological aspects	• Assumes organizational registers or surveys are available such that they identify umbrella organizations from other CSOs
Potential usefulness	• Measures concentration of CSO umbrella organizations • Indicates degree of intermediary organizational structure among CSOs
Potential limitations	• Definition of umbrella organization may be complex and not replicated in data structure
Suggested modifications	
Links to other measures	• Number of CSOs per 100,000 population (size) • Membership (size) • CSO formation (space) • Freedom of association (JHU measure and qualitative review) (space)

ASSESSMENT OF DATA QUALITY AND AVAILABILITY

Method of data collection	• Organizational registers • Organizational surveys
Data provider	• Public agencies • Large umbrella organizations themselves
Data set description	
Access to data	• Varied
Frequency of data collection	• Irregular

COMMENTS

With some modification, the indicator can be applied to field-level data, as well as to specific case studies.

REVENUE

INDICATOR NAME INDEX OF PHILANTHROPIC GIVING

Brief definition	Composite measure of giving to civil society organizations using three variables : time (volunteering), money and in-kind donations, relative to government social spending
Dimension	STRUCTURE–REVENUE
Unit of measurement	

Type of indicator: ☒ preferred   ☐ standard   ☐ optional

Unit of analysis: ☐ micro (variation)   ☐ meso (variation)   ☒ macro

METHODOLOGICAL DESCRIPTION AND UNDERLYING DEFINITIONS

Measurement and methodological aspects	• Based on two kinds of information: (i) estimates of giving, volunteering and in-kind donations derived from representative population surveys; and (ii) measures of government social spending from government outlays in national income accounts
Potential usefulness	• Resource mobilization measure of CSOs relative to expenditure • Measures current and expected donor behaviour
Potential limitations	• Some degree of universal comparability, but varying survey design, definitions and frequency may limit comparability cross-nationally and across time • Monetary equivalents
Suggested modifications	• Modify by country to capture cultural differences and non-Western applications
Links to other measures	• Other giving measures (revenue) • Marketization (revenue) • Volunteering (size) • Volunteering in advocacy CSOs relative to volunteering in service-providing CSOs (composition) • Tax incentives (space)

ASSESSMENT OF DATA QUALITY AND AVAILABILITY

Method of data collection	• Population surveys • Government outlays in national income accounts
Data provider	• National statistical offices • Individual researchers/country specific
Access to data	• Good – published for some countries
Frequency of data collection	• Population surveys typically every two to three years • National income accounts (annual)

COMMENTS

With some modification, the indicator can be applied to field-level data (meso level), as well as to specific case studies (micro level).

INDICATOR NAME PHILANTHROPIC GIVING INDEX (PGI)

Brief definition	Measure of the climate for philanthropic giving and fundraising in the US
Dimension	STRUCTURE–REVENUE
Unit of measurement	

Type of indicator: ☒ preferred ☐ standard ☐ optional

Unit of analysis: ☐ micro (variation) ☐ meso (variation) ☒ macro

METHODOLOGICAL DESCRIPTION AND UNDERLYING DEFINITIONS

Measurement and methodological aspects	• 23 questions: 1–6 Likert type, used to compute PGI and related indexes; 7–20 related to success or failure of fundraising vehicles; 21–22 yes not reorganizational involvement in capital campaigns; and 23 narrative
Potential usefulness	• Measures current and expected donor behaviour • No significant time lags • Ties donor behaviour to solicitation strategies
Potential limitations	• Data for US only
Modifications required	
Links to other measures	• Public-sector dependency (revenue) • Marketization (revenue) • Volunteering (size) • Tax incentives (space) • Other giving measures (revenue)

ASSESSMENT OF DATA QUALITY AND AVAILABILITY

Method of data collection	• Expert survey of fundraising experts in six areas: arts, culture, humanities; PEAI (public benefit, environment, animal and international); education; health; human services; and religion
Data provider	• Indiana University Center on Philanthropy
Access to data	• Good – published
Frequency of data collection	• Semi-annual

COMMENTS

Source: www.philanthropy.iupui.edu/
Background information:
Kaplan, A E (1999); Keirouz, K S et al (1999); Gronbjerg, K (1994); Independent Sector (2002); Renz et al (1995)

INDICATOR NAME VALUE OF VOLUNTEER INPUT

Brief definition	Imputed monetary valuation (IMV) of unpaid work in CSOs compared to paid work in CSOs relative to non-profit operating expenditures (NPOE) or relative to GDP
Dimension	STRUCTURE–REVENUE
Unit of measurement	IMV of unpaid work relative to the value of paid work as a percentage of NPOE or GDP

Type of indicator:	[X] preferred	[ ] standard	[ ] optional
Unit of analysis:	[ ] micro (variation)	[ ] meso (variation)	[X] macro

METHODOLOGICAL DESCRIPTION AND UNDERLYING DEFINITIONS

Measurement and methodological aspects	• The total number of *volunteers* equals the percentage of the sample reported to have volunteered multiplied by the total adult population. For example, if 20 per cent of respondents reported to have volunteered, and the population in your country is 10 million, then the estimated number of volunteers would be 20 per cent x 10 million or 2 million plus/minus sampling error. • The total number of *volunteer hours* can be calculated by multiplying the percentage of the sample population volunteering in each area by the average number of volunteer hours in each area. For example, if 10 per cent of respondents reported volunteering a total of five hours per month in a certain field and the population in your country is 10 million, then the estimated number of volunteer hours would be 1 million x 5 = 5 million hours (plus/minus sampling error) for this particular field. • To calculate the number of *full-time equivalent volunteers*, divide the total number of volunteer hours by a factor representing the assumed number of annual hours worked by full-time employees. This number should be available from the statistical office in your country. • The *imputed value of volunteer input* is obtained by multiplying the total number of hours volunteered by the average gross hourly earnings for private non-agricultural employees. This estimate is usually increased by a percentage to approximate the cost of fringe benefits and the like. Both numbers should be available from statistical offices. Thus, the general approach taken is that of an assumed 'replacement wage'. • The IMV is then the numerator and the NPOE *or* GDP is the denominator. NPOE is preferred because it reflects cost, whereas GDP reflects value added.
Potential usefulness	• Allows for an estimate of the volunteer contribution to national economies in terms of total labour input and the associated cost to NPOE or the value added to GDP • Enables cross-national comparisons in volunteering patterns and reliance on voluntary labour
Potential limitations	• Computing monetary equivalents • Social desirability effects • No checks and balances in population surveys for over- and under-reporting • Possible subjective distortions from confounding voluntary work with membership participation • Some degree of universal comparability, but varying survey design, definitions and frequency may limit comparability cross-nationally and across time
Suggested required	• Further testing of suitability of shadow wages • Determine comparability and substitutability of paid staff and volunteers across different income groups and tasks
Links to other measures	• Public-sector dependency (revenue) • Marketization (revenue) • Volunteering (size) • Volunteering in advocacy CSOs relative to volunteering in service-providing CSOs (composition)

ASSESSMENT OF DATA QUALITY AND AVAILABILITY

Method of data collection	• Population surveys
Data provider	• National statistical offices
Access to data	• Coverage and availability of population census data good for some countries
Frequency of data collection	• Typically every two to three years

COMMENTS

Source: Archambault, Anheier and Sokolowski (1998)
Background information: Institute for Volunteering Research (for the UK: www.ivr.org.uk/institute.htm); United Nations Office of Volunteering (www.iyv.org/); Independent Sector (for the US: www.independentsector.org)
With some modification, the indicator can be applied to field-level data, as well as to specific case studies.

INDICATOR NAME MARKETIZATION

Brief definition	Inflows of spendable resources received by civil society organizations during the year from fees and charges (business and commercial income) relative to inflows of spendable resources from other sources (public-sector payments and private giving)
Dimension	STRUCTURE–REVENUE
Unit of measurement	Inflows from fees and payments as a share of CSOs' spendable resources (percentage)

Type of indicator: [X] preferred   [ ] standard   [ ] optional

Unit of analysis: [ ] micro (variation)   [ ] meso (variation)   [X] macro

METHODOLOGICAL DESCRIPTION AND UNDERLYING DEFINITIONS

Measurement and methodological aspects	• Spendable resources funds not intended for capital expenditures or endowments • To calculate inflows of spendable resources, collect information on actual monetary flows from specific sources as described above using statistical offices, tax authorities, relevant government ministries and specialized agencies, and umbrella organizations
Potential usefulness	• Indicator of resource dependency • Reveals information about funding patterns and relationships between sectors
Potential limitations	• Some degree of universal comparability, but varying survey design, definitions and frequency may limit comparability cross-nationally and across time
Suggested modifications	
Links to other measures	• Public-sector dependency (revenue) • Index of Philanthropic Giving (revenue) • Foundation giving as share of total CSO revenue (revenue) • Corporate giving as a share of total CSO revenue (revenue) • CSO financing (space) • CSO formation (space)

ASSESSMENT OF DATA QUALITY AND AVAILABILITY

Method of data collection	• National income accounts • National tax data • Organizational surveys • Country-specific data sources
Data provider	• National tax and statistical offices • Country specific/relevant government ministries • Individual researchers
Access to data	• National income accounts: good – published for some countries • Organizational surveys irregular
Frequency of data collection	• National income accounts annual, quarterly, monthly • Organizational surveys irregular

COMMENTS

• Fees and charges: fees for service, dues, proceeds from sales of products and investment income
• Public-sector payments: grants and contracts, statutory transfers and third-party payments
• Philanthropy or private giving: foundation giving, business or corporate donations and individual giving
With some modification, the indicator can be applied to field-level data, as well as to specific case studies.

INDICATOR NAME PUBLIC SECTOR DEPENDENCY

Brief definition	Inflows of spendable resources received by CSOs during the year from public-sector payments relative to inflows of spendable resources from other sources (fees and charges and private giving)
Dimension	STRUCTURE–REVENUE
Unit of measurement	Public-sector payments as a share of CSOs' inflows of spendable resources (percentage)

Type of indicator: ☐ preferred ☒ standard ☐ optional

Unit of analysis: ☐ micro (variation) ☐ meso (variation) ☒ macro

METHODOLOGICAL DESCRIPTION AND UNDERLYING DEFINITIONS

Measurement and methodological aspects	• Spendable resources funds not intended for capital expenditures or endowments • To calculate inflows of spendable resources, collect information on actual monetary flows from specific sources as described above using statistical offices, tax authorities, relevant government ministries and specialized agencies, and umbrella organizations
Potential usefulness	• Indicator of resource dependency • Reveals information about funding patterns and relationships between sectors
Potential limitations	• Some degree of universal comparability, but varying survey design, definitions and frequency may limit comparability cross-nationally and across time
Suggested modifications	• In-kind contributions from the public sector could also be used as a variation
Links to other measures	• Marketization (revenue) • Index of Philanthropic Giving (revenue) • Foundation giving as share of total CSO revenue (revenue) • Corporate giving as share of total CSO revenue (revenue) • CSO financing (space) • CSO formation (space)

ASSESSMENT OF DATA QUALITY AND AVAILABILITY

Method of data collection	• National income accounts • National tax data • Organizational surveys • Country-specific data sources
Data provider	• National tax and statistical offices • Country specific/relevant government ministries • Individual researchers
Access to data	• National income accounts: good – published for some countries • Organizational surveys irregular
Frequency of data collection	• National income accounts annual, quarterly, monthly • Organizational surveys irregular

COMMENTS

• Public-sector payments: grants and contracts, statutory transfers and third-party payments. Following UN conventions, 'public sector' here refers to all branches and levels of government, including the executive, judicial, administrative and regulatory activities of federal, state, local or regional political entities. This includes quasi-governmental entities, such as social insurance funds, and international and intergovernmental bodies, such as the UN, the World Bank and other multilateral and bilateral institutions.
• Fees and charges: fees for service, dues, proceeds from sales of products and investment income
• Philanthropy or private giving: foundation giving, business or corporate donations and individual giving
With some modification, the indicator can be applied to field-level data, as well as to specific case studies.

INDICATOR NAME INDIVIDUAL GIVING

Brief definition	Individual giving as a percentage of personal income
Dimension	STRUCTURE–REVENUE
Unit of measurement	Amount of individual giving relative to individual income

Type of indicator: ☐ preferred ☒ standard ☐ optional

Unit of analysis: ☐ micro (variation) ☐ meso (variation) ☒ macro

METHODOLOGICAL DESCRIPTION AND UNDERLYING DEFINITIONS

Measurement and methodological aspects	• Individual giving is defined as direct contributions by individuals and contributions made through 'federated fundraising' campaigns, such as workplace giving
Potential usefulness	• Basic measure of philanthropic engagement
Potential limitations	• Underestimates 'high-level' giving and irregular giving • Data on individual giving limited: incomplete data available in *some* developed and transition countries (very limited in developing countries) from individuals who itemize taxes (see 'Method of data collection') and CSO tax returns; but no reliable data series available on individual giving based upon solid data collection over time • Data collection on private contributions from individuals and religious institutions weakest area of giving data • If household surveys conducted, three potential limitations: people tend to forget how much they give to a CSO in a given period of time; people tend to over-claim, fearing to admit that they have given nothing or very little; and giving to CSOs shows dramatic seasonal variations and greatly increases after national or international disasters reported in the media • Some degree of universal comparability, but varying survey design, definitions and frequency may limit comparability cross-nationally and across time (especially definition of CSO)
Suggested modifications	• Account for over- and under-reporting
Links to other measures	• Index of Philanthropic Giving (revenue) • Individual CSO donations per capita (revenue) • Other giving measures (revenue) • Volunteering (size) • Participation (size) • Membership (size) • Membership in advocacy CSOs relative to membership in service-providing CSOs (composition) • Volunteering in advocacy CSOs relative to volunteering in service-providing CSOs (composition) • CSO financing (space) • CSO formation (space) • Tax incentives (space)

ASSESSMENT OF DATA QUALITY AND AVAILABILITY

Method of data collection	• National tax data (for example, in the US, National Taxonomy of Exempt Entities and Internal Revenue Service; CSO (1990) tax returns) • Individual giving surveys/family expenditure surveys (population survey) • Country-level surveys
Data provider	• National tax and statistical offices • Country specific/individual researchers
Access to data	• Good
Frequency of data collection	• Tax data collected annually • Population surveys irregular

COMMENTS

Background information: Independent Sector and the Urban Institute (2002); Rosenberg (1996); Wolff (1995)

With some modification, the indicator can be applied to field-level data, as well as to specific case studies.

INDICATOR NAME CORPORATE GIVING

Brief definition	Corporate giving as a percentage of corporate profits
Dimension	STRUCTURE–REVENUE
Unit of measurement	Amount of corporate giving relative to corporate profits

Type of indicator: ☐ preferred ☒ standard ☐ optional

Unit of analysis: ☐ micro (variation) ☐ meso (variation) ☒ macro

METHODOLOGICAL DESCRIPTION AND UNDERLYING DEFINITIONS

Measurement and methodological aspects	• Corporate giving is defined as cash, sponsorship, secondment, gifts in-kind, enterprise agencies, training schemes, administrative support, and joint promotions (see 'Comments' for more information)
Potential usefulness	• Indicator of resource dependency • Reveals information about funding patterns and relationships between sectors • Indicator of corporate social responsibility in some countries
Potential limitations	• Coverage and availability of data on direct corporate giving limited (for example, no disclosure is required in the US) • Imputing monetary value for non-cash corporate giving
Suggested modifications	• Account for over- and under-reporting
Links to other measures	• Index of Philanthropic Giving (revenue) • Corporate giving as a percentage of corporate profits (revenue) • Corporate social responsibility programmes as share of corporate profits (revenue) • Other giving measures (revenue) • CSO financing (space) • CSO formation (space) • Tax incentives (space)

ASSESSMENT OF DATA QUALITY AND AVAILABILITY

Method of data collection	• National tax data (for example, in the US, Foundation tax returns – Form 990) • Surveys of corporate giving
Data provider	• National tax and statistical offices • Country specific/individual researchers
Access to data	• Tax data good for most developed countries (but captures a limited portion of corporate giving)
Frequency of data collection	• Tax data collected annually • Surveys of corporate giving irregular

COMMENTS

See Hazell and Whybrew (1993); Saxon-Harrold (1987); Foundation Center (www.fdncenter.org)
Note: motivations for corporate giving usually: (i) influence legislation and policy; (ii) build public and community relations; and (iii) improve quality of life in locales in which they operate
With some modification, the indicator can be applied to field-level data, as well as to specific case studies.

INDICATOR NAME INDIVIDUAL CSO DONATIONS PER CAPITA

Brief definition	Funds given to CSOs per capita
Dimension	STRUCTURE–REVENUE
Unit of measurement	Monetary

Type of indicator:	☐ preferred	☒ standard	☐ optional
Unit of analysis:	☐ micro (variation)	☐ meso (variation)	☒ macro

METHODOLOGICAL DESCRIPTION AND UNDERLYING DEFINITIONS

Measurement and methodological aspects	• Estimated sum of donations divided by population size • In sample survey, sum of donations divided by sample size
Potential usefulness	• Basic measure of philanthropic engagement
Potential limitations	• Some degree of universal comparability, but varying survey design, definitions and frequency may limit comparability cross-nationally and across time • Data on individual giving limited: incomplete data available in *some* developed and transition countries (very limited in developing countries) from individuals who itemize taxes (see 'Method of data collection') and CSO tax returns; but no reliable data series available on individual giving based upon solid data collection over time • If household surveys conducted, three potential limitations: people tend to forget how much they give to a CSO in a given period of time; people tend to over-claim, fearing to admit that they have given nothing or very little; and giving to CSOs shows dramatic seasonal variations and greatly increases after national or international disasters reported in the media
Suggested modifications	• Account for over and under-reporting
Links to other measures	• Index of Philanthropic Giving (revenue) • Individual giving (revenue) • Other giving measures (revenue) • Volunteering (size) • CSO financing (space) • CSO formation (space) • Tax incentives (space)

ASSESSMENT OF DATA QUALITY AND AVAILABILITY

Method of data collection	• Population/household survey • National tax data
Data provider	• National statistical offices/census bureau • Itemized individual tax returns
Access to data	• Good – published for some countries
Frequency of data collection	• Population/household surveys every five to ten years • Tax data collected annually

COMMENTS

INDICATOR NAME VOLUNTEER HOURS IN CSOS PER CAPITA

Brief definition	Number of hours volunteered in CSOs per capita
Dimension	STRUCTURE–REVENUE
Unit of measurement	Volunteer hours in CSOs per capita

Type of indicator: ☐ preferred   ☒ standard   ☐ optional

Unit of analysis: ☐ micro (variation)   ☐ meso (variation)   ☒ macro

METHODOLOGICAL DESCRIPTION AND UNDERLYING DEFINITIONS

Measurement and methodological aspects	• Total number of hours volunteered divided by sample/population size • Assumes cross-national definition of volunteering
Potential usefulness	• Easy to understand • Widely available indicator of social engagement
Potential limitations	• Some degree of universal comparability, but varying survey design, definitions and frequency may limit comparability cross-nationally and across time • Limited data availability in some countries
Suggested modifications	• Modify to capture cultural differences and non-Western applications (for example, countries with large, informal household sectors where unpaid work is not necessarily equivalent to volunteering)
Links to other measures	• Index of Philanthropic Giving (revenue) • Individual CSO donations per capita (revenue) • Other giving measures (revenue) • Volunteering (size) • Tax incentives (space)

ASSESSMENT OF DATA QUALITY AND AVAILABILITY

Method of data collection	• Population survey • Organizational survey of CSOs
Data provider	• National statistical offices/census bureau
Access to data	• Good – published for some countries
Frequency of data collection	• Population/household surveys every five to ten years • Volunteering more frequent

COMMENTS

INDICATOR NAME FOUNDATION GIVING AS A SHARE OF TOTAL CSO REVENUE

Brief definition	Inflows of spendable resources received by CSOs during the year from foundation grants relative to inflows of spendable resources from other sources (public sector payments, fees and charges, and other private giving [corporations])
Dimension	STRUCTURE–REVENUE
Unit of measurement	Foundation grants as a share of CSOs' inflows of spendable resources (percentage)

Type of indicator:	☐ preferred	☐ standard	☒ optional
Unit of analysis:	☐ micro (variation)	☐ meso (variation)	☒ macro

METHODOLOGICAL DESCRIPTION AND UNDERLYING DEFINITIONS

Measurement and methodological aspects	• Add total grant disbursements by foundations in given year and relate this sum to the total operating expenditure or revenue of CSO
Potential usefulness	• Indicator of resource dependency • Reveals information about funding patterns and relationships between sectors
Potential limitations	• Some degree of universal comparability, but varying survey design, definitions and frequency may limit comparability cross-nationally and across time
Suggested modifications	• Foundation grants may be reported for grant period and not for particular years; grants from abroad may not be included
Links to other measures	• Index of Philanthropic Giving (revenue) • Marketization (revenue) • Public-sector dependency (revenue) • Other giving measures (revenue) • Foundation density (size) • CSO financing (space) • CSO formation (space) • Tax incentives (space)

ASSESSMENT OF DATA QUALITY AND AVAILABILITY

Method of data collection	• National income accounts • Organizational surveys of foundations • Directories • Country-specific data sources
Data provider	• National statistical offices • Foundation directories • Individual researchers/ country specific (in the US, for example, see the Foundation Center, www.fdncenter.org; in Europe, see the European Foundation Center, www.efc.be, or Charities Aid Foundation, www.cafonline.com)
Access to data	• National income accounts: good – published for some countries • Organizational surveys irregular
Frequency of data collection	• National income accounts annual, quarterly, monthly • Organizational surveys irregular

COMMENTS

• Fees and charges: fees for service, dues, proceeds from sales of products and investment income
• Public-sector payments: grants and contracts, statutory transfers and third-party payments
• Philanthropy or private giving: foundation giving, business or corporate donations and individual giving
With some modification, the indicator can be applied to field-level data, as well as to specific case studies.

INDICATOR NAME CORPORATE GIVING AS A SHARE OF TOTAL CSO REVENUE

Brief definition	Inflows of spendable resources received by civil society organizations during the year from corporations relative to inflows of spendable resources from other sources (public-sector payments, fees and charges, and other private giving [foundations])
Dimension	STRUCTURE–REVENUE
Unit of measurement	Corporate donations to CSOs as a share of CSOs' inflow of spendable resources (percentage)

Type of indicator:	☐ preferred	☐ standard	☒ optional
Unit of analysis:	☐ micro (variation)	☐ meso (variation)	☒ macro

METHODOLOGICAL DESCRIPTION AND UNDERLYING DEFINITIONS

Measurement and methodological aspects	• Adds total of disbursements of donated funds by corporations to CSOs in given year and relates this sum to the total operating expenditure or revenue of CSO
Potential usefulness	• Indicator of resource dependency • Reveals information about funding patterns and relationships between sectors
Potential limitations	• Some degree of universal comparability, but varying survey design, definitions and frequency may limit comparability cross-nationally and across time • Corporate giving and sponsoring may be closely related and mixed up in available data
Suggested modifications	
Links to other measures	• Index of Philanthropic Giving (revenue) • Marketization (revenue) • Public-sector dependency (revenue) • Other giving measures (revenue) • Foundation density (size) • CSO financing (space) • CSO formation (space) • Tax incentives (space)

ASSESSMENT OF DATA QUALITY AND AVAILABILITY

Method of data collection	• National income accounts • Organizational surveys of corporations • Country-specific data sources
Data provider	• National statistical offices • Individual researchers/country specific
Access to data	• National income accounts: good – published for some countries • Organizational surveys irregular
Frequency of data collection	• National income accounts annual, quarterly, monthly • Organizational surveys irregular

COMMENTS

• Fees and charges: fees for service, dues, proceeds from sales of products and investment income
• Public-sector payments: grants and contracts, statutory transfers and third-party payments
• Philanthropy or private giving: foundation giving, business or corporate donations and individual giving
With some modification, the indicator can be applied to field-level data, as well as to specific case studies.

INDICATOR NAME CORPORATE SOCIAL RESPONSIBILITY (CSR) PROGRAMMES AS A SHARE OF CORPORATE PROFITS

Brief definition	CSR programmes relative to corporate profits
Dimension	STRUCTURE–REVENUE
Unit of measurement	Cost of CSR programmes as a share of corporate profits

Type of indicator:	☐ preferred		☐ standard		☒ optional
Unit of analysis:	☐ micro (variation)		☐ meso (variation)		☒ macro

METHODOLOGICAL DESCRIPTION AND UNDERLYING DEFINITIONS

Measurement and methodological aspects	• Adds total cost of social responsibility programmes by corporations and relates this sum to the total reported profits
Potential usefulness	• Measure of actual commitment on behalf of corporations
Potential limitations	• Costs may be over-reported; at the same time, activities of smaller corporations may go unreported
Suggested modifications	• Correct for over- and under-reporting
Links to other measures	• Corporate giving as percentage of corporate profits (revenue) • Corporate giving as share of total CSO revenue (revenue) • Other giving measures (revenue) • Tax incentives (space)

ASSESSMENT OF DATA QUALITY AND AVAILABILITY

Method of data collection	• Organizational surveys • Annual reports • Tax data
Data provider	• Statistical offices • Individual researchers
Access to data	• Limited in some countries
Frequency of data collection	• Irregular; could be annual for some countries

COMMENTS

VALUES: MACRO INDICATORS

INDICATOR NAME TRUST

Brief definition	Generalized trust in people by CSO members relative to adult population
Dimension	VALUES
Unit of measurement	Percentage difference between CSO member and adult population

Type of indicator:	☒ preferred	☐ standard	☐ optional
Unit of analysis:	☐ micro (variation)	☐ meso (variation)	☒ macro

METHODOLOGICAL DESCRIPTION AND UNDERLYING DEFINITIONS

Measurement and methodological aspects	• Representative, national samples used in World Values Survey (covers over 40 societies; 70 per cent of world's population; more in 2000–2001) and similar population surveys • WVS question: 'Generally speaking, would you say that most people can be trusted or that you can't be too careful in dealing with people?' • Relates trust by members of CSO to trust in population generally
Potential usefulness	• Standardized, cross-cultural measure of trust in society
Potential limitations	• Broad conception of trust • WVS data limited to macro-level CSD view; use similar population surveys for regional-level applications
Suggested modifications	• Trust in particular groups • Trust in CSOs as measured by take-up/use of services (as a separate indicator)
Links to other measures	• Confidence (use as related optional indicator if 'trust' used as preferred indicator) (values) • Tolerance (values)

ASSESSMENT OF DATA QUALITY AND AVAILABILITY

Method of data collection	• Population survey
Data provider	• World Values Survey • National survey firms
Access to data	• Good – published
Frequency of data collection	• Every three to five years; more frequently in most developed countries

COMMENTS

Depending upon sample size, data can be broken down to regional levels.

INDICATOR NAME TOLERANCE

Brief definition	Tolerance levels by CSO members relative to adult population
Dimension	VALUES
Unit of measurement	Percentage difference between CSO member and adult population

Type of indicator: ☒ preferred ☐ standard ☐ optional

Unit of analysis: ☐ micro (variation) ☐ meso (variation) ☒ macro

METHODOLOGICAL DESCRIPTION AND UNDERLYING DEFINITIONS

Measurement and methodological aspects	• Representative, national samples used in World Values Survey (covers over 40 societies; 70 per cent of world's population; more in 2000–2001) and similar population surveys • WVS question: 'On this list are various groups of people. Could you please sort out any that you would not like to have as neighbours?' Groups for the 1990–1993 WVS: people of a different race; left-wing and right-wing extremists; Muslims; Jews; Hindus; immigrants/foreign workers; people who have AIDS; and homosexuals.
Potential usefulness	• Standardized, cross-cultural measure of tolerance in society
Potential limitations	• WVS data limited to macro-level CSD view; use similar population surveys for regional-level applications
Suggested modifications	• Adjust answer categories ('groups') to situation in country
Links to other measures	• Confidence (use as related optional indicator if 'trust' used as preferred indicator) (values) • Trust (values)

ASSESSMENT OF DATA QUALITY AND AVAILABILITY

Method of data collection	• Population survey
Data provider	• World Values Survey • National survey firms
Access to data	• Good – published
Frequency of data collection	• Every three to five years; more frequent in most developed countries

COMMENTS

Depending upon sample size, data can be broken down to regional levels.

INDICATOR NAME INCREASE IN NUMBER OF CSOS WITH CODE OF CONDUCT/ETHICS

Brief definition	Increase in number of CSOs with explicit code of conduct/ethics over previous year
Dimension	VALUES
Unit of measurement	Percentage increase

Type of indicator:	☒ preferred		☐ standard		☐ optional
Unit of analysis:	☐ micro (variation)		☐ meso (variation)		☒ macro

METHODOLOGICAL DESCRIPTION AND UNDERLYING DEFINITIONS

Measurement and methodological aspects	
Potential usefulness	• Provides information about *organizational* values to complement information collected on individual values in civil society
Potential limitations	Data for international organizations may soon be available in the *Yearbook of International Organizations* (UIA, 1905–1999/2000); otherwise, data collection could be time-consuming and expensive
Suggested modifications	
Links to other measures	• Expected corrupt behaviour (values) • Confidence (use as related optional indicator if 'trust' used as preferred indicator) (values) • Trust (values) • Tolerance (values) • Corruption Perceptions Index (space)

ASSESSMENT OF DATA QUALITY AND AVAILABILITY

Method of data collection	• Organizational surveys of CSOs (such as the *Yearbook of International Organizations*) • Annual reports
Data provider	• Individual researcher/country specific
Access to data	• Varied
Frequency of data collection	• Irregular; but a system could be developed for the CSD

COMMENTS

Transparency International is also developing a TI Code of Ethics Project: see www.transparency.org/building_coalitions/ethics.html

INDICATOR NAME EXPECTED CORRUPTION/CORRUPT BEHAVIOUR AMONG CSO
MEMBERS RELATIVE TO ADULT POPULATION

Brief definition	Expectation of corruption/corrupt behaviour among members of CSOs relative to expectations of adult population in everyday life
Dimension	VALUES
Unit of measurement	Percentage difference between CSO member and adult population

Type of indicator:	☐ preferred	☒ standard	☐ optional
Unit of analysis:	☐ micro (variation)	☐ meso (variation)	☒ macro

METHODOLOGICAL DESCRIPTION AND UNDERLYING DEFINITIONS

Measurement and methodological aspects	• Representative, national samples used in World Values Survey (covers over 40 societies; 70 per cent of world's population; more in 2000–2001) and similar population surveys • WVS question: 'How widespread do you think bribe-taking and corruption are in this country?'
Potential usefulness	
Potential limitations	• WVS data limited to macro-level CSD view; use similar population surveys for regional-level applications
Suggested modifications	
Links to other measures	• Confidence (use as related optional indicator if 'trust' used as preferred indicator) (values) • Trust (values) • Tolerance (values) • Corruption Perceptions Index (space)

ASSESSMENT OF DATA QUALITY AND AVAILABILITY

Method of data collection	• Population survey
Data provider	• Individual researcher/country specific • World Values Survey
Access to data	• Good – published
Frequency of data collection	• Every three to five years; more frequent in most developed countries

COMMENTS

Depending upon sample size, data can be broken down to regional levels.

INDICATOR NAME CONFIDENCE

Brief definition	Confidence in selected institutions among CSO members relative to adult population
Dimension	VALUES
Unit of measurement	Percentage difference between CSO members and adult population

Type of indicator:	☐ preferred	☒ standard	☐ optional
Unit of analysis:	☐ micro (variation)	☐ meso (variation)	☒ macro

METHODOLOGICAL DESCRIPTION AND UNDERLYING DEFINITIONS

Measurement and methodological aspects	• Use as related indicator if 'trust' used as preferred indicator • WVS question: 'I am going to name a number of institutions. For each one, could you tell me how much confidence you have in them: is it a great deal of confidence, quite a lot of confidence, not very much confidence or none at all?' Major social institutions chosen for this indicator (from the 1990–1993 WVS): the legal system, major companies, the social security system and the political system. • Representative national samples used in World Values Survey (covers over 40 societies; 70 per cent of world's population; more in 2000–2001) and similar population surveys
Potential usefulness	• Provides complement to 'trust' indicator because civil society located in the space around the institutions covered in the World Values Survey
Potential limitations	• Civil society and CSOs not explicit category in most surveys • WVS data limited to macro-level CSD view; use similar population surveys for regional-level applications • World Values survey biased towards public institutions
Suggested modifications	
Links to other measures	• Trust (values) • Expected corrupt behaviour (values) • Membership (size) • Participation (size) • Membership in human rights organizations (values)

ASSESSMENT OF DATA QUALITY AND AVAILABILITY

Method of data collection	• Population survey
Data provider	• World Values Survey • National survey firms
Access to data	• Good – published
Frequency of data collection	• Every three to five years; more frequent in developed countries

COMMENTS

INDICATOR NAME MEMBERSHIP IN HUMAN RIGHTS ORGANIZATIONS (HROS)

Brief definition	Membership in HROs as an indicator of commitment to human values
Dimension	VALUES
Unit of measurement	Membership in HROs among CSO members relative to population levels

Type of indicator:	☐ preferred		☐ standard		☒ optional
Unit of analysis:	☐ micro (variation)		☐ meso (variation)		☒ macro

METHODOLOGICAL DESCRIPTION AND UNDERLYING DEFINITIONS

Measurement and methodological aspects	• Membership data in World Values Survey: adult membership in human rights groups • Includes membership in the following types of organizations (based on 1990–1993 WVS): local community action on issues such as poverty, employment, housing and racial equality; developing world growth or human rights; peace movements. WVS question: 'Please look carefully at the following list of voluntary organizations and activities and say which, if any, you belong to.' • Representative, national samples used in World Values Survey (covers over 40 societies; 70 per cent of world's population; more in 2000–2001) and similar population surveys
Potential usefulness	• Behavioural habits (such as membership in organizations) are important predictors of human values, and volunteering and contributing patterns
Potential limitations	• WVS data limited to macro-level CSD view; use similar population surveys for regional-level applications
Suggested modifications	• Choose those organizations in the country, region or case where the CSD is being applied with an interest in the well-being of the population (such as those focused on minorities or asylum-seekers)
Links to other measures	• Membership (size) • Participation (size) • Freedom of Association (JHU measure and qualitative review) (space) • Post-material versus material value dispositions (values)

ASSESSMENT OF DATA QUALITY AND AVAILABILITY

Method of data collection	• Population survey
Data provider	• World Values Survey • National survey firms
Access to data	• Good – published
Frequency of data collection	• Every three to five years; more frequent in most developed countries

COMMENTS

Depending upon sample size, data can be broken down to regional levels.

INDICATOR NAME MATERIAL VERSUS POST-MATERIAL VALUE DISPOSITIONS

Brief definition	Measurement of the intergenerational shift in material versus post-material value dispositions across 12 dimensions to capture how people engage/will engage in society; shows how CSO members differ from population at large
Dimension	VALUES
Unit of measurement	Percentage difference between CSO member and adult population

Type of indicator: ☐ preferred ☐ standard ☒ optional

Unit of analysis: ☐ micro (variation) ☐ meso (variation) ☒ macro

METHODOLOGICAL DESCRIPTION AND UNDERLYING DEFINITIONS

Measurement and methodological aspects	• Representative, national samples used in World Values Survey (covers over 40 societies; 70 per cent of world's population; more in 2000–2001) and similar population surveys
	• WVS question: 'There's a lot of talk these days about what the aims of this country should be for the next ten years. On this card are listed some of the goals which different people would give top priority. Would you please say which one of these you consider the most important?' 12 goals/dimensions rated:
	  1 materialist (survival needs – physical and economic security): rising prices, economic growth, stable economy, maintain order, fight crime and strong defence forces;
	  2 post-materialist (belonging, self-expression, intellectual and aesthetic satisfaction): more say on the job, less impersonal society, more say in government, ideas count, freedom of speech, more beautiful cities;
	• The polarization between material and post-material tends to be a phenomenon of societies that have undergone high levels of economic development and not a phenomenon limited to Western societies; see Inglehart (1997, pp124–130).
	• Ranking method measures value *priorities*. Shift from material to post-material values indicates how people engage/will engage in society ('one's value *priorities* are a genuine and crucial aspect of one's motivation', Inglehart, 1997, p115).

Potential usefulness	• Although controversial, this indicator provides a rich picture of how people engage in society • World Values Survey provides standardized, cross-cultural measure of materialist and post-materialist value dispositions
Potential limitations	• WVS data limited to macro-level CSD view
Suggested modifications	
Links to other measures	• Trust (values) • Confidence (values) • Volunteering (size and composition indicators) • Membership (size and composition indicators)	• Index of Philanthropic Giving (revenue) • Expected corrupt behaviour (values) • Membership in human rights organizations (values)

ASSESSMENT OF DATA QUALITY AND AVAILABILITY

Method of data collection	• Population survey
Data provider	• World Values Survey • National survey firms
Access to data	• Good – published
Frequency of data collection	• Every three to five years; more frequent in most developed countries

COMMENTS

Sources: Inglehart (1997); Inglehart, Basañez and Moreno (1998)

SPACE: MACRO INDICATORS

INDICATOR NAME THE JOHNS HOPKINS NON-PROFIT LAW INDEX

Brief definition	Legal features that might affect the willingness or ability of citizens to use, establish and operate non-profit organizations
Dimension	SPACE
Unit of measurement	Composite average score based on the assessment of legal experts

Type of indicator: ☒ preferred   ☐ standard   ☐ optional

Unit of analysis: ☐ micro (variation)   ☐ meso (variation)   ☒ macro

METHODOLOGICAL DESCRIPTION AND UNDERLYING DEFINITIONS

Measurement and methodological aspects	• The following 24 legal features are used in the JHU Law Index:
	  1 Demand-side indicators: (i) non-distribution constraint; (ii) personal benefit restrictions; (iii) reporting requirements; (iv) public availability of information; (v) governance; (vi) fundraising regulation;
	  2 General legal posture: (i) right of association; (ii) allowable purposes; and (iii) allowable political activities;
	  3 Formation: (i) unincorporated organizations permitted; (ii) membership requirements; (iii) capital requirements; (iv) government right to appoint board members; (v) government discretion in granting legal personality; and (vi) appeal procedures;
	  4 Financing: (i) broadness of organizational tax exemptions; (ii) income tax exemptions; (iii) real estate/property tax exemption; (iv) stamp and other duties; (v) indirect tax exemption (eg sales tax, VAT); (vi) unrelated business activities; (vii) organizational tax benefits for donations; (viii) tax benefits for individuals; and (ix) tax benefits for corporations
	• Each feature is assigned a value of 0, 1 or 2 by legal experts in each country
	• Scores are then summed and averaged to yield an aggregate score in each section ('demand-side', 'general legal posture', 'formation' and 'financing')
	• A full composite score of 8 for all sections is possible for the law index
	• In addition, index scores are compared with the size of the non-profit sector using share of total employment in the sector to measure the enabling quality of the legal environment on the development of the non-profit sector

Potential usefulness	• Measurement of the degree of enablement provided by the fiscal and regulatory system
Potential limitations	• Scoring systems blur finer distinctions, especially as laws (and their application) vary widely • JHU data on non-profit organizations (NPOs) may not cover all organizations included in the CIVICUS definition of a CSO
Suggested modifications	• Not all features may apply in the context of specific countries • This indicator can be used in its entirety or broken down into separate indicators. For example, see 'Tax incentives', 'Freedom of association', 'CSO formation' and 'CSO financing' indicators.
Links to other measures	• Freedom of association (JHU measure and qualitative review) (space) • Tax incentives (space) • Civil liberties (space) • Corruption Perceptions Index (space)

ASSESSMENT OF DATA QUALITY AND AVAILABILITY

Method of data collection	• Index scores based on composite average scores from legal expert assessments • Comparison of index scores with size of the non-profit sector
Data provider	• The Johns Hopkins University, Institute for Policy Studies
Access to data	• Good – published for some countries
Frequency of data collection	• Infrequent but can be updated easily

COMMENTS

Source: Salamon and Toepler (2000) *The Johns Hopkins Non-profit Law Index* (www.jhu.edu/~ccss/pubs/pdf/ccsswp17.pdf)
With further development, the indicator can be applied to field-level data, as well as to specific case studies.

INDICATOR NAME USAID LEGAL ENVIRONMENT INDICATOR

Brief definition	Legal status of NGOs
Dimension	SPACE
Unit of measurement	Composite average score based on the assessment of legal experts

Type of indicator:	[X] preferred		[ ] standard		[ ] optional
Unit of analysis:	[ ] micro (variation)		[ ] meso (variation)		[X] macro

METHODOLOGICAL DESCRIPTION AND UNDERLYING DEFINITIONS

Measurement and methodological aspects	• Six to ten legal experts are asked a set of questions covering seven legal features of NGOs • Legal experts: USAID recommends drawing upon donors, NGO assistance implementers, representatives of NGO support centres, and representatives of local NGOs in chief sub-sectors such as women's, environmental or human rights groups. In some instances, it may be appropriate to select a larger group in order to reflect the diversity and breadth of the sector; but a significantly larger group may make consensus-building more difficult. Furthermore, at least 50 per cent of the expert group should be local nationals. After initial assessments, a USAID working group meets to review rankings and score sheets, and compares them with the expert's overview statement, other countries' rankings and prior years' scores. The working group may return to experts for clarification/justification if deemed necessary. • See the full assessment of the USAID NGO Sustainability Indicator in the impact dimension for more details on USAID's methodology
Potential usefulness	• Measurement of the degree of support provided to NGOs by the legal and regulatory system
Potential limitations	• Composite scoring systems blur finer distinctions, especially as laws (and their application) vary widely • Subjectivity of perception measures • USAID data on NGOs may not cover all organizations and entities included in the CIVICUS definition of a CSO
Suggested modifications	• Country-specific context must be taken into account • Development of legal expert assessments for field/meso and case/micro applications
Links to other measures	• JHU Law Index (space) • Freedom of association (JHU measure and qualitative review) (space) • Tax incentives (space) • Civil liberties (space) • Corruption Perceptions Index (space)

ASSESSMENT OF DATA QUALITY AND AVAILABILITY

Method of data collection	• Index scores based on composite average scores from legal expert assessments
Data provider	• USAID, Europe and Eurasia Democracy and Government Unit (NGO Sustainability Index)
Access to data	• Good for some countries– published for Central and Eastern European and former Soviet Union countries
Frequency of data collection	• Annual (since 1998)

COMMENTS

Source: USAID (2000); see also
www.usaid.gov/regions/europe_eurasia/dem_gov/ngoindex/index.htm
With further development, the indicator can be applied to field-level data, as well as to specific case studies.

INDICATOR NAME CORRUPTION PERCEPTIONS INDEX (CPI) (TRANSPARENCY INTERNATIONAL)

Brief definition	Measures perceptions of corruption within countries, which draws on 17 different polls and surveys from 9 independent institutions carried out among business people, the general public and country analysts
Dimension	SPACE
Unit of measurement	Composite index

Type of indicator:	☒ preferred	☐ standard	☐ optional
Unit of analysis:	☐ micro (variation)	☐ meso (variation)	☒ macro

METHODOLOGICAL DESCRIPTION AND UNDERLYING DEFINITIONS

Measurement and methodological aspects	• Surveys used to form index use different sampling frames and various methodologies, and combine assessments from the past three years to reduce abrupt variation in scoring • 99 countries covered • Corruption defined as the misuse of public power for private benefit – for example, bribing of public officials, kickbacks in public procurement or embezzlement of public funds • Scoring: 0–10, where 10 is high; for CSD, 0 = 0%, 1 = 10%, 2= 20%…10 = 100%
Potential usefulness	• Basic indicator of corruption in society
Potential limitations	• Emphasis on business and public sector
Suggested modifications	• For CSD, use as a measure of the enabling environment provided by the overall fiscal and regulatory environment for civil society
Links to other measures	• Expected corruption/corrupt behaviour (values) • Freedom of Association (JHU measure and qualitative review) (space)

ASSESSMENT OF DATA QUALITY AND AVAILABILITY

Method of data collection	• Surveys of business people from nine different organizations
Data provider	• Transparency International
Access to data	• Good – published
Frequency of data collection	• Annual since 1995

COMMENTS

Source: Lambsdorff, G J (1998; 1999a; 1999b); see also www.transparency.org/cpi/index.html and www.gwdg.de/~uwww/ for previous indices

Definition of corruption (Transparency International): The abuse of public office for private gain. The surveys used in compiling the CPI tend to ask questions in line with the misuse of public power for private benefits, with a focus, for example, on bribing of public officials or giving and taking of kickbacks in public procurement.

INDICATOR NAME TAX INCENTIVES (FROM JHU LAW INDEX)

Brief definition	Tax and financing features that might affect the willingness or ability of citizens to use, establish and operate CSOs based on the JHU Non-profit Law Index
Dimension	SPACE
Unit of measurement	Composite average score based on the assessment of legal experts

Type of indicator:	☐ preferred	☒ standard	☐ optional
Unit of analysis:	☐ micro (variation)	☐ meso (variation)	☒ macro

METHODOLOGICAL DESCRIPTION AND UNDERLYING DEFINITIONS

Measurement and methodological aspects	• The following 15 legal features measured: 1 Financing: (i) broadness of organizational tax exemptions; (ii) income tax exemptions; (iii) real estate/property tax exemption; (iv) stamp and other duties; (v) indirect tax exemption (eg sales tax, VAT); (vi) unrelated business activities; (vii) organizational tax benefits for donations; (viii) tax benefits for individuals; and (ix) tax benefits for corporations 2 Demand-side indicators: (i) non-distribution constraint; (ii) personal benefit restrictions; (iii) reporting requirements; (iv) public availability of information; (v) governance; (vi) fundraising regulation • Each feature is assigned a value of 0, 1 or 2 by a legal experts in each country • Scores are then summed and averaged to yield an aggregate score in 'Financing' and 'Demand-side indicators' • A full composite score of 4 is possible • Note: see the full assessment of the JHU Non-profit Law Index above
Potential usefulness	• Measurement of the degree of enablement provided by the fiscal and regulatory system • Provides insight regarding CSOs' prospects for self-sustainability
Potential limitations	• Scoring systems blur finer distinctions, especially as laws (and their application) vary widely • JHU data on NPOs may not cover all organizations included in the CIVICUS definition of a CSO
Suggested modifications	• Apply within country-specific context of tax and legal system
Links to other measures	• JHU Law Index (space) • Freedom of association (JHU measure and qualitative review) (space) • Civil liberties (space) • Corruption Perceptions Index (space)

ASSESSMENT OF DATA QUALITY AND AVAILABILITY

Method of data collection	• Index scores based on composite average scores from legal expert assessments
Data provider	• The Johns Hopkins University, Institute for Policy Studies
Access to data	• Good – published for some countries
Frequency of data collection	• Irregular but can be updated easily

COMMENTS

Source: Salamon and Toepler (2000) *The Johns Hopkins Non-profit Law Index* (www.jhu.edu/~ccss/pubs/pdf/ccsswp17.pdf)
With further development, the indicator can be applied to field-level data, as well as to specific case studies.

INDICATOR NAME FREEDOM OF ASSOCIATION (FROM JHU LAW INDEX INDICATOR)

Brief definition	Indicator of the legal features in a country that might affect the willingness or ability of citizens to establish and operate CSOs based on the JHU Non-profit Law Index
Dimension	SPACE
Unit of measurement	Composite average score based on the assessment of legal experts

Type of indicator:	☐ preferred	☒ standard	☐ optional
Unit of analysis:	☐ micro (variation)	☐ meso (variation)	☒ macro

METHODOLOGICAL DESCRIPTION AND UNDERLYING DEFINITIONS

Measurement and methodological aspects	• The following nine legal features are used from the JHU Law Index:
	  1 General legal posture: (i) right of association; (ii) allowable purposes; and (iii) allowable political activities;
	  2 Formation: (i) unincorporated organizations permitted; (ii) membership requirements; (iii) capital requirements; (iv) government right to appoint board members; (v) government discretion in granting legal personality; and (vi) appeal procedures
	• Each feature is assigned a value of 0, 1 or 2 by legal experts in each country
	• Scores are then summed and averaged to yield an aggregate score in 'general legal posture' and 'formation'
	• A full composite score of 4 is possible
	• Note: see the full assessment of the JHU Non-profit Law Index above.

Potential usefulness	• Measurement of the degree of enablement provided by the fiscal and regulatory system • Shows level of support for citizen organization and the degree to which the law upholds this right
Potential limitations	• Scoring systems blur finer distinctions, especially as laws (and their application) vary widely • JHU data on NPOs may not cover all organizations included in the CIVICUS definition of a CSO
Suggested modifications	• Country-specific modification might be needed depending on the type of legal system
Links to other measures	• JHU Law Index (space) • Freedom of association (qualitative review) (space) • Tax incentives (space) • Civil liberties (space) • Corruption Perceptions Index (space)

ASSESSMENT OF DATA QUALITY AND AVAILABILITY

Method of data collection	• Index scores based on composite average scores from legal expert assessments
Data provider	• The Johns Hopkins University, Institute for Policy Studies
Access to data	• Good – published for some countries
Frequency of data collection	• Irregular but can be updated easily

COMMENTS

Source: Salamon and Toepler (2000) *The Johns Hopkins Non-profit Law Index* (www.jhu.edu/~ccss/pubs/pdf/ccsswp17.pdf)
With further development, this indicator can be applied to field-level data, as well as to specific case studies.

INDICATOR NAME CIVIL LIBERTIES (FREEDOM HOUSE)

Brief definition	Freedom to develop views, institutions and personal autonomy apart from the state
Dimension	SPACE
Unit of measurement	Standards-based rating of countries' civil liberties based on the judgement of Freedom House

Type of indicator: ☐ preferred   ☒ standard   ☐ optional

Unit of analysis: ☐ micro (variation)   ☐ meso (variation)   ☒ macro

METHODOLOGICAL DESCRIPTION AND UNDERLYING DEFINITIONS

Measurement and methodological aspects	• Covers four areas: freedom of expression (2 indicators); associational and organizational rights (3 indicators); rule of law and human rights (4 indicators); and personal autonomy and economic rights (5 indicators)

Civil liberties – Freedom House

Category	Raw points	Degree of freedom	CSD conversion
1	50–56	1–2.5 'free'	100%
2	42–49		83%
3	34–41		67%
4	26–33	3–5.5 'partly free'	50%
5	17–25		33%
6	9–16	5.5–7 'not free'	17%
7	0–8	Least free	0%

	• Freedom House does not maintain a culture-bound view of democracy and civil rights. To reach its conclusions, the survey team employs a broad range of international sources of information, including both foreign and domestic news reports, NGO publications, think-tank and academic analyses, and individual professional contacts • All countries covered
Potential usefulness	• Highlights need for explicitly multidimensional approach to human rights measurement
Potential limitations	• Scales not disaggregated • Does not account for the diverse political and cultural factors that affect the interpretation of human rights
Suggested modifications	• Disaggregated data
Links to other measures	• Freedom of association (JHU measure and qualitative review) (space) • JHU Non-profit Law Index (space) • USAID Legal Environment Indicator (space) • Tax incentives (space) • Corruption Perceptions Index (space)

ASSESSMENT OF DATA QUALITY AND AVAILABILITY

Method of data collection	• Aggregated data set of civil liberties based on responses to a check-list and judgements of survey team at Freedom House (standards-based survey ratings)
Data provider	• Freedom House
Access to data	• Aggregated data published annually
Frequency of data collection	• Annual

COMMENTS

Source: Karatnycky, A and the Freedom House Survey Team (2001); see also
www.freedomhouse.org/research/freeworld/2001/methodology3.htm
With further development, this indicator can be applied to field-level data, as well as to specific case studies.

INDICATOR NAME POLITICAL FREEDOM INDEX (PFI)

Brief definition	Individual political freedom in society is measured by integrity of self, rule of law, political participation, freedom of expression and equality before the law
Dimension	SPACE
Unit of measurement	Simple average of five clusters (1–100)

Type of indicator:	☐ preferred	☒ standard	☐ optional
Unit of analysis:	☐ micro (variation)	☐ meso (variation)	☒ macro

METHODOLOGICAL DESCRIPTION AND UNDERLYING DEFINITIONS

Measurement and methodological aspects	• PFI = simple average score of five clusters: (1) integrity of self; (2) rule of law; (3) political participation; (4) freedom of expression; and (5) equality before the law (note: in the published UNDP version, clusters 1 and 2 are merged) • Each cluster is related to a set of indicators for which qualitative and quantitative data can be gathered. The individual indicators are correlates of the individual human rights in the UN Universal Declaration of Human Rights. • Measuring clusters: individual indicators within a cluster contribute to the overall value for that cluster. Their value (between 1–100) is determined by the judgement of an intersubjective groups of experts. Thus, there is an implicit weighting function within each cluster. • PFI country averages are reported, as well as individual cluster scores to enable alternative weighting systems.
Potential usefulness	• Easy to understand and communicate
Potential limitations	• May blur finer distinctions, especially in non-Western countries • **Outdated data – only published in 1992**
Suggested modifications	• Develop a similar checklist and standards system based on checklists of human rights questions and sources for data on political freedom (see sources below under 'Comments') • Contextualize data/scores with the history and background of the country
Links to other measures	• Freedom of association (JHU measure and qualitative review) (space) • JHU Non-profit Law Index (full) (space) • Civil liberties (space) • Membership and participation (structure) • Corruption Perceptions Index (space) • Tax incentives (space)

ASSESSMENT OF DATA QUALITY AND AVAILABILITY

Method of data collection	• Index scores based on composite average scores from standard indicators and expert assessments
Data provider	• UNDP (1992) *Human Development Report 1992*
Access to data	• Good – published
Frequency of data collection	• Only published once (1992)

COMMENTS

Sources: Desai (1992); UNDP (1992, Box 2.2, p31 for checklists of human rights questions and 'Sources for Data on Political Freedom: Technical Annex 3', p104)
Other sources for information on political freedom and human rights:
Barsh (1993); Desai and Redfern (1995); Karatnycky, A and the Freedom House Survey Team (2001); Gastil (1987); Humana (1992); Mitchell and McCormick (1988, pp476–498); Schmid and Jongman (1994); Taylor and Jodice (1983); Transparency International (1999–2000)

INDICATOR NAME FREEDOM OF ASSOCIATION (QUALITATIVE REVIEW)

Brief definition	Qualitative review of laws related to free association
Dimension	SPACE
Unit of measurement	Composite index

Type of indicator:	☐ preferred		☐ standard		☒ optional
Unit of analysis:	☐ micro (variation)		☐ meso (variation)		☒ macro

METHODOLOGICAL DESCRIPTION AND UNDERLYING DEFINITIONS

Measurement and methodological aspects	• Use with either Freedom of association–JHU indicator or USAID Legal Environment Indicator
	• Requires separate survey or expert polling
	• Possible questions :
	  1 Does the law code in your country guarantee and promote the free assembly, speech and association of citizens?
	  2 Freedom of association is embodied in the constitution or legal tradition of your country and protected effectively by government/state

Potential usefulness	• Shows the degree to which the law upholds the right of free association • A qualitative measure enables finer distinctions – particularly with non-Western applications
Potential limitations	• Data collection may be time consuming and expensive
Suggested modifications	
Links to other measures	• Freedom of association (JHU measure) (space) • USAID Legal Environment Indicator (space) • JHU Law Index (space) • Tax incentives (space) • Civil liberties (space) • Corruption Perceptions Index (space)

ASSESSMENT OF DATA QUALITY AND AVAILABILITY

Method of data collection	• Sample survey or expert polling • Qualitative assessment to be used with macro-level space indicators
Data provider	• In-country researchers
Access to data	• Country specific
Frequency of data collection	None yet – to be developed, but could be run on a regular basis

COMMENTS

This indicator may be captured in a stakeholder survey.

Brief definition	The degree of ease and accessibility of CSOs formation
Dimension	SPACE
Unit of measurement	Composite average score based on the assessment of legal experts

Type of indicator:	☐ preferred	☐ standard	☒ optional
Unit of analysis:	☐ micro (variation)	☐ meso (variation)	☒ macro

METHODOLOGICAL DESCRIPTION AND UNDERLYING DEFINITIONS

Measurement and methodological aspects	• The following six legal features are used from the JHU Law Index: Formation: (i) unincorporated organizations permitted; (ii) membership requirements; (iii) capital requirements; (iv) government right to appoint board members; (v) government discretion in granting legal personality; and (vi) appeal procedures; • Each feature is assigned a value of 0, 1 or 2 by legal experts in each country • Scores are then summed and averaged to yield an aggregate score in 'general legal posture' and 'formation' • A full composite score of 2 is possible • Note: see the full assessment of the JHU Non-profit Law Index above.
Potential usefulness	• Shows the level of government acceptance of/support for citizens to organize and represent their interests
Potential limitations	• Scoring systems blur finer distinctions, especially as laws (and their application) vary widely • JHU data on NPOs may not cover all organizations included in the CIVICUS definition of a CSO
Suggested modifications	• Country-specific modification might be needed depending upon the type of legal system • This indicator could be captured in a stakeholder survey using the above 'formation' questions and other questions regarding the timeliness, transparency, cost of registration and operation where the unit of measurement would be the percentage of respondents or experts valuing CSO registration as positive
Links to other measures	• Freedom of association (JHU measure and qualitative review) (space) • USAID Legal Environment Indicator (space) • JHU Law Index (space) • Tax incentives (space) • CSO financing (space) • Civil liberties (space) • Corruption Perceptions Index (space)

ASSESSMENT OF DATA QUALITY AND AVAILABILITY

Method of data collection	• Index scores based on composite average scores from legal expert assessments
Data provider	• The Johns Hopkins University, Institute for Policy Studies
Access to data	• Good – published for some countries
Frequency of data collection	• Irregular but can be updated easily

COMMENTS

Source: Salamon and Toepler (2000) *The Johns Hopkins Non-profit Law Index*
(www.jhu.edu/~ccss/pubs/pdf/ccsswp17.pdf)

INDICATOR NAME CSO FINANCING

Brief definition	What are the financing regulations for CSOs?
Dimension	SPACE
Unit of measurement	Composite average score based on the assessment of legal experts

Type of indicator:	☐ preferred		☐ standard		☒	optional
Unit of analysis:	☐ micro (variation)		☐ meso (variation)		☒	macro

METHODOLOGICAL DESCRIPTION AND UNDERLYING DEFINITIONS

Measurement and methodological aspects	• The following nine legal features are used from the JHU Law Index: Financing: (i) broadness of organizational tax exemptions; (ii) income tax exemptions; (iii) real estate/property tax exemption; (iv) stamp and other duties; (v) indirect tax exemption (eg sales tax, VAT); (vi) unrelated business activities; (vii) organizational tax benefits for donations; (viii) tax benefits for individuals; and (ix) tax benefits for corporations • Each feature is assigned a value of 0, 1 or 2 by legal experts in each country • Scores are then summed and averaged to yield an aggregate score in 'general legal posture' and 'formation' • A full composite score of 2 is possible • Note: see the full assessment of the JHU Non-profit Law Index above
Potential usefulness	• Shows the level of government acceptance of/support for citizens organization • Provides insight into CSOs' prospects for self-sustainability
Potential limitations	• Scoring systems blur finer distinctions, especially as laws (and their application) vary widely • JHU data on NPOs may not cover all organizations included in the CIVICUS definition of a CSO
Suggested modifications	• Country-specific modification might be needed depending on the type of legal system • This indicator could be captured in a stakeholder survey using the above 'fundraising' questions and other questions regarding the timeliness, transparency, cost of registration and operation where the unit of measurement would be the percentage of respondents or experts valuing CSO registration as positive
Links to other measures	• Freedom of association (JHU measure and qualitative review) (space) • USAID Legal Environment Indicator (space) • JHU Law Index (space) • Tax incentives (space) • CSO formation (space) • Civil liberties (space) • Corruption Perceptions Index (space)

ASSESSMENT OF DATA QUALITY AND AVAILABILITY

Method of data collection	• Index scores based on composite average scores from legal expert assessments
Data provider	• The Johns Hopkins University, Institute for Policy Studies
Access to data	• Good – published for some countries
Frequency of data collection	• Irregular but can be updated easily

COMMENTS

Source: Salamon and Toepler (2000) *The Johns Hopkins Non-profit Law Index* (www.jhu.edu/~ccss/pubs/pdf/ccsswp17.pdf)

INDICATOR NAME CSO FUNDRAISING

Brief definition	What is the range of revenue/fundraising sources permitted under the law?
Dimension	SPACE
Unit of measurement	Index score based on composite average scores from expert assessments

Type of indicator:	☐ preferred	☐ standard	☒ optional
Unit of analysis:	☐ micro (variation)	☐ meso (variation)	☒ macro

METHODOLOGICAL DESCRIPTION AND UNDERLYING DEFINITIONS

Measurement and methodological aspects	• Requires expert polling or separate survey (to be developed)
Potential usefulness	• Shows the level of government acceptance of/support for citizens organization • Provides insight into CSOs' prospects for self-sustainability • A qualitative measure enables finer distinctions – particularly with non-Western applications
Potential limitations	• Data collection may be time consuming and expensive
Suggested modifications	
Links to other measures	• Freedom of association (JHU measure and qualitative review) (space) • USAID Legal Environment Indicator (space) • JHU Law Index (space) • Tax incentives (space) • Civil liberties (space) • Corruption Perceptions Index (space)

ASSESSMENT OF DATA QUALITY AND AVAILABILITY

Method of data collection	• Qualitative assessments to be used with macro-level space indicators (sample survey or expert polling)
Data provider	• In-country researchers
Access to data	• Country specific
Frequency of data collection	• None yet – to be developed, but could be run on a regular basis

COMMENTS

For possible questions, see USAID (2000; also www.usaid.gov/regions/europe_eurasia/dem_gov/ngoindex/index.htm) and Salamon and Toepler (2000) *The Johns Hopkins Non-profit Law Index* (also www.jhu.edu/~ccss/pubs/pdf/ccsswp17.pdf)

INDICATOR NAME GOVERNANCE (FROM WORLD BANK GOVERNANCE RESEARCH INDICATORS DATASET)

Brief definition	Traditions and institutions that determine how authority is exercised in a particular country
Dimension	SPACE
Unit of measurement	Composite average scores from expert assessments and cross-country surveys; percentage conversion by CCS

Type of indicator:	☐ preferred	☐ standard	☒ optional
Unit of analysis:	☐ micro (variation)	☐ meso (variation)	☒ macro

METHODOLOGICAL DESCRIPTION AND UNDERLYING DEFINITIONS

Measurement and methodological aspects	The following six governance components are used in the World Bank Governance Dataset: 1 Voice and accountability: extent to which citizens can participate in the selection of governments (political process, civil liberties, political rights); 2 Political instability and violence: perceptions of the likelihood that the government in power will be destabilized or overthrown by possibly unconstitutional and/or violent means; 3 Government effectiveness: perceptions of the quality of public service provision, bureaucracy, competence of civil servants, independence of civil service from political pressures and the credibility of government's commitment to policies (or 'inputs require for government to produce and implement good policies')(note: a variation – civil society effectiveness – could be used for the CSD either as a separate indicator or as part of a stakeholder survey) 4 Regulatory burden: incidence of market-unfriendly policies 5 Rule of law: extent to which agents (citizens and government) have confidence and abide by the rules of society; and 6 Graft/corruption: the exercise of public power for private gain. Various indicators are assigned to the six components listed above and are converted to a common unit. Next to the common unit estimate, the dataset also includes standard errors and a list of indicators used for each component. Because such a large number of indicators of varying scales are aggregated, large standard errors result and, therefore, no precise ranking is inferred by the authors. Instead, the 'traffic light' approach is used whereby countries are grouped into three broad categories: countries in 'governance crisis', countries 'at risk', and countries 'not at risk'. This approach reveals possible vulnerabilities but avoids a tight ranking system. For the CSD, we convert the World Bank estimates to percentages for illustrative purposes (see conversion table below). See also www.worldbank.org/wbi/governance/dataset for the entire range provided in the traffic light approach. The governance dataset can be used as a single indicator or broken down into individual indicators, such as 'voice and accountability', 'rule of law' or 'graft/corruption' (note: only those in bold are particularly relevant to the CSD).
Potential usefulness	• Although imprecise, each individual indicator assigned to the governance components listed above provides some useful information or signal about the state of governance
Potential limitations	• No precise rankings can be inferred from this dataset due to standard errors associated with each indicator estimate
Suggested modifications	
Links to other measures	• Corruption Perceptions Index (space) • Freedom of association (JHU measure and qualitative review) (space) • USAID Legal Environment Indicator (space) • JHU Law Index (space) • Tax incentives (space) • Civil liberties (space)

ASSESSMENT OF DATA QUALITY AND AVAILABILITY

Method of data collection	• Polls of experts and cross-country surveys
Data provider	• World Bank (1999) based on 1997–1998 data
Access to data	• Published
Frequency of data collection	• Published once in 1999 but expected to continue

COMMENTS

World Bank Worldwide Governance Research Indicators Dataset:
www.worldbank.org/wbi/governance/datasets.htm#dataset2001; see also Kaufmann et al (1999a; 1999b)
for background papers and Harvard CID-World Bank DataMart (2000) for a database of quantitative and
descriptive data on cross-country differences in political social institutions

World Bank Governance (raw score)	CSD conversion (%)
−2.5	0
−2.4	2
−2.3	4
−2.2	6
−2.1	8
−2	10
−1.9	12
−1.8	14
−1.7	16
−1.6	18
−1.5	20
−1.4	22
−1.3	24
−1.2	26
−1.1	28
−1	30
−0.9	32
−0.8	34
−0.7	36
−0.6	38
−0.5	40
−0.4	42
−0.3	44
−0.2	46
−0.1	48
0	50
0.1	52
0.2	54
0.3	56
0.4	58
0.5	60
0.6	62
0.7	64
0.8	66
0.9	68
1	70
1.1	72
1.2	74
1.3	76
1.4	78
1.5	80
1.6	82
1.7	84
1.8	86
1.9	88
2	90
2.1	92
2.2	94
2.3	96
2.4	98
2.5	

IMPACT: MACRO INDICATORS

INDICATOR NAME FULFILLED COMMITMENT INDEX (FCI)

Brief definition	Degree to which goals/commitments set by national representatives of CSOs have progressed
Dimension	IMPACT
Unit of measurement	Standards-based ratings based on 'progress' and 'regression'

Type of indicator:	☒ preferred	☐ standard	☐ optional
Unit of analysis:	☐ micro (variation)	☐ meso (variation)	☒ macro

METHODOLOGICAL DESCRIPTION AND UNDERLYING DEFINITIONS

Measurement and methodological aspects	• FCI is a progress chart developed by Social Watch to illustrate the evolution of countries with respect to 13 commitments assumed by governments at the World Summit on Social Development (WSSD) and the Fourth World Conference on Women in Beijing (FWCW). It will be used in the CSD to measure CSO commitments. • One to two indicators can be chosen as proxies for each commitment. For example, if CSOs' representatives commit to improving primary education, one to two indicators could be chosen to monitor primary school enrolment. • Calculation of progress indices: a table for each commitment will show the value of the indicator(s) for the year x, the value for the last year available, the value that should be reached by the year x+8, and the goal to be reached by the year x+10. • Ratings (1-5, where 5 is high): significant regression; regression; standing still; progress but not enough; and progress at good pace or goal achieved. The ratings can then be converted to percentages for the CSD (see below).
Potential usefulness	• Can be used to complement 'CSOs' share in output' indicator • Use as a proxy in CIVICUS–CCS report to illustrate construction of CSD
Potential limitations	• It will be very difficult for CSOs to agree on a shared set of goals and commitments because they represent such diverse constituents
Suggested modifications	• Use FCI and have CSO leaders/representatives rank their contribution to change (link with perceived impact survey)
Links to other measures	• CSOs' share in output (impact) • Perceived impact survey (impact)

ASSESSMENT OF DATA QUALITY AND AVAILABILITY

Method of data collection	• Household surveys, demographic and health surveys, school censuses, literacy surveys, population surveys and national accounts
Data provider	• National or field-level representatives of CSOs • National statistical offices • International comparative indicators (UN, World Bank)
Access to data	• To be developed • Could be regular once system is in place
Frequency of data collection	• Should be applied annually; of greatest use to CSO leaders and policy-makers

COMMENTS

See Social Watch (www.socialwatch.org/2000/eng/chartings/stepsforward.htm) for more information on the FCI
With some modification, the indicator can be applied to field-level data, as well as to specific case studies.

CSD CONVERSION FOR THE FCI

Social watch (raw score)	CSD conversion (%)	Social watch (raw score)	CSD conversion (%)
1	0.0	3	50.0
1.1	2.5	3.1	52.5
1.2	5.0	3.2	55.0
1.3	7.5	3.3	57.5
1.4	10.0	3.4	60.0
1.5	12.5	3.5	62.5
1.6	15.0	3.6	65.0
1.7	17.5	3.7	67.5
1.8	20.0	3.8	70.0
1.9	22.5	3.9	72.5
2	25.0	4	75.0
2.1	27.5	4.1	77.5
2.2	30.0	4.2	80.0
2.3	32.5	4.3	82.5
2.4	35.0	4.4	85.0
2.5	37.5	4.5	87.5
2.6	40.0	4.6	90.0
2.7	42.5	4.7	92.5
2.8	45.0	4.8	95.0
2.9	47.5	4.9	97.5
		5	100.0

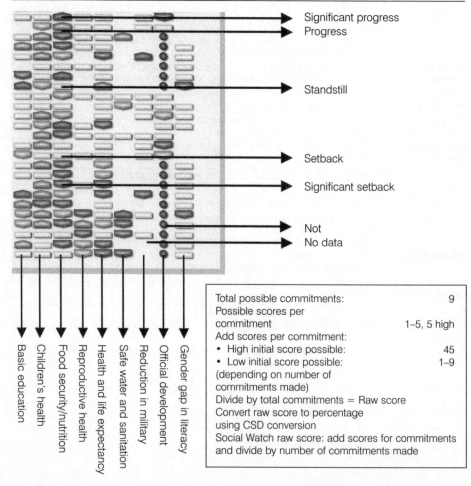

Significant progress
Progress

Standstill

Setback

Significant setback

Not
No data

Basic education
Children's health
Food security/nutrition
Reproductive health
Health and life expectancy
Safe water and sanitation
Reduction in military
Official development
Gender gap in literacy

Total possible commitments:	9
Possible scores per commitment	1–5, 5 high

Add scores per commitment:
- High initial score possible: 45
- Low initial score possible: 1–9

(depending on number of commitments made)
Divide by total commitments = Raw score
Convert raw score to percentage
using CSD conversion
Social Watch raw score: add scores for commitments
and divide by number of commitments made

INDICATOR NAME USAID NGO SUSTAINABILITY INDEX

Brief definition	Degree of improvement in the sustainability of NGOs
Dimension	IMPACT
Unit of measurement	Index score based on composite average scores from expert assessments

Type of indicator:	☒	preferred	☐	standard	☐	optional
Unit of analysis:	☐	micro (variation)	☐	meso (variation)	☒	macro

METHODOLOGICAL DESCRIPTION AND UNDERLYING DEFINITIONS

Measurement and methodological aspects	• Indicators in the following seven dimensions are analysed by six to ten sectoral experts for each dimension: legal environment; organizational capacity; financial viability; advocacy; public image; service provision; and NGO infrastructure. Taken together, these dimensions provide a basic description of what a sustainable NGO sector should look like. Individually, these dimensions provide a reasonable measure of impact over time, and a basis for identifying both needs and opportunities in a strategic planning process. • Sectoral experts: USAID recommends drawing upon donors, NGO assistance implementers, representatives of NGO support centres, and representatives of local NGOs in chief sub-sectors, such as women's, environmental or human rights groups. In some instances, it may be appropriate to select a larger group in order to reflect the diversity and breadth of the sector; but a significantly larger group may make consensus-building more difficult. Furthermore, at least 50 per cent of the expert group should be local nationals. • After initial assessments, a USAID working group meets to review rankings and score sheets, and compares them with the expert's overview statement, other countries' rankings and prior years' scores. The working group may return to experts for clarification/justification if deemed necessary. • Compare most recent index with previous year to use as an improvement indicator • See Appendix B.1 for scoring instructions
Potential usefulness	• Measure of NGO sustainability
Potential limitations	• Composite scoring systems may blur finer distinctions • Subjectivity of perception measures • USAID data on NGOs may not cover all organizations and entities included in the CIVICUS definition of a CSO
Suggested modifications	• Country-specific context must be taken into account • Development of legal expert assessments for field/meso and case/micro applications • This indicator can be used in its entirety or broken down into separate indicators: legal environment (see space); organizational capacity; financial viability; advocacy; public image; service provision; and NGO infrastructure in space, structure–revenue and composition, and impact
Links to other measures	• Fulfilled Commitment Index (impact) • Tax incentives, CSO formation, CSO fundraising, freedom of association (space)

ASSESSMENT OF DATA QUALITY AND AVAILABILITY

Method of data collection	• Sectoral expert assessments
Data provider	• USAID, Europe and Eurasia Democracy and Government Unit (NGO Sustainability Index)
Access to data	• Good for some countries – published for Central and Eastern European and former Soviet Union countries
Frequency of data collection	• Annual (since 1997)

COMMENTS

Source: USAID (2000: www.usaid.gov/regions/europe_eurasia/dem_gov/ngoindex/index.htm)
With further development, the indicator can be applied to field-level data, as well as to specific case studies (see 'Perceived impact survey by representatives in field' and '...by representatives or members of CSO' in Table 4)

INDICATOR NAME MEDIA COVERAGE OF CSOS

Brief definition	Share of articles/segments relevant to CSOs in key newspapers in given period
Dimension	IMPACT
Unit of measurement	Percentage of articles/segments

Type of indicator: ☒ preferred   ☐ standard   ☐ optional

Unit of analysis: ☐ micro (variation)   ☐ meso (variation)   ☒ macro

METHODOLOGICAL DESCRIPTION AND UNDERLYING DEFINITIONS

Measurement and methodological aspects	• Requires separate survey or input by clipping service • Content analytic techniques apply
Potential usefulness	• Public awareness is a prerequisite to support • Useful for micro/event applications of the CSD • Directly affects ability of CSOs to recruit members, volunteers and monetary support
Potential limitations	• Media coverage may not be a suitable indicator of public support or awareness in some countries • May be a misleading indicator if there is a flurry of articles/segments over a short period of time as an issue gains visibility, and then nothing occurs as the media moves to other issues
Suggested modifications	• Requires country-specific definition of what newspapers to include • Measuring other media outlets (print, radio, television, internet) may be useful, as well
Links to other measures	• Perceived Impact Survey (impact) • Membership and participation (structure)

ASSESSMENT OF DATA QUALITY AND AVAILABILITY

Method of data collection	• Commercial monitoring service • Monitoring by relevant CSOs or umbrella organizations
Data provider	• Commercial monitoring service • Monitoring by relevant CSOs or umbrella organizations
Access to data	• Could be regular once system is in place
Frequency of data collection	• Should be applied at regular intervals to be of greatest use to CSO leaders and policy-makers

COMMENTS

With some modification, the indicator can be applied to field-level data, as well as to specific case studies.

INDICATOR NAME CHANGE IN HUMAN DEVELOPMENT INDEX (HDI) OVER
PREVIOUS PERIOD

Brief definition	A composite index of human development in a country using three variables: life expectancy at birth to capture longevity; adult literacy and combined enrolment to capture educational attainment; and real GDP per capita to capture standard of living
Dimension	IMPACT
Unit of measurement	Percentage change

Type of indicator:	☐ preferred	☒ standard	☐ optional
Unit of analysis:	☐ micro (variation)	☐ meso (variation)	☒ macro

METHODOLOGICAL DESCRIPTION AND UNDERLYING DEFINITIONS

Measurement and methodological aspects	Each index = Actual x_1 – Minimum x_1/Maximum x_1 – Minimum x_1 (see technical note in *Human Development Report*) • Life expectancy index: life expectancy at birth • Educational attainment index: adult literacy, two-thirds weight; combined enrolment, one third weight • Adjusted real GDP per capita (PPP$) index Use percentage change from previous period (previous period depends upon what time periods are used in other dimensions)
Potential usefulness	• Widely available and accepted indicator of well-being in society
Potential limitations	• Validity: HDI does not measure the impact of civil society and CSOs directly
Suggested modifications	• Use change in HDI and have CSO leaders/representatives rank their contribution to change; link with perceived impact survey and FCI
Links to other measures	• CSO share of total output (impact) • Fulfilled Commitment Index (impact) • Change in Gini (impact) • Perceived Impact Survey (impact)

ASSESSMENT OF DATA QUALITY AND AVAILABILITY

Method of data collection	• Population surveys • Household surveys • National income accounts • Ministries of education and health reports
Data provider	• UNDP *Human Development Report* (ongoing annual publication)
Access to data	• Good – published
Frequency of data collection	• Annual

COMMENTS

Why use HDI? To measure impact of civil society and CSOs on society. If civil society and CSOs have a significant impact, than we should see a change in the HDI (or some other measure of well-being) – CSOs should have a *redistribution effect*.
• Are large civil societies associated with higher HDI rankings (see attached graphs)?
• Do variations in size of civil society/CSOs correspond to variations in impact (proxied by HDI?) over time?
• Other possible measures of well-being in society: Physical Quality of Life Index (Morris, 1979); Dasgupta's Quality of Life Index (1993)

INDICATOR NAME CSO SHARE IN TOTAL OUTPUT BY FUNCTIONAL FIELD (NOTE: MESO AND MICRO INDICATOR ONLY)

Brief definition	CSO share in total output by functional field relative to public and for-profit sectors
Dimension	IMPACT
Unit of measurement	Percentage of output by functional field

Type of indicator:	☐ preferred	☒ standard	☐ optional
Unit of analysis:	☐ micro (variation)	☐ meso (variation)	☒ macro

METHODOLOGICAL DESCRIPTION AND UNDERLYING DEFINITIONS

Measurement and methodological aspects	• Four criteria identified key activity and output measures for data collection on non-profit, for-profit and government providers: 1 The activities must relate to the categories of organizations that are of most interest to users. 2 They must be inherently linked with the purpose and primary activity of the organizations. 3 They must be relatively conveniently available on a sectoral basis not only for non-profit providers but also for government and for-profit providers. 4 They must be relatively unambiguous and relatively easy to grasp conceptually. • See Appendix B.3 for type and definition of non-profit sector output and capacity measures by International Classification of Non-profit Organizations (ICNPO) groups (note space for 'additional measures as applicable')
Potential usefulness	• Illustrates the contribution of CSOs to society and the role that they play in relation to government and for-profits in particular fields
Potential limitations	• Output measures are difficult to define with precision because significant differences exist among countries in the way that various activities and outputs are measured
Suggested modifications	• Country-specific applications are best
Links to other measures	• Perceived Impact Survey/Stakeholder Survey (impact/all dimensions) • Fulfilled Commitment Index (impact)

ASSESSMENT OF DATA QUALITY AND AVAILABILITY

Method of data collection	• Statistical offices • Organizational surveys
Data provider	• Varied • **Johns Hopkins Comparative Non-profit Sector Project (JHCNSP)**
Access to data	• Good for some countries
Frequency of data collection	• Some output data is available on an annual basis; others are more irregular

COMMENTS

For more information, see JHCNSP (www.jhu.edu/~cnp/)

INDICATOR NAME CHANGE IN GINI COEFFICIENT OVER PREVIOUS PERIOD

Brief definition	Gini coefficient: an expression showing the degree of inequality in society in a frequency distribution, such as personal income, family income or household income, or expenditure
Dimension	IMPACT
Unit of measurement	Percentage change

Type of indicator:	☐ preferred	☒ standard	☐ optional
Unit of analysis:	☐ micro (variation)	☐ meso (variation)	☒ macro

METHODOLOGICAL DESCRIPTION AND UNDERLYING DEFINITIONS

Measurement and methodological aspects	G = area between Lorenz curve and 45° line/area above 45° line • Lorenz curve = a graphical representation showing the degree of inequality of a frequency distribution in which the cumulative percentages of a population in a given society are plotted against the cumulative percentage of income in that society. A straight line rising at an angle of 45° from the start on the graph will indicate perfect equality (for example, if 10 per cent of the population earns 10 per cent of the income, and 20 per cent of the population earns 20 per cent of the income, and so on). However, perfect equality is never the case, and the actual frequency distribution is represented by the Lorenz curve. • The cumulative percentages of population and income are usually arranged by decile or quintile
Potential usefulness	• Widely available and accepted indicator of inequality in society • Could be used to test whether income becomes more equal or unequal in the distribution of resources from civil society
Potential limitations	• Validity: Gini does not measure the impact of civil society and CSOs directly
Suggested modifications	• Use change in Gini and have CSO leaders/representatives rank their contribution to change; link with perceived impact survey and FCI
Links to other measures	• CSOs' share of total output (impact) • Fulfilled Commitment Index (impact) • Change in HDI (impact) • Perceived Impact Survey (impact)

ASSESSMENT OF DATA QUALITY AND AVAILABILITY

Method of data collection	• Population surveys • Household surveys • National income accounts
Data provider	• UN • **World Bank** • **National statistical offices**
Access to data	• Good – published
Frequency of data collection	• Annual

COMMENTS

INDICATOR NAME PERCEIVED IMPACT SURVEY

Brief definition	Contribution of civil society (or CSOs) in solving specific social, economic and political problems
Dimension	IMPACT
Unit of measurement	Average rank/range of perceived impact

Type of indicator:	☐ preferred	☒ standard	☐ optional
Unit of analysis:	☐ micro (variation)	☐ meso (variation)	☒ macro

METHODOLOGICAL DESCRIPTION AND UNDERLYING DEFINITIONS

Measurement and methodological aspects	• Requires expert survey • Delphi method applies: see Chapter 5 for more information on the Delphi method
Potential usefulness	• Indicator of aspects of civil society considered important by experts • Provides preliminary parameters of the impact of civil society for which there are no other estimates currently available
Potential limitations	• Subjectivity of perception measures • Small sample size
Suggested modifications	• Country and context-specific application are best
Links to other measures	• Fulfilled Commitment Index (impact) • Media coverage of CSOs (impact) • Change in HDI (impact) • CSOs' share in total output (impact)

ASSESSMENT OF DATA QUALITY AND AVAILABILITY

Method of data collection	• Expert survey
Data provider	• In-country researchers
Access to data	• None yet – survey to be designed
Frequency of data collection	• Could be regular once system is in place

COMMENTS

With some modification, the indicator can be applied to field-level data, as well as to specific case studies.

INDICATOR NAME SUBJECTIVE WELL-BEING

Brief definition	Levels of subjective well-being in society
Dimension	IMPACT
Unit of measurement	Share of adults who are 'satisfied' with their lives

Type of indicator:	☐ preferred	☐ standard	☒ optional
Unit of analysis:	☐ micro (variation)	☐ meso (variation)	☒ macro

METHODOLOGICAL DESCRIPTION AND UNDERLYING DEFINITIONS

Measurement and methodological aspects	• Representative, national samples used in World Values Survey (covers over 40 societies; 70 per cent of world's population; more in 2000–2001) and similar population surveys • WVS question: 'Generally speaking, how satisfied are you with your life as a whole: satisfied, reasonably satisfied, not very satisfied, or not at all satisfied?'
Potential usefulness	• Standardized, cross-cultural measure of subjective well-being in society
Potential limitations	• WVS data limited to macro-level CSD view; use similar population surveys for regional-level applications
Suggested modifications	• Subjective well-being in particular groups and at the meso and micro levels
Links to other measures	• Change in HDI over period (impact) • Change in Gini (impact) • Perceived Impact Survey (impact)

ASSESSMENT OF DATA QUALITY AND AVAILABILITY

Method of data collection	• Population survey
Data provider	• World Values Survey • National survey firms
Data set description	• Population survey
Access to data	• Good – published
Frequency of data collection	• Every three to five years; more frequent in most developed countries

COMMENTS

See Diener, E and Suh, M (eds) (1999) *Subjective Well-Being in Global Perspective*. Cambridge: MIT Press

With some modification, the indicator can be applied to field-level data, as well as to specific case studies.

Examples of Specific Methodologies

B.1 USAID NGO Sustainability Index Scoring Dimensions and Indicators

Instructions to experts: please provide a short summary of the NGO situation in your country, approximately one quarter to one half of a page long. This summary should include general information, such as the number of NGOs that are operating; what types of NGOs; in what sector are the NGOs the strongest; etc. This description will be quantified by your overall country rating.

1 LEGAL ENVIRONMENT

— REGISTRATION. Is there a favourable law on NGO registration? Are NGOs easily able to register and operate?
— OPERATION. Is the internal management, scope of permissible activities, financial reporting, and/or dissolution of NGOs well detailed in current legislation? Does clear legal terminology preclude unwanted state control over NGOs? Are NGOs protected from the possibility of the state dissolving an NGO for political/arbitrary reasons?
— ADMINISTRATIVE IMPEDIMENTS AND STATE HARASSMENT. Are NGOs and their representatives allowed to operate freely within the law? Are they free from harassment by the central government, local governments and tax police? Can they freely address matters of public debate and express criticism?
— LOCAL LEGAL CAPACITY. Are there local lawyers who are trained in, and familiar with, NGO law? Is legal advice available to NGOs in the capital city and in secondary cities?
— TAXATION. Do NGOs receive any sort of tax exemption? Do individual or corporate donors receive tax deductions? Do NGOs have to pay taxes on grants? Do NGOs enjoy exemptions or deductions on grants or endowment income?
— EARNED INCOME. Does legislation exist that allows NGOs to earn income from the provision of goods and services? Are NGOs allowed legally to compete for government contracts/procurements at the local and central levels?

2 ORGANIZATIONAL CAPACITY

— CONSTITUENCY BUILDING. Do NGOs actively seek to build constituencies for their initiatives? (Please note that constituency building is a very important topic. We request that you discuss this in some detail with your expert group, and be certain to address constituency building activities and/or capacity in your country overview.)
— STRATEGIC PLANNING. Do most NGOs have a clearly defined mission? Do most NGOs incorporate strategic planning techniques in their decision-making process?
— INTERNAL MANAGEMENT STRUCTURE. Is there generally a clearly defined management structure within the NGOs, including a recognized division of responsibilities between the board of directors and staff members? Do leading NGOs in a variety of sectors make this distinction?
— NGO STAFFING. Is there a permanent, paid staff in leading NGOs? Are potential volunteers sufficiently recruited and engaged?
— TECHNICAL ADVANCEMENT. Do NGOs' resources generally allow for modernized basic office equipment (relatively new computers and software, functional fax machines, internet access, etc)?

3 FINANCIAL VIABILITY

— LOCAL SUPPORT. Do NGOs raise a significant percentage of their funding from local sources? Are NGOs able to draw upon a core of volunteer and non-monetary support from their communities and constituencies? Are there local sources of philanthropy?
— DIVERSIFICATION. Do NGOs raise a significant percentage of their funding from local sources? Do NGOs generally have multiple/diverse sources of funding? Do most NGOs have enough resources to remain viable for the short-term future?
— FINANCIAL MANAGEMENT SYSTEMS. Are there sound financial management systems in place?
— FUNDRAISING. Have many NGOs cultivated a loyal core of financial supporters? Do NGOs engage in any sort of membership outreach and constituency development programmes?
— EARNED INCOME. Do revenues from services, products or rent from assets supplement the income of NGOs? Do government and/or local businesses contract with NGOs for services? Do membership-based organizations such as unions typically collect dues?

4 ADVOCACY

— COOPERATION WITH LOCAL AND FEDERAL GOVERNMENT. Are there direct lines of communication between NGOs and policy-makers? Are NGOs able to influence public policy at the central/federal level and at the local level?

— POLICY ADVOCACY INITIATIVES. Have NGOs formed issue-based coalitions and conducted broad-based advocacy campaigns? Have these campaigns been effective at the local level and/or national level at effective policy change?

— POLITICAL LOBBYING EFFORTS. Are there mechanisms and relationships for NGOs to participate in the political process? Are NGOs comfortable with the concept of lobbying and advocacy? Have there been any lobbying successes at the policy level? Have NGOs led efforts to raise awareness of problems or increased support for a particular position?

— LOCAL ADVOCACY FOR LEGAL REFORM. Is there awareness in the wider NGO community on how a favourable legal and regulatory framework can enhance NGO effectiveness and sustainability? Is there a local NGO advocacy effort to promote legal reforms that will benefit NGOs, local philanthropy, etc?

5 SERVICE PROVISION

— RANGE OF GOODS AND SERVICES. Do many NGOs produce basic social services, such as health, education, relief, housing, water or energy? Do some NGOs also produce goods and services in other areas, such as economic development, environmental protection or governance and empowerment? Overall, is their 'product line' diversified?

— COMMUNITY RESPONSIVENESS. Do the goods and services that NGOs produce reflect the needs and priorities of their constituents and communities?

— CONSTITUENCIES AND CLIENTELE. Are those goods and services that go beyond basic social needs provided to a constituency broader than NGOs' own memberships? Are some products, such as publications, workshops or expert analysis, marketed to other NGOs, academia, churches or government?

— COST RECOVERY. When NGOs provide goods and services, do they recover any of their costs? Do they have knowledge of the market demand – and the ability of distinct constituencies to pay – for those products?

— GOVERNMENT RECOGNITION AND SUPPORT. Does the government, at the national and/or local level, recognize the value that NGOs can add in providing basic social services? Do they provide grants or contracts to NGOs to enable them to provide such services? (Please note that government recognition and support is a very important topic for NGO sustainability. We request that you discuss this in some detail with your expert group, and be certain to address constituency building activities and/or capacity in your country overview.)

6 INFRASTRUCTURE

— INTERMEDIARY SUPPORT ORGANIZATIONS (ISOs) AND NGO RESOURCE CENTRES. Are there ISOs and NGO resource centres throughout the country that provide local NGOs with access to information, technology, training and technical assistance? Do they earn some of their operating revenue from earned income (such as fees for service) and other locally generated sources?

— LOCAL GRANT-MAKING ORGANIZATIONS. Do local community foundations and/or ISOs provide grants from either locally raised funds or re-granting international donor funds to address locally identified needs and projects?

— NGO COALITIONS. Do NGOs share information with each other? Is there a network in place that facilitates such information sharing? Is there an organization or committee through which the sector promotes its interests?

— TRAINING. Are there capable local NGO management trainers? Is basic NGO management training available in the capital city and in secondary cities? Is more advanced specialized training available in areas such as strategic management, accounting, financial management, fundraising, volunteer management and board development? Are training materials available in local languages?

— INTERSECTORAL PARTNERSHIPS. Are there examples of NGOs working in partnership, either formally or informally, with local business, government and the media to achieve common objectives? Is there awareness among the various sectors of the possibilities for, and advantages of, such partnerships?

7 PUBLIC IMAGE

— MEDIA COVERAGE. Do NGOs enjoy positive media coverage at the local and national level? Is a distinction made between public service announcements and corporate advertising? Does the media provide positive analysis of the role that NGOs play in civil society?

— PUBLIC PERCEPTION OF NGOs. Does the general public have a positive perception of NGOs? Does the public understand the concept of an NGO? Is the public supportive of NGO activity overall?

— GOVERNMENT/BUSINESS PERCEPTION OF NGOs. Do the business sector and local and central government officials have a positive perception of NGOs? Do they rely on NGOs as a community resource, or as a source of expertise and credible information?

— PUBLIC RELATIONS. Do NGOs publicize their activities or promote their public image? Have NGOs developed relationships with journalists to encourage positive coverage?

— SELF-REGULATION. Have NGOs adopted a code of ethics or tried to demonstrate transparency in their operations? Do leading NGOs publish annual reports?

Scoring instructions for each dimension

Step 1

With an NGO expert group, discuss each indicator of the seven dimensions and score it on the following four-point scale. Fractional scores are permitted:

1   The indicator in question is lacking or not implemented/utilized. Such absence poses a serious constraint on NGO sectoral sustainability.
2   The indicator in question is lacking or not implemented/utilized, constraining the NGO sector's sustainability to some degree.
3   The indicator in question is present and implemented/utilized to the degree that it has a somewhat positive impact on the NGO sector's sustainability.
4   The indicator in question is present and well enough implemented/ utilized to nurture the NGO sector's sustainability.

Step 2

For each dimension, add up all of the indicator scores, which yield your raw sum.

Step 3

Average the indicator scores for that dimension by dividing your working sum by the number of indicators you scored. Round if necessary to the nearest one tenth. (This step is necessary because the various dimensions have different numbers of indicators.)

Step 4

For each dimension, convert your average score into the final seven-point index rating scale by looking it up on the following table:

Table AB.1 *Dimension Rating Conversion*

Average score	Dimension rating
3.6 to 4.0	1
3.2 to 3.5	2
2.8 to 3.1	3
2.4 to 2.7	4
1.9 to 2.3	5
1.5 to 1.8	6
1.0 to 1.4	7

Definition of dimension ratings

1   While the needed reforms and/or the NGO sector's development are not complete, the local NGO community recognizes which reforms or developments are still required, and has a plan and the ability to pursue

them itself. Model NGOs can be found in cities and towns, in all regions of a country and in numerous different sectors.

2   The environment is enabling and the local NGO community demonstrates a commitment to pursuing needed reforms and to developing its professionalism. Foreign assistance continues to accelerate or facilitate these developments. Model NGOs can be found in most large cities, in most regions of a country, and in a variety of sectors and issues.

3   Foreign assistance is able to accelerate or facilitate reform because the environment is generally enabling and/or local progress and commitment to developing the aspect in question are strong. An enabling environment includes a government open to reform (legal), a growing economy (financial), some decentralization of governing structures (advocacy) or an independent media (image). NGOs in regional centres and in four or five sectors are beginning to mature.

4   Progress in the aspect in question is hampered by the factors cited above, but, to a lesser degree, perhaps by a stagnant rather than a contracting economy; a passive rather than hostile government; a disinterested rather than controlled or reactionary media; or a community of good-willed but inexperienced activities. While NGOs in the capital city or in three or four sectors are progressing, others lag far behind.

5   Programmatic success in developing the local capacity or facilitating progress in the aspect in question is hampered by a contracting economy; an authoritarian leader; highly centralized governance structure; a controlled or reactionary media; or a low level of capacity, will or interest on the part of the NGO community. The absorptive capacity of the NGO sector is limited – perhaps limited geographically to the capital city or, sectorally, to two or three areas of activity or policy issues.

6   Little progress has occurred since the Soviet era; one problem or constraint has been replaced by another. Facilitating the development of local capacity is severely limited by a hostile authoritarian regime; state-controlled media; brain drain; and/or a small or highly fractured community of activists with very little capacity or experience in organizing and initiating activities, in running organizations, and/or little interest in doing so.

7   Erosion or no change has occurred since the Soviet era. A war, with its human and material costs, depleted economy, highly divided society or totalitarian regime and the like, has set the development of the sector back.

Source: USAID (2000, pp12–22)

B.2 Production of Welfare (POW) Model: Performance and Indicator Domains

Economy
- Resource inputs
- Expenditures
- Average costs

Effectiveness (service provision)
- Final outcomes
- Recipient satisfaction
- Output volume
- Output quality

Choice/pluralism
- Concentration
- Diversity

Efficiency
- Intermediate output efficiency
- Final outcome efficiency

Equity
- Redistributive policy consistency
- Service targeting
- Benefit-burden ratios
- Accessibility
- Procedural equity

Participation
- Membership/volunteers
- Attitudes

Advocacy
- Advocacy resource inputs
- Advocacy intermediate outputs

Innovation
- Reported innovations
- Barriers and opportunities

B.3. Examples of Non-Profit Sector Output and Capacity Measures by International Classification of Non-profit Organizations (ICNPO) Groups[1]

Field	Target measure	Coverage/Definition
Culture and Arts	Number of attendees of the performing arts	**Performing Arts:** dramatic, operatic, orchestral, dance and other artistic performances in a theatre, concert room, pavilion or outdoor arena. Includes both 'high culture' and folk culture.
	Visitors of museums	**Museums:** a permanent institution open to the public, which acquires, conserves, researches, communicates and exhibits, for purposes of study, education and enjoyment, material evidence of man and his environment.
	Volumes in libraries	**Libraries:** any organized collection of printed books and periodicals or any other graphic or audio-visual materials, and the services of a staff to provide and facilitate the use of such materials as are required to meet the informational, research, educational or recreational needs of its users. **Volumes:** any printed or manuscript work contained in one binding or portfolio.
Education	Number of students enrolled in primary and secondary schools	**Primary schools:** facilities that provide basic elementary instruction of a general nature. Included are primary schools, elementary schools, grammar schools and basic schools. **Secondary schools:** facilities that provide

		general or specialized instruction based upon at least four years' previous instruction at the primary level, and which do not primarily aim at preparing the student directly for a given trade or occupation. Included are high schools, middle schools, lyceums or gymnasiums.
	Number of students in college and universities	**Number of persons** enrolled full time in a school for systematic instruction that requires, as a minimum condition of admission, the successful completion of education at the secondary level or its equivalents. Included are general and technical universities, teachers' colleges and higher professional schools.
	Number of post-graduate degrees awarded	**Post-graduate degree:** a degree such as a MSc or PhD awarded to persons who already posses a first university degree (or equivalent qualification).
Health	Patient days in in-patient hospitals	**Patient days:** number of patients admitted to in-patient hospitals during the most recent year multiplied by the average hospital stay in days.
	Number of residents in nursing homes for the frail elderly	**Frail elderly:** individual, 65 years or older, suffering from health problem that requires long-term nursing care and medical attention. **Nursing homes:** facilities offering living arrangements and extensive personal nursing care and in-house health services by physicians and nurses.
	Day care places for the handicapped (disabled)	**Handicap:** means the loss or limitation of opportunities to take part in life of community on an equal level with others. **Disabled:** A person may be disabled by physical, intellectual or sensory impairment, medical condition or mental illness. It may be permanent or transitory.
	Litres of blood collected	
Social Services	Residents in residential care facilities for the *elderly* other than nursing homes	**Residential care facilities:** primarily domiciliary facilities offering living arrangements, which may include some limited form of nursing care and health care supervision. **Elderly:** Pertaining to one later in life, typically older than 65.
	Pre-school children in child day-care facilities	**Child day-care facilities:** facilities providing supervision and instruction preceding the primary educational level – for example, kindergartens and nursery schools, as well as infant classes for children between the ages of two to six. Excluded are nursery play centres for children below the age of two.
	Residents in residential care facilities for juveniles	**Residential care facilities:** primarily domiciliary facilities offering living arrangements, which may include some limited form of nursing care and health care supervision. **Juveniles:** young persons between the ages of 12 and 18.

Environ-ment	Areas under protection	**Areas** under some form of environmental protection in square kilometres, generally parkland, preservation areas, refuges, etc.
	Membership in environmental, ecological and animal rights associations	
Housing	Number of dwelling units constructed or rehabilitated	**Dwelling unit:** a group of rooms or single room occupied or intended for occupancy as separate living quarters. Not included are transient accommodations, barracks for workers and institutional-type quarters, as well as businesses, offices and warehouses. **Rehabilitated:** refers to major and full-scale rehabilitation of dwelling units only.
	Number of occupants	**Number of occupants:** number of people occupying a dwelling unit constructed or managed.
Develop-ment	Number and amount of credit for micro-enterprises	**Micro-enterprises:** business having less than 20 employees. **Self-employed:** working proprietors of unincorporated businesses, own-account workers, member of producers' cooperatives and unpaid family workers.
Employ-ment	Trainees in adult training programmes and continuing education programs	**Adult training:** training provided for a person who has already occupied or who is occupying a dependent or independent position of employment. **Continuing education:** a comprehensive term referring to all forms and types of education pursued by those who have left formal education at any point and who entered employment and/or assumed adult responsibilities. **Vocational training** (often refers to apprentice programmes): the systematic development of the attitudes, knowledge and skill pattern required for a job.
Civic	Number of members in civic associations	**Civic associations:** programmes and services to encourage civic mindedness.
Inter-national	Share of social development budget or international assistance budget going to non-profit organizations	**International assistance:** grants or loans (at concessional financial terms; at least 25 per cent grant element) given for the promotion of economic development and welfare.
	Volume of food aid delivered internationally	**Food aid:** the transfer from donor to recipient countries of food commodities on a totally grant basis or on highly concessional terms.

Source: Salamon and Anheier (1997–1999), *Project Manual*, The Johns Hopkins Comparative Non-profit Sector Project, Baltimore: Johns Hopkins Institute for Policy Studies

Data Sources and Other Indicators[*]

C.1 Data Sources on the Internet

International data sources

Business Environment Risk Intelligence (BERI)	www.beri.com
Centre for International Development and Conflict Management (CIDCM); see Conflict Research Datasets and *Peace and Conflict 2003* report	www.cidcm.umd.edu
Cross-National Time Series Data Archive (CNTS)	www.databanks.sitehosting.net
Economics Departments, Institutes and Research Centres in the World (EDIRC)	www.edirc.repec.org
Economist Intelligence Unit (EIU)	www.eiu.com
Freedom House (country rankings for civil and political liberties)	www.freedomhouse.org
Global Audit (for information on democracy and monitoring emerging economies)	www.globalaudit.org
Global Barometer	www.globalbarometer.org
Global Civil Society Yearbook	www.lse.ac.uk/depts/global/yearbook
Global Reach (Global Internet Statistics)	www.global-reach.biz
International Association for Official Statistics (IAOS)	www.singstat.gov.sg/IAOS/index.html
International Centre for Not-for-Profit Law	www.icnl.org
International Civil Aviation Organization	www.icao.org
International Crime Victim Survey (ICVS)	www.unicvi.it/icvs
International Energy Agency Statistics	www.iea.org/statist
International Federation of Data Organizations (IFDO)	www.ifdo.org
International Institute for Democracy and Electoral Assistance (Voter Turnout Index)	www.idea.int/vt.index.cfm
International Institute for Management Development (World Competitiveness Yearbook)	www02.imd.ch/wcy/index.cfm
International Labour Organization (ILO)	www.ilo.org
ILO Business and Social Initiatives Database (BASI)	www.oracle02.ilo.org/dyn/basi/vpisearch.first
International Monetary Fund (IMF)	www.imf.org
IMF Dissemination Standards Bulletin Board	www.dsbb.imf.org
International Organization for Migration	www.iom.int
International Social Survey Programme	www.issp.org
International Statistical Institute	www.cbs.nl/isi

Source	URL
International Telecommunication Union	www.itu.int
Internet Traffic Report	www.internettrafficreport.com
Inter-Parliamentary Union	www.ipu.org
Interstate Statistical Committee of the Commonwealth of Independent States	www.cisstat.com
Johns Hopkins University Comparative Non-Profit Sector Project (JHCNSP)	www.jhu.edu/~cnp
Lijphart Election Archive	www.dodgson.ucsd.edu/lij
Online Sourcebook on Decentralization and Local Development	www.ciesin.org/decentralization
Organization for Economic Cooperation and Development (OECD)	www.oecd.org
PARtnerships In Statistics for development in the 21st Century	www.paris21.org
Polity Project Data Archive	www.weber.ucsd.edu/~kgledits/Polity.html
PopNet	www.popnet.org
Population Reference Bureau (PRB)	www.prb.org
Protest Net	www.protest.net
Social Watch (Progress of fulfilled commitments, country reports, development indicators in English, French and Spanish)	www.socialwatch.org
Statistical Data Locator (Nanyang Technological University)	www.ntu.edu.sg/library/stat/statdata.htm
Transparency International (Corruption Perceptions Index)	www.transparency.org
UN Human Settlements Programme (UN-Habitat)	www.unhabitat.org
UN Conference on Trade and Development (UNCTAD)	www.unctad.org
UN Crime and Justice Information Network (UNCJIN)	www.odccp.org/uncjin.html
UN Department of Economic and Social Affairs (UN-DESA) (see UNSD for statistics)	www.un.org/esa/desa.htm
UN Development Programme (UNDP)	www.undp.org
Human Development Reports (HDR)	www.undp.org/hdro
UN Educational, Scientific and Cultural Organization (UNESCO) Institute for Statistics	www.uis.unesco.org
UN International Programme for the Development of Communication (IPDC) (UNESCO)	www.unesco.org/webworld/ipdc
UN Food and Agriculture Organization (FAO)	www.fao.org
UN High Commission for Human Rights (UNHCHR)	www.unhchr.ch
UN High Commission for Refugees (UNHCR)	www.unhcr.ch
UN Industrial Development Organization (UNIDO) (Industrial Statistics)	www.unido.org
UN Interregional Crime and Justice Research Institute	www.unicri.it
UN Office for Drug Control and Crime Prevention (UN-ODCCP)	www.odccp.org/crime_prevention.html

International data sources

UN Population Information Network (POPIN)	www.un.org/popin
UN Research Institute for Social Development (UNRISD) (Research Programme)	www.unrisd.org/engindex/research.htm
UN Statistics Division (UNSD)	www.un.org/Depts/unsd
UN University-World Institute for Development Economics Research (WIDER) (see UNU-WIDER)	
Income Inequality Database)	www.wider.unu.edu
UN Women Watch	www.un.org/womenwatch/resources
Union of International Associations	www.uia.org
United Nations Economic Commission for Europe – links to national statistics (by country)	www.unece.org./stats/links.htm
University of California, San Diego, Social Science Data Collection	www.ssdc.ucsd.edu
University of Michigan with links to statistical agencies worldwide	www.lib.umich.edu/govdocs/stforeig.html
Uppsala Conflict Data Project (UCDP)	www.pcr.uu.se
World Bank Data	www.worldbank.org/data
World Bank Data Group on Governance	www.worldbank.org/wbi/governance/datasets.htm
	www.econ.worldbank.org
Research Group	www.worldbank.org/lsms
Living Standards Measurement Study	
World Economic Forum (for the Global Competitiveness Survey – GCS)	www.weforum.org
World Health Organization Statistical Information System (WHOIS)	www.3.who.int/whois
World Tourism Organization	www.world-tourism.org
World Trade Organization (WTO)	www.wto.org
World Values Survey	wvs.isr.umich.edu

Regional data sources

Centro de Investigaciones Sociológicas (CIS) Databank (in English and Spanish)	www.cis.es
European Central Bank Statistics	www.ecb.int
European Public Opinion Polls, including candidate countries Eurobarmeter (CCEB),	
Eurobarometer and Europinion (CTS)	www.europa.eu.int/comm/public_opinion
EUROSTAT (Statistical Office of the European Communities)	www.europa.eu.int/comm/eurostat
Latinóbarometro	www.latinobarometro.org
New Democracies Barometer	www.cspp.strath.ac.uk/catalog4_0.html
Social Science Data Archives	www.ssda.anu.edu.au
US Agency for International Development (USAID) NGO Sustainability Index (for Central and Eastern Europe)	www.usaid.gov/regions/europe_eurasia/dem_gov
WHO Regional Offices for Europe	www.who.dk/countryinformation

National data sources

Center on Philanthropy (US)	www.philanthropy.iupui.edu
Foundation Center (US)	www.fdncenter.org
Independent Sector (US)	www.independentsector.org
Index of National Civil Health (US)	www.puaf.umd.edu/civicrenewal
Institute for Volunteering Research (UK)	www.ivr.org.uk/institute.htm

C.2 Other Possible Data Sources by Dimension

INDICATORS BY DIMENSION	SOURCES
Structure	
Organizational capacity	USAID NGO Sustainability Index, Appendix A:
Financial viability	www.usaid.gov/regions/europe_eurasia/dem_gov/ngoindex/index.htm
NGO infrastructure	
Networks and cooperation	
Impact	
CSO effectiveness	Similar to 'Government effectiveness' in Governance (from World Bank Governance Research Indicators Dataset), Appendix A: www.worldbank.org/wbi/governance/datasets.htm
Public image	USAID NGO Sustainability Index
Service provision	
Voter turnout	International Institute for Democracy and Electoral Assistance –Voter Turnout Index www.idea.int/vt
Social capital measure	Sum of memberships multiplied by trust, World Values Survey: wvs.isr.umich.edu
Space	
Advocacy	USAID NGO Sustainability Index, Appendix A www.usaid.gov/regions/europe_eurasia/dem_gov/ngoindex/index.htm
Rule of law	Governance (from World Bank Governance Research Indicators Dataset), Appendix A: www.worldbank.org/wbi/governance/datasets.htm
Graft/corruption	• Governance (from World Bank Governance Research Indicators Dataset), Appendix A: www.worldbank.org/wbi/governance/datasets.htm • Corruption Perceptions Index, Transparency International, Appendix A: www.transparency.org/cpi
Extent to which government policies are judged supportive by national CSO representatives	See stakeholder survey approach in Chapter 5

Note: * URLs updated April 2003

Notes

Foreword

1 See www.civicus.org.
2 See *From Impossibility to Reality: A Reflection Paper on the CIVICUS CSI Pilot Phase* by Volkhart 'Finn' Heinrich and Kumi Naidoo; *Improving the Understanding and Strength of Civil Society: The Contribution of the CIVICUS Civil Society Index* by Volkhart 'Finn' Heinrich; both are available on the CIVICUS website.
3 Volkhart 'Finn' Heinrich is a project manager at CIVICUS and Kumi Naidoo is the secretary general and CEO of CIVICUS.

Chapter 3

1 The basic idea to use a graphical approach to present multidimensional information was developed by Social Watch (2000) using the Equity Diamond.

Chapter 4

1 Of course, we can offer neither a full interpretation nor an explanation of the various case studies. This would go well beyond the purpose of the present chapter and would require, in each case, a far more detailed analysis. However, we will, on occasion, point to interesting findings and highlight aspects that warrant further exploration and discussion.
2 We had access to two versions of the World Values Survey (WVS) when designing the illustrative examples for this chapter. One version contains waves 1 to 3 (ie 1981–1984, 1990–1993 and 1995–1997) and the other waves 1 to 2. Some countries are included in one version but not in the other, and some countries are included/excluded from certain survey questions in different waves. In order to provide examples of the multiple uses of the CSD, such as over time and cross-sectional, we used both versions of the WVS in this chapter (see World Values Study Group, 1994; 1999).
3 Warren (1999, p14) suggests that 'Trust is a way of describing the way groups of individuals presume the good will of others with respect to shared interests, as well as the divisions of knowledge necessary to make use of explicit rules for collective action.'

Figure sources. **4.1a:** Paid employment (Salamon et al, 1993b); Fulfilled commitment index (Social Watch, 2000); Voice and accountability (World Bank, 1999); Trust among members (World Values Study Group, 1994). **4.1b:** Paid employment (Salamon et al, 1999b); Membership, tolerance and trust (World Values Study Group, 1994); Fulfilled commitment index (Social Watch, 2000); Change in HDI (UNDP, 2000); Voice and accountability (World Bank, 1999); Civil liberties (Freedom House, 2001). **4.1c:** Paid employment (Salamon, et al, 1999b); Volunteering (Independent Sector, 2000); Membership, trust, tolerance, confidence and subjective well-being (World Values Study Group, 1994); Fulfilled commitment index (Social Watch, 2000); Change in HDI (UNDP, 2000); Voice and accountability (World Bank, 1999); Civil liberties (Freedom House, 2001); Political freedom index (Desai, 1994). **4.1d:** Paid employment and operating expenditures (Salamon et al, 1999b); Volunteering (Independent Sector, 2000); Membership, trust, tolerance, confidence, membership in human rights organizations and subjective well-being (World Values Study Group, 1994); Fulfilled commitment index (Social Watch, 2000); Change in HDI (UNDP, 2000); Gini index of inequality (World Bank, 2000); Voice and accountability (World Bank, 1999); Civil liberties (Freedom House, 2001); Political freedom index (Desai, 1994) Corruption (Transparency International, 1999–2000). **4.1e:** Public sector dependency and marketization (Volkhart, 2001); Trust, tolerance, confidence and subjective well-being (World Values Study Group, 1999); Gini index of inequality (World Bank, 2000); Corruption (Transparency International, 1999–2000); Civil liberties (Freedom House, 2001). **4.1f:** Paid employment (Salamon et al, 1999b); Membership, tolerance, trust and subjective well-being (World Values Study Group, 1999); Fulfilled commitment index (Social Watch, 2000); Civil liberties (Freedom House, 2001); Voice and accountability (World Bank, 1999). **4.2a:** Membership, trust and subjective well-being (World Values Study Group, 1999); Civil liberties (Freedom House, 2001). **4.2b:** Paid employment (Salamon et al, 1999b); Membership, trust, confidence and subjective well-being (World Values Study Group, 1994); Change in HDI (UNDP, 2000); Civil liberties (Freedom House, 2001); Corruption (Transparency International, 1999–2000). **4.2c:** Membership, trust and subjective well-being (World Values Study Group, 1999); Civil liberties (Freedom House, 2001). **4.2d-1:** Paid employment (Salamon et al, 1999b); Membership, trust, confidence and subjective well-being (World Values Study Group, 1999); Fulfilled commitment index (Social Watch, 2000); Civil liberties (Freedom House, 2001); Corruption (Transparency International, 1999–2000). **4.2e:** Membership and trust among members (World Values Study Group, 1999); Change in HDI (UNDP, 2000); Voice and accountability (World Bank, 1999). **4.3a:** Paid employment (Salamon et al, 1999b); Membership, confidence, trust and subjective well-being (World Values Study Group, 1999); Fulfilled commitment index (Social Watch, 2000); Voice and accountability (World Bank, 1999); Civil liberties (Freedom House, 2001). **4.3b:** Paid employment (Salamon et al, 1999b); Membership, confidence, trust and subjective well-being (World Values Study Group, 1999); Fulfilled commitment index (Social Watch, 2000); Voice and accountability (World Bank, 1999); Civil liberties (Freedom House, 2001). **4.3c:** Paid employment (Salamon et al, 1999b); Trust (World Values Study Group, 1999); Gini (WIDER-UNU, 2000); Civil liberties (Freedom House, 2001).

Chapter 5

1   Readers unfamiliar with these terms may consult any introductory textbook on social science research methodology.
2   Helmut Anheier assisted in developing the Johns Hopkins Comparative Non-profit Sector Project, particularly in its methodological dimensions, and served as its co-director between 1990 and 1999.
3   The Johns Hopkins Comparative Non-profit Sector Project is currently conducting a large qualitative assessment of the impact of non-profit organizations, using an abbreviated version of the Delphi method suggested below in the section on Stakeholder Surveys.

Chapter 6

1   Note that all information and data presented in this chapter is based on material published in the *CIVICUS Index on Civil Society Occasional Paper Series*, vol 1 (3–11), in which results of the pilot study first appeared. Readers interested in following up on the sources can download the full country reports at the following website: www.civicus.org.

2   Naidoo and Heinrich (2001) offer a more complete description and assessment of the pilot testing.

3   The following description is based on Yury Zagoumennov (2001) *Belarus Civil Society: In Need of a Dialogue*. We are grateful to the Belarus team for being able to refer to their case study material.

4   The following description is based on Don K Embuldeniya (2001) *Exploring the Health, Strength, and Impact of Canada's Civil Society*. We are grateful to the Canadian team for being able to refer to their case study material.

5   The following description is based on Gojko Bezovan (2001) *Croatian Civil Society: On the Path to Becoming a Legitimate Public Actor*. We are grateful to the Croatian team for being able to refer to their case study material.

6   The following description is based on Aire Trummal and Mikko Lagerspetz (2001) *The Profile of Estonian Civil Society*. We are grateful to the Estonian team for being able to refer to their case study material.

7   The following description is based on Maria Isabel Verduzco and Aguirre Reveles (2001) *The CIVICUS Index of Civil Society Project in Mexico*. We are grateful to the Mexican team for being able to refer to their case study material.

8   The following description is based on Association of NGOs in Aotearoa and New Zealand Social and Civic Policy Institute (2001) *Aotearoa/New Zealand Civil Society: A Framework for Government–Civil Society Dialogue*. We are grateful to the New Zealand team for being able to refer to their case study material.

9   The following description is based on Adnan Sattar Rabia Baig (2001) *Civil Society in Pakistan*. We are grateful to the Pakistan team for being able to refer to their case study material.

10 The following description is based on Phiroshaw Camay and Anne Gordon (2001) *Two Commas and a Full Stop*. We are grateful to the South African team for being able to refer to their case study material.

11 The following description is based on Svitlana Kuts et al (2001) *Deepening the Roots of Civil Society in Ukraine: Findings From an Innovative and Participatory Assessment Project on the Health of Ukrainian Civil Society*. We are grateful to the Ukrainian team for being able to refer to their case study material.

Appendix B

1   Definitions used by the Johns Hopkins Project are based on standard international statistical sources, such as UNESCO's *Statistical Yearbook*, reports from several international statistical agencies, such as the OECD and the World Bank, the statistical offices from several countries participating in the project, and the Oxford English Dictionary.

References

Anheier, H K, Glasius, M and Kaldor, M (2001) 'Introducing Global Civil Society'. In H K Anheier, M Glasius and M Kaldor (eds) *Global Civil Society 2001*. Oxford University Press, Oxford

Anheier, H and Kendall, J (eds) (2001) *Third Sector Policy at the Crossroads: An International Nonprofit Analysis*. Routledge, London

Anheier, H K and Kendall J (2002) 'Trust and the Voluntary Sector' *British Journal of Sociology*, Volume 53, Issue 3, 343–362

Anheier, H K, and Salamon, L M (eds) (1998) *The Nonprofit Sector in the Developing World*. Manchester University Press, Manchester

Anheier, H K and Salamon, L M (2003) 'The Nonprofit Sector in Comparative Perspective'. In W W Powell and R Steinberg (eds) *The Nonprofit Sector: A Research Handbook*. New Haven, Yale University Press

Anheier, H K and Seibel, W (2001) *The Nonprofit Sector in Germany*. Manchester University Press, Manchester

Archambault, E (1996) *The Nonprofit Sector in France*. Manchester University Press, Manchester

Archambault, E, Anheier, H K and Sokolowski, W (1998) 'The Monetary Value of Volunteer Time: A Comparative Analysis of France, Germany and the United States', Paper presented at the Review of Income and Wealth Conference, Lillehammer, Norway

Association of NGOS in Aotearoa and New Zealand Social and Civic Policy Insitute (2001) *Aotearoa/New Zealand Civil Society: A Framework for Government–Civil Society Dialogue*. Civicus Index on Civil Society Occasional Paper Series, Volume 1, Issue 5

Baig, A S R (2001) *Civil Society in Pakistan*. Civicus Index on Civil Society Occasional Paper Series, Volume 1, Issue 11

Barsh, R L (1993) 'Measuring Human Rights: Problems of Methodology and Purpose', *Human Rights Quarterly* Volume 15(1), 87–121

Bezovan, G (2001) *Croatian Civil Society: On the Path to Becoming a Legitimate Public Actor*. Civicus Index on Civil Society Occasional Paper Series, Volume 1, Issue 4

Camay, P and Gordon, A (2001) *Two Commas and a Full Stop*. Civicus Index on Civil Society Occasional Paper Series, Volume 1, Issue 9

Clark, J (2003) *Worlds Apart: Civil Society and the Battle for Ethical Globalization*. Earthscan/Kumarian, London

Cohen, J L and Arato, A (1997) *Civil Society and Political Theory*. Cambridge University Press, Cambridge

Coleman, J (1990) *Foundations of Social Theory*. Harvard University Press, Cambridge, Massachusetts

Commission on the Future of the Voluntary Sector (1996) *Meeting the Challenge of Change: Voluntary Action in the 21st Century*. NCVO, London

Dahrendorf, R (1959) *Class and Class Conflict in Industrial Society*. Routledge and Kegan Paul, London

Dahrendorf, R (1991) 'Die gefährdete Civil Society'. In K Michalski (ed) *Europa und die Civil Society*. Castelgandolfo-Gespräche, Stuttgart

Dahrendorf, R (1995) 'Über den Bürgerstatus'. In B van den Brink and W van Reijen (eds) *Bürgergesellschaft, Recht und Demokratie*. Suhrkamp, Frankfurt am Main

Dasgupta, P (1993) *An Inquiry into Well-Being and Destitution*. Oxford University Press, Oxford, Clarendon Press, New York

Dasgupta, P and Serageldin, I (2000) *Social Capital: A Multifaceted Perspective*. World Bank, Washington, DC

Davis, J (1985) *The Logic of Causal Order*. Sage, Series on Quantitative Applications in the Social Sciences, Volume 55, London

Deakin, N (2001) *In Search of Civil Society*. Palgrave, Basingstoke

Deguchi, M (2001) 'The distortion between institutionalised and noninstitutionalised NPOs: New policy initiatives and nonprofit organisations in Japan'. In H K Anheier and J Kendall (eds) *Third sector policy at the crossroads: An international nonprofit analysis*. Routledge, London

Desai, M (1994) *Measuring Political Freedom*. Discussion Paper 10, Centre for the Study of Global Governance, LSE, London

Desai, M and Redfern, P (eds) (1995) *Global Governance: Ethics and Economics of the World Order*. Pinter Publishers, London

Deutsch, K W (1963) *The Nerves of Government*. The Free Press, New York

Development Cooperation Directorate, Organization for Economic Cooperation and Development (OECD) (2001) *Partnerships In Statistics for Development in the 21st Century*. www.paris21.org, OECD, Paris

Diener, E and Suh, M (eds) (1999) *Subjective Well-Being in Global Perspective*. MIT Press, Cambridge

Edwards, M and Gaventa, J (eds) (2001) *Global Citizen Action*. Lynne Rienner Publishers, Boulder, Co

Edwards, B, Foley, M W and Diani, M (2001) *Beyond Tocqueville: Civil Society and the Social Capital Debate in Comparative Perspective*. University Press of New England, Hanover

Eisner, R (1994) *The Misunderstood Economy: What Counts and How to Count It*. Harvard Business School Press, Boston

Elias, N (1994) *The Civilizing Process*. Blackwell, Oxford

Embuldeniya, D K (2001) *Exploring the Health, Strength, and Impact of Canada's Civil Society*. Civicus Index on Civil Society Occasional Paper Series, Volume 1, Issue 8

Enquettekommission des Deutschen Bundestages (2002) *Zivilgesellschaft und buergerschaftliches Engagement*. Leske and Budrich, Berlin

Etzioni, A (1971) *The Active Society: A Theory of Societal and Political Processes*. Collier-Macmillan, London

Ferlie, E (1996) (ed) *The New Public Management in Action*. Oxford University Press, Oxford

Forbes, D P (1998) 'Measuring the unmeasurable: empirical studies of nonprofit organisation effectiveness', *Nonprofit and Voluntary Sector Quarterly* (NVSQ), Volume 27(2), 159–182

Freedom House (FH) (2001) *Country Ratings*. Freedom House, www.freedom house.org/ratings/index.htm.

Galtung, J (1992) 'Theory Formation in Social Research: a Plea for Pluralism'. In E Oyen (ed) *Comparative Methodology. Theory and Practice in International Social Research*. Sage, London

Gaskin, K and Davis Smith, J (1997) *A New Civic Europe? A Study of the Extent and Role of Volunteering*. The National Centre for Volunteering, London

Gastil, R D and Sussman, L R (1987) *Freedom in the World: Political Rights and Civil Liberties, 1986–1987*. Greenwood Press, New York

Gellner, E (1994) *Conditions of Liberty: Civil Society and Its Rivals*. Hamish-Hamilton, London

Glasius, M et al (2002) *Global Civil Society*. Oxford University Press, Oxford

Glasius, M and Kaldor, M (2002) 'The State of Global Civil Society: Before and After September 11'. In M Glasius, M Kaldor and H K Anheier (eds) *Global Civil Society 2002*. Oxford University Press, Oxford

Gramsci, A (1971) 'State and Civil Society'. In Q Hoare and G N Smith (eds and translators) *Selections of the Prison Notebooks of Antonio Gramsci*. Lawrence and Wishart, London

Gronbjerg, K (1994) *Understanding Nonprofit Funding*. Jossey-Bass, San Francisco, CA

Habermas, J (1992). *Faktizität und Geltung*. Suhrkamp, Frankfurt am Main

Halman, L (2001) *The European Values Study: A Third Wave*. Source Book of the 1999/2000 European Values Study Surveys. Tilburg University Press, Tilburg

Harvard Center for International Development (CID)–World Bank DataMart (2000) www.paradocs.pols.columbia.edu/datavine/MainPage.jsp

Hazell, R and Whybrew, T (eds) (1993) *Measuring the Voluntary Sector: The Fnders' Perspective*. Association of Charitable Foundations, Charities Aid Foundation, Corporate Responsibility Group

Heinrich, V and Naidoo, K (2001) 'From Impossibility to Reality: A Reflection and Position Paper on the CIVICUS Civil Society Index 1999–2001', *Civicus Index on Civil Society Occasional Paper Series*. CIVICUS World Alliance for Citizen Participation, Washington, DC, http://www.civicus.org/new/media/CIVICUSPositionPaper1.pdf

Herman, R and Renz, D (1997) 'Multiple Constituencies and the Social Construction of Nonprofit Effectiveness', *Nonprofit and Voluntary Sector Quarterly* (NVSQ), Volume 26, 185–206

Holloway, R (2001) *Assessing Civil Society – Handbook for the use of the Civil Society Index*. CIVICUS, Washington, DC

Huizinga, J (1954) *The Waning of the Middle Ages*. Doubleday, New York

Humana, C (ed) (1992) *World Human Rights Guide, 3rd Edition*. Oxford University Press, New York

Independent Sector (1994) *Giving and Volunteering in the United States: Findings from a National Survey*. Independent Sector, Washington, DC

Independent Sector (2000) *Giving and Volunteering Survey*. www.independentsector.org/GandV/s_volu.htm

Independent Sector (2002) *Giving and Volunteering in the United States 2001*. Independent Sector, Washington, DC (7th biennially report; see www.independentsector.org/GandV/default.htm)

Independent Sector and the Urban Institute (2002) *The New Nonprofit Almanac and Desk Reference*. Independent Sector, Washington, DC (see www.independent sector.org/programs/research/na01main.html)

Inglehart, R (1997) *Modernization and Postmodernization: Cultural, Economic, and Political Change in 43 Societies*. Princeton University Press, Princeton, NJ

Inglehart, R, Basañez, M and Moreno, A (1998) *Human Values and Beliefs: A Cross-Cultural Sourcebook: Political, Religious, Sexual, and Economic Norms in 43 Societies: Findings from the 1990–1993 World Values Survey*. The University of Michigan Press, Ann Arbor, Michigan

International Centre for Not-for-profit Law (ICNL) and the World Bank (1997) *Handbook on Good Practice for Laws Relating to Nongovernmental Organizations*. ICNL, Washington, DC (see also www.icnl.org/handbook/)

Jongman, A J and Schmid, A P (eds) (1994) *Monitoring Human Rights: Manual for Assessing Country Performance*. PIOOM, Leiden

Kaldor, M (2003) *Global Civil Society*. Polity Press, London

Kaplan, A E (1999) *Giving USA 1999: The Annual Report on Philanthropy for the Year 1998*. AAFRC Trust for Philanthropy, New York

Karatnycky, A and the Freedom House Survey Team (2001) *Freedom in the World: The Annual Survey of Political Rights and Civil Liberties, 2000–2001*. Freedom House, New York

Kaufmann, D, Kraay, A and Zoido-Lobatón, P (1999a) *Governance Matters.* World Bank Policy Research Working Paper 2196, World Bank, Washington, DC (www.worldbank.org/wbi/governance/pubs/govmatters.htm)

Kaufmann, D, Kraay, A and Zoido-Lobatón, P (1999b) *Aggregating Governance Indicators.* World Bank Policy Research Working Paper 2195. World Bank, Washington, DC (www.worldbank.org/wbi/governance/pubs/aggindicators.htm)

Kaviraj, S and Khilnani, S (eds) (2001) *Civil Society: History and Possibilities.* Cambridge University Press, Cambridge

Keane, J (1998) *Civil Society: Old Images, New visions.* Polity Press, Cambridge, UK

Keane, J (2001) 'Concepts of Global Civil Society'. In H Anheier, M Glasius and M Kaldor (eds) *Global Civil Society 2001*, Oxford University Press, Oxford

Keirouz, K, Grimm, J, and Steinberg, R (1999) 'The Philanthropic Giving Index: A New Indicator of the Climate for Raising Funds', *Nonprofit and Voluntary Sector Quarterly*, Volume 28(4), 491-499, December

Keirouz, K S (1999) 'Public Perceptions and Confidence in Indiana Nonprofit Organizations: Based on the Indiana Poll November–December 1998', Indiana University, Center on Philanthropy, Indianapolis, IN

Kendall, J and Knapp, M (1999) 'Evaluation of the Voluntary (Nonprofit) Sector: Emerging Issues'. In D Lewis (ed) *International Perspectives on Voluntary Action: Reshaping the Third Sector.* Earthscan, London

Kendall, J and Knapp, M (2000) 'Measuring the Performance of Voluntary Organisations', *Public Management* Volume 2(1), 105–132

Knapp, M R J, Hardy, B and Forder, J (2001) 'Commissioning for Quality: Ten Years of Social Care Markets in England', *Journal of Social Policy,* Volume 30(2), 283–306

Kuts, S et al (2001) *Deepening the Roots of Civil Society in Ukraine. Findings From an Innovative and Participatory Assessment Project on the Health of Ukrainian Civil Society,* Civicus Index on Civil Society Occasional Paper Series, Volume 1, Issue 10

Lambsdorff, G J (1999a) *Corruption in Empirical Research: A Review.* Transparency International Working Paper, Transparency International (www.transparency.org/working_papers/lambsdorff/lambsdorff_eresearch.html)

Lambsdorff, G J (1999b) *The Transparency International Corruption Perceptions Index 1999: Framework Document.* Transparency International (www.transparency.org/cpi/1999/cpi_framework.html)

Le Grand, J (1999) 'Competition, Collaboration or Control? Tales from the British National Health Service', *Health Affairs,* Volume 18, 27–37

McLaughlin, K, Osborne, S P and Ferlie, E (eds) (2002) *New Public Management: Current Trends and Future Prospects.* Routledge, London

Mitchell, N J and McCormick , J M (1988) 'Economic and Political Explanations of Human Rights Violations', *World Politics,* Volume 40, 476–498

Morris, M D (1979) *Measuring the Condition of the World's Poor: The Physical Quality of Life Index.* Pergamon Press, New York

Mulgan, G (1999) 'Government and the Third Sector: Building a More Equal Partnership. In H K Anheier (ed) *Third Way – Third Sector,* Report No 1. Centre for Civil Society, London School of Economics, pp17–22

Murray, V (2000) 'Evaluating the Impact of Public–Private Partnerships: a Canadian Experience'. In S P Osborne (ed) *Public–Private Partnerships: Theory and Practice in International Perspective.* Routledge, London

Naidoo, K and Tandon, R (1999) 'The Promise of Civil Society'. In K Naidoo and B Knight (eds) *Civil Society at the Millennium.* Kumarian Press, Bloomfield, CT

Olvera Rivera, A (2001) *Sociedad civil, gobernabilidad democrática, espacios públicos y democratización: los contornos de un proyecto.* Sociedad Civil y Gobernabilidad en México Universidad Veracruzana, Mexico

Osborne, S P (1998) 'Organizational Structure and Innovation in UK Voluntary Social Welfare Organizations: Applying the Aston Measures', *Voluntas,* Volume 9(4), 345–362

Paton, R (1998) *Performance Measurement, Benchmarking and Public Confidence.* Charities Aid Foundation, London

Perrow, C (2001) 'Organisational Theory and the Non-Profit Form'. In H K Anheier (ed) *Organisational Theory and the Non-Profit Form,* Report No 2. Centre for Civil Society, London School of Economics, London

Plowden, W (2001) *Next Steps in Voluntary Action.* Centre for Civil Society, London School of Economics and NCVO, London

Putnam, R D (2000) *Bowling Alone: The Collapse and Survival of American Community.* Simon and Schuster, New York

Putnam, R (ed) (2002) *Democracies in Flux.* Oxford University Press, Oxford

Rosenberg, C N (1996) *Wealthy and Wise: A Summary.* Claude Rosenberg, Jr, San Francisco, CA

Salamon, L M (1994) 'The Rise of the Nonprofit Sector', *Foreign Affairs,* Volume 74(3), 111–124

Salamon, L M (1995) *Partners in Public Service.* Johns Hopkins University Press, Baltimore

Salamon, L M (2002) *The State of Nonprofit America.* Brookings, Washington, DC

Salamon, L M and Anheier, H K (1996) *The Emerging Nonprofit Sector.* Manchester University Press, Manchester

Salamon, L M and Anheier, H K (eds) (1997) *Defining the Non-profit Sector: A Cross-National Analysis.* Manchester University Press, Manchester

Salamon, L M, Anheier, H K, List, R, Toepler, S, Sokolowski, S W and associates (1999a) *Global Civil Society: Dimensions of the Non-profit Sector.* Johns Hopkins University, Institute for Policy Studies, Center for Civil Society Studies, Baltimore, Maryland

Salamon, L M, Anheier, H K and associates (1999b) *The Emerging Sector Revisited: A Summary – Revised Estimates.* Johns Hopkins University, Institute for Policy Studies, Center for Civil Society Studies, Baltimore, Maryland

Salamon, L M and Toepler, S (2000) *The Influence of the Legal Environment on the Development of the Nonprofit Sector.* Center for Civil Society Studies Working Paper Number 17. Johns Hopkins Center for Civil Society Studies, Baltimore (JHU Law Index)

Saxon-Harrold, S K E (1987) *The Charitable Behaviour of the British People: A National Survey of Patterns and Attitudes to Charitable Giving.* Charities Aid Foundation, Tonbridge, Kent

Sirianni, C and Friedland, L (2000) *Civic Innovation in America: Community Empowerment, Public Policy and the Movement for Civic Renewal.* University of California, Berkeley

Social Watch (2000) *Social Watch 2000.* Social Watch, www.socialwatch.org/2000/eng/chartings/stepsforward.htm and www.socwatch.org.uy/2000/eng/chartings/methodology.htm for methodology

Strategy Unit (2002) *Private Action, Public Benefit. A Review of Charities and the Wider Not-For-Profit Sector.* Cabinet Office, London

Taylor, C L and Jodice, D A (1983) *World Handbook of Political and Social Indicators, 3rd edition.* Yale University Press, New York

Transparency International (TI) (1999–2000) *The 2000 Corruption Perceptions Index (CPI).* www.transparency.org/cpi/2000/cpi2000.html

Trummal, A and Lagerspetz, M (2001) *The Profile of Estonian Civil Society.* Civicus Index on Civil Society Occasional Paper Series, Volume 1, Issue 6

Tufte, E R (1999) *The Visual Display of Quantitative Information.* Graphics Press, Cheshire, Connecticut, 17th edition

Union of International Associations (UIA) (1905–1999/2000) *Yearbook of International Organizations.* K G Saur, Munich

United Nations (UN) (1993) *System of National Accounts.* United Nations, New York (see also www.un.org/Depts/unsd/sna/sna1-en.htm)

United Nations Development Programme (UNDP) (1992) *Global Dimensions of Human Development: Human Development Report 1992.* Oxford University Press, New York and Oxford (see, in particular, Chapter 2, 'Political Freedom and Human Development', and 'Technical Annex 3', p104)

UNDP (2000) *Human Development Report 2000: Human Rights and Human Development.* United Nations, New York (www.undp.org/hdr2000/english/book/back1.pdf)

UNDP (2002) *Human Development Report.* United Nations, New York

United Nations Statistics Division (UNSD) (2000) *COMTRADE Database* (Trade in Cultural Goods). United Nations, New York

United Nations Statistical Division (National Accounts) (2002) *Handbook on Nonprofit Institutions.* United Nations, New York

University of California, San Diego (UCSD) (2001a) *Social Science Data Collection,* www.ssdc.ucsd.edu

University of California, San Diego (UCSD) (2001b). *Lijphart Election Archive, Social Sciences and Humanities Library,* www.dodgson.ucsd.edu/lij

USAID, Bureau for Europe and Eurasia, Office of Democracy and Governance (2000) *The 1999 NGO Sustainability Index.* USAID, Washington, DC (available for 1998, 1999, 2000: www.usaid.gov/regions/europe_eurasia/dem_gov/ngoindex/index.htm)

Verba, S, Schlozman, K L and Brady, H (1995) *Voice and Equality: Civil Voluntarism in American Politics.* Harvard University Press, Cambridge, Massachusetts

van der Vijver, F and Leung, K (1997) *Methods and Data Analysis for Cross-Cultural Research.* Sage, Thousand Oaks

Verduzco, M and Reveles, A (2001) *The CIVICUS Index of Civil Society Project in Mexico.* Civicus Index on Civil Society Occasional Paper Series, Volume 1, Issue 7

Volkhart, F H (2001). 'The Roles of NGOs in Strengthening the Foundations of South African Democracy', *Voluntas,* Volume 12(1), 1–15

Warren, M E (ed) (1999) *Democracy and Trust.* Cambridge University Press, Cambridge

Wolff, E N (1995) *Top Heavy: A Study of the Increasing Inequality of Wealth in America.* Twentieth Century Fund Press, New York

World Bank (1999) *Worldwide Governance Research Indicators Dataset,* www.worldbank.org/wbi/governance/datasets.htm#dataset

World Bank (2000) *World Development Indicators.* World Bank, Washington, DC, www.worldbank.org/data/wdi2000/pdfs/tab2_8.pdf

World Bank (2000) *World Development Report.* World Bank, Washington, DC

World Institute for Development Economics Research (WIDER)–United Nations University (UNU) (2000) *UNU/WIDER-UNDP World Income Inequality Database WWW,* Version 1.0, www.wider.unu.edu/wiid/wiid.htm

World Values Study Group (1994) *World Values Survey, 1981–1984 and 1990–1993.* CD-ROM, CPSR version. Institute for Social Research, Inter-university Consortium for Political and Social Research, Ann Arbor, Michigan

World Values Study Group (1999) *World Values Survey, 1981–1984, 1990–1993 and 1995–1997.* CD-ROM, Cumulative File for the First 3 Waves. Institute for Social Research, Inter-university Consortium for Political and Social Research, Ann Arbor, Michigan.

Zagoumennov, Y (2001) *Belarus Civil Society: In Need of a Dialogue.* Civicus Index on Civil Society Occasional Paper Series, Volume 1, Issue 3

Index